50 Hikes in New England

50 *Hikes*
In New England

First Edition

Marty Basch

THE COUNTRYMAN PRESS
A division of W. W. Norton & Company
Independent Publishers Since 1923

To Jan,
Thanks for the smiles over the miles

AN INVITATION TO THE READER
Over time trails can be rerouted, and signs and
landmarks altered. If you find that changes have
occurred on the routes described in this book,
please let us know so that corrections may be
made in future editions. The author and publisher
also welcome other comments and suggestions.
Address all correspondence to:
    Editor, 50 Hikes Series
    The Countryman Press
    500 Fifth Avenue
    New York, NY 10110

Maps by Michael Borop,
© The Countryman Press
Book design by Glenn Suokko
Text composition by Eugenie S. Delaney
Interior photographs by the author unless
otherwise credited

The Countryman Press
www.countrymanpress.com

A division of W. W. Norton & Company, Inc.,
500 Fifth Avenue, New York, NY 10110
www.wwnorton.com

10 9 8 7 6 5 4 3 2

Acknowledgments

Hiking is something I discovered after moving to New Hampshire back when I had hair and the benign trek to the wondrous ledges atop West Rattlesnake over Squam Lake hooked me. Since then I've logged countless steps over numerous miles across New England's mountains with awe, wonder, and sometimes second thoughts as wind, rain, thunder, and more often foil the most well-intentioned plans.

The hiking community is a tight one, and the years have been kind to me, connecting me with hikers now friends, colleagues, and commiserators. Along the way I've been linked to many people who have tolerated me and my questions—Doug Mayer, Mike Micucci, Peter Crane, Rob Burbank, Steve Smith, Mike Dickerman, Jim Crawford, and Steve Finch. That's a list of colorful characters. They all have passion, guidance, and knowledge. I am honored and humbled they have shared it with me. Though none of us knew it, it all led in some way to this book.

There's nothing like local knowledge and a number of people shared their backyard expertise. I'm grateful to Sugarloaf's Ethan Austin (Carrabassett Valley), Sunday River's Darcy Morse (Grafton Notch), Okemo's Bonnie MacPherson (Ludlow area), and Karen Boushie of Smugglers' Notch (Stowe area) for their invaluable assistance. Thanks again to Nancy Marshall Communications—namely Nancy Marshall, Charlene Williams, and Rose Whitehouse. They smoothed the way into Maine's scenic wonders known as Acadia National Park and Baxter State Park.

Gear is dear to hikers, and over the miles I had a chance to try some new equipment. Thanks to Sue Killoran for connecting me with Tecnica, keeping my feet comfortable over the miles in their boots, and also to Ingrid Niehaus for hooking me up with trusty Mountainsmith packs.

At The Countryman Press thanks go to editorial director Kermit Hummel. He somehow hiked to my website and and initiated contact. After a few e-mails, this project was born. Thanks for making the trip. Also words of thanks go to Doug Yeager, Lisa Sacks, and Laura Stiers.

Of course, there is my hiking honey, Jan Basch. We have spent much time in the outdoors and on the trails. Not only does she love me, she trusts me. Go figure. I'm one lucky man.

50 Hikes in New England at a Glance

HIKE	CITY, STATE	DISTANCE (miles)	DIFFICULTY
1. Walkabout Trail	Chepachet, RI	2, 6, or 8	Easy to Moderate
2. George B. Parker Woodland	Coventry, RI	7	Moderate (Strenuous for some)
3. Stepstone Falls	West Greenwich, RI	3.4	Easy
4. Mount Tom Trail and Cliffs	Exeter, RI	4.2	Moderate
5. Breakheart Pond Loop	West Greenwich, RI	6.3	Moderate
6. Mount Tom State Park Tower	Litchfield, CT	1	Easy
7. Devil's Hopyard State Park	East Haddam, CT	2.6	Easy to Moderate (for some)
8. The Wolf Den at Mashamoquet Brook State Park	Pomfret Center, CT	4	Moderate
9. Cobble Mountain	Kent, CT	6.4	Moderate to Strenuous
10. Bear Mountain	Salisbury, CT	6.7	Strenuous
11. Monument Mountain	Great Barrington, MA	2.8	Easy to Moderate
12. Northfield Mountain	Northfield, MA	3.1	Moderate
13. Mount Tom State Reservation	Holyoke, MA	5.1	Moderate to Strenuous
14. Mount Toby	Sunderland, MA	3	Moderate
15. Mount Watatic	Ashburnham, MA	3	Moderate
16. Pine Cobble	Williamstown, MA	3.2	Moderate
17. Wachusett Mountain	Princeton, MA	3.2	Moderate
18. Alander Mountain	South Egremont, MA	5	Moderate to Strenuous
19. Mount Everett and Mount Race	South Egremont, MA	7.2	Strenuous
20. Mount Greylock	Williamstown, MA	8	Strenuous
21. West Rattlesnake	Holderness, NH	1.8	Easy
22. Mount Willard	Crawford Notch, NH	3.2	Easy to Moderate
23. Welch-Dickey Loop	Waterville Valley, NH	4.4	Moderate
24. Boulder Loop	Albany, NH	3.1	Easy to Moderate
25. North and Middle Sugarloaf	Twin Mountain, NH	3.2	Easy to Moderate

TIME	ELEVATION GAIN (feet)	COMMENTS
1 to 5 hours depending on distance	200	Lovely forested trek with reservoir views
4 hours	200	Woodsy Audubon ramble
2 hours	150	Peaceful jaunt to waterfall
2 hours	400	Cliffs afford hillside views
3½ hours	240	Nice trail mix and soothing pond
1 hour	400	Beautiful stone tower; family friendly
2 hours	300	Falls, small covered bridge, and picnic area
2½ to 3 hours	300	Explore a cool cave and rock formations
4 hours	700	Diverse loop with rock scramble and vistas
4 to 5 hours	1560	Rolling landscape from Connecticut's highest
2 hours	720	View peaceful Housatonic River Valley
2 hours	690	Ledge overlook; lots to do
4 hours	650	Good hawk watching and sweeping vistas
2½ to 3 hours	900	Fire tower affords fine views
2 hours	600	Little peak, big rewards
2 hours	1000	Nice piece of the Berkshires
3 hours	930	Balance Rock along the way; plenty on top
3½ to 4 hours	840	Wild Bay State feel
5 hours	2200	Prominent peaks with a challenge
5 to 6 hours	2390	Southern New England's highest
1 hour	450	Stunning lake views; fall in love with hiking here
2 hours	900	Harder side of easy with great vistas
3 hours	1800	Twice the fun on two mountains
2 hours	950	Tower above the Kancamagus Highway
2½ hours	1100	Enchanting rock formations

50 Hikes in New England at a Glance

HIKE	CITY, STATE	DISTANCE (miles)	DIFFICULTY
26. Mount Chocorua	Albany, NH	7.6	Moderate
27. North Moat	North Conway, NH	10	Strenuous
28. Mount Eisenhower	Crawford Notch, NH	6.6	Moderate to Strenuous
29. Franconia Ridge	Franconia State Park, NH	8.9	Strenuous
30. Mount Washington	Twin Mountain, NH	9.2	Strenuous
31. Mount Tom	Woodstock, VT	3.2	Easy
32. White Rocks Overlook and Ice BedsTrail	Wallingford, VT	1.8	Easy
33. Gile Mountain	Norwich, VT	1.4	Easy
34. Wheeler Mountain	Barton, VT	2.6	Moderate
35. Lye Brook Falls	Manchester, VT	4.6	Moderate
36. Mount Ascutney	Windsor, VT	6.4	Moderate
37. Mount Hunger	Waterbury Center, VT	4	Strenuous
38. Okemo Mountain	Ludlow, VT	6	Moderate
39. Camel's Hump	Huntington Center, VT	4.8	Strenuous
40. Mount Mansfield	Underhill Center, VT	5.6	Strenuous
41. Table Rock	Grafton Notch State Park, ME	2.4	Easy to Moderate
42. Cadillac Mountain	Bar Harbor, ME	4.4	Moderate
43. The Bubbles	Bar Harbor, ME	1.6	Moderate
44. Pleasant Mountain	Bridgton, ME	5.8	Moderate
45. Tumbledown Pond	Roxbury, ME	3	Moderate
46. Old Speck	Graton Notch State Park, ME	7.6	Strenuous
47. Blueberry and Speckled Mountains	Gilead, ME	8.6	Moderate to Strenuous
48. South Turner Mountain	Baxter State Park, ME	4	Moderate to Strenuous
49. The Bigelows	Carrabassett Valley, ME	13.5	Strenuous
50. Mount Katahdin	Baxter State Park, ME	10.4	Very Strenuous

TIME	ELEVATION GAIN (feet)	COMMENTS
5 hours	2250	Scale the rocky cone
7 hours	2750	Lofty look at Mount Washington Valley
5 hours	2750	4,000-footer with big summit cairns
8 hours	3900	Classic White Mountains ridge
9 hours	3800	New England's mighty mountain
1½ hours	600	In-town delight for all generations
1½ hours	450	Unique chance to touch summer ice
1 hour	400	Fire tower ramble
2½ hours	715	Peer above lakes and into Canada
3 hours	740	Pretty waterfall and thought-provoking rock slide
5 hours	2400	Isolated Vermont landmark mountain
4 hours	2290	Scramble to dramatic overlook
4 hours	1900	Tower provides glimpse above ski trails
4 hours	2300	Dizzying panorama
4½ to 5 hours	2550	Vermont's highest
2 hours	900	Good family trek with scrambles to ledge
3 hours	1450	Where the mountains meet the sea
2 hours	550	Engaging Acadia National Park hike
4 hours	1800	Low-lying mountain above ponds, farms, and fields
3 hours	1500	Kind of a ledgy alpine beach area
6 to 6½ hours	2650	Brawny peak with observation tower
6 hours	2550	Wilderness White Mountain National Forest trek
4 hours	1700	Watch for moose
10 hours or multi-day	3600	Big, bad, and beautiful
9 to 10 hours	4200	Wicked remote, challenging, and awesome

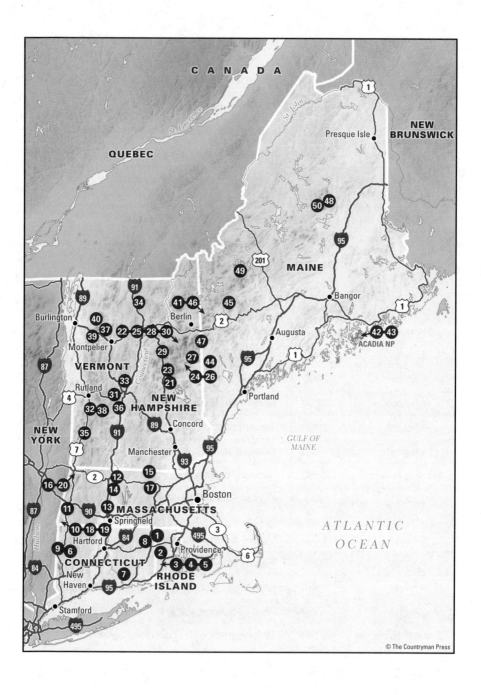

Contents

Introduction

New England is my adopted home, and it is on its trails I find beauty, challenges, peace, and camaraderie.

Some of the most eye-catching areas are off its bucolic roadways and on pathways over stoic mountains, along rocky ridges, through wonderful woods, and more.

I've hiked all over the region. Often hikes are the reason I travel. But I also hike when I'm traveling, planning ahead to do a hike as I'm heading between Point A and Point B.

I invite you to use these pages as a guide to a rich collection of hikes around the region with exhilarating vistas, lush forests, stunning peaks, and exquisite waterways in national forests, state parks, wilderness areas, and other preserved lands.

Each trip is rated by difficulty from easy to strenuous and comes with vivid descriptions that include detailed maps, photos, distances, and directions. Every hike, whether benign or rugged, starts and ends from the same trailhead. They range in length from an easy mile to a vigorous thirteen.

The guide contains trips for all levels of hikers and ages, from new trekkers to hiking enthusiasts looking for suggestions in parts of New England they might not have considered.

The hikes revolve around popular regional destinations for each state, and also, with the exception of Rhode Island (tiny Jerimoth Hill is just a leg-stretcher), include a trip to the highest peak in each state. Fledgling hikers can see their progress in attempting to reach those high points over every state.

Many hikes involve pieces of legendary trails like the Appalachian Trail and Long Trail.

There are ten hikes for each of the northern New England states and Massachusetts, while Connecticut and Rhode Island each have five. New Hampshire hikes are in the White Mountains and Lakes Region. Vermont hikes are generally in the southern and central Green Mountains, and Northeast Kingdom. Maine has pods in the western area (White Mountains, Carrabassett Valley), Baxter State Park, and Acadia National Park. In Massachusetts, the hikes are in central and western areas of the state, including the Berkshires, while Connecticut has hikes throughout the state, including the popular western side. There are western Rhode Island hikes too that could funnel into Connecticut, and Connecticut into Massachusetts.

Hikers tend to be territorial. Once they like a spot, say the White Mountains, it becomes their second home. I know all about it. The Whites are my home. It's easy to become a listaholic when it comes to hiking. I became one during the time I hiked the Appalachian Mountain Club's White Mountain Four Thousand Footers. But I've also come to embrace guidebooks. They are a list unto themselves, offering a selection of hikes to do while also allowing people to multitask as day trippers, overnighters, paddlers, bikers, and shoppers in places they've never visited.

New England draws hikers from all over the Northeast and Canada. On the trails, there are hikers from Boston, Hartford, New York, Portland, Providence, Manchester,

Burlington, and other urban areas. Canadians come south to hike the peaks, enjoying a land of cheap gas, tobacco, and alcohol.

Up and down the eastern seaboard, hikers are drawn to New England's hills. So please enjoy this regional sampler of hiking hits.

Perhaps we'll meet on the trail.

USING THIS BOOK

The 50 hikes in this book offer a variety of destinations, terrain, and scenery. Consider it a passport to the region, and only a piece (though a tasty piece) of what there is to hike in New England.

Each hike starts with an informational section that contains nuggets and news that not only give you particulars about the hike but also are helpful in terms of deciding if the hike is for you and what kind of time frame and terrain to expect.

The hike's difficulty is rated as easy, moderate, or strenuous. Up front, this is a very subjective method. But the terrain is noted, and characteristics like steepness, exposure, length of hike, and elevation gain are taken into consideration.

Time of hike is also a subjective measure. This is merely a suggestion. Hikers, depending on terrain, can often move about 2 miles per hour. Again, this is based on steepness, terrain, etc. What takes an hour for one person may take 90 minutes for another.

The elevation gain is a measurement between the hike's low and high points. This is a gauge to help you get a sense of the terrain.

The trails used in the hike are provided in the informational section too. This can be a helpful tool for those who might want to jot down the names or enter them into a phone instead of reaching into a pack for a book while on the trail.

Directions to the hikes are found here.

Please consider that some roads may be dirt, and the possibility exists that certain remote roadways may be closed in certain seasons.

Each hike also contains a map with identifying features like the trailhead, parking, etc. The US Geological Survey (USGS) quadrant generally covers the area. There is also an additional information source like a state park or national forest headquarters to use too.

BEFORE YOU GO

Planning and preparation are paramount, given the ever-changing weather and terrain in New England.

- Choose a hike that's good for everyone. Think weakest link in the chain, and gear the hike to that person.
- Check the weather before you go. Absolutely, positively a must. Warm and sunny at the trailhead can turn to cold, dark, and stormy higher up. Don't be afraid to turn back.
- Hike in daylight. Start the hike early enough and have a time frame. If need be, turn around before reaching the summit or destination. Be cognizant of the season, as hours of daylight are different throughout the year.

As simple as it sounds, have a backpack and be sure it contains these items:

- Water: General rule is two quarts per person, but take into consideration the weather and duration of the hike.
- Food: Always have some. Could be a snack, fruit, or nuts. If you're out for a while, pack a lunch too.
- Extra clothing: Rain and wind gear work wonders. So does a fleece pullover or vest. Hats and gloves too. The treks to New England's higher summits absolutely require it.

- Sunglasses and sunscreen: Protection is the name of the game, all year.
- Insect repellant: Same thing. Bugs are pesky.
- Knife (or multi-tool containing one): Invaluable.
- Waterproof matches and a lighter: And put those matches in something waterproof too.
- Light source: Flashlight is good, headlamp is better as it leaves hands free.
- First aid kit: With items like bandages, gauze, and moleskin. OTC painkillers are good.
- Map and compass: Know how to use them, as GPS and cellphones aren't always reliable in the mountains and hills.

BASIC HIKING SAFETY

Knowledge is key on the trails. The old-school Scouting mantra of being prepared still holds true today for every hiker, whether child or adult. Though hiking is a glorious way to get away from the grind and pressures of modern-day society, it doesn't mean your brain goes on vacation.

Quite the opposite.

It's time to think.

Just as skiers and snowboarders have a code telling them how to behave on the trails, so do hikers.

In New Hampshire, the New Hampshire Fish and Game Department—instrumental in the search and rescue (and recovery) of hikers in the Granite State—and the White Mountain National Forest teamed up to design a mountain safety education program called hikeSafe.

The program, unveiled in May 2003, focuses on hiker safety for day hikers, backpackers, group leaders, summer camps, and campground users.

The campaign is a valuable aid for hikers, whether they are hitting the trails in the White Mountains of New Hampshire or in the hills of Rhode Island.

The organizations came up with the Hiker Responsibility Code, similar to the Skier's Responsibility Code.

The principles are geared to create self-aware hikers recognizing that things can go wrong on the trails.

The Code says:

You are responsible for yourself, so be prepared:

1. With knowledge and gear. Become self-reliant by learning about the terrain, conditions, local weather, and your equipment before you start.
2. To leave your plans. Tell someone where you are going, the trails you are hiking, when you will return, and your emergency plans.
3. To stay together. When you start as a group, hike as a group, end as a group. Pace your hike to the slowest person.
4. To turn back. Weather changes quickly in the mountains. Fatigue and unexpected conditions can also affect your hike. Know your limitations and when to postpone your hike. The mountains will be there another day.
5. For emergencies. Even if you are headed out for just an hour, an injury, severe weather, or a wrong turn could become life threatening. Don't assume you will be rescued; know how to rescue yourself.
6. To share the hiker code with others.

MORE SAFETY SUGGESTIONS

There are many hazards along the trail, from possible wildlife encounters to slipping on a rock. But the number one potential pitfall is arguably the weather. New England's weather is notorious for change, so being safety-conscious tends to ensure a more pleasurable experience.

Lightning

"When thunder roars, head indoors" is a common slogan heard across the land. But that phrase isn't always practical for hikers in New England, a region where lightning storms are a fact of life year-round and certainly during spring through early fall.

Of course, the best advice is to know the day's forecast and chose a hike accordingly. Do not take a foreboding forecast lightly.

Also, forecasts aren't always spot-on. Keep an eye to the sky while in the outdoors to avoid being caught in any fast- or slow-moving storms.

Many hikes in this book are above treeline, with more exposure to severe elements. Be cognizant of the weather forecast, in particular the afternoon, as many storms come in during that time.

It's best to avoid water, open spaces, higher ground, and metal objects like fences and wires.

Hikers caught in a storm despite all good intentions should crouch down with feet together to reduce contact with the ground and try to stay at least 15 feet away from other people.

Hypothermia

Hypothermia is the cooling of the body core temperature because of heat loss. It can happen year-round, particularly on those days of rain and wind when the temperature is between 40 and 60 degrees.

The key is recognizing the symptoms.

Those in the search-and-rescue business call it the "umbles."

As moderate hypothermia overtakes someone, they start to mumble their speech. Then they start to grumble and whine a bit. They fumble and bumble, having trouble with things like backpack straps or zippers as they shiver and behave irrationally. Walking could lead to a stumble, like being intoxicated, and even a tumble.

The end result of these symptoms can be death.

Prevention is also key. To prevent heat loss, keep hands and head covered. Forget cotton. Dress in layers starting with wicking underwear. Drink plenty of water and eat lots of food to get those heat-generating calories. Take rest stops to avoid perspiration. Carry emergency gear, like a foam pad for sitting, a good insulated jacket or sleeping bag for warmth, and extra food and water.

If someone is exhibiting symptoms, get them warm and dry. Get them food and water. Get them moving.

NEW ENGLAND'S SEASONS

The region's weather changes abruptly with the season, and many storms have altered the mountain landscape. Also, each season has its own challenges, whether from nature or man.

Spring hiking

Spring is very shifty. It's often a time for all four seasons in a day. Higher-elevation trips may be more wintry.

And it's also time for that territorial wonder—mud season.

Mud season is one of those regional phenomena found in areas with harsh winters like New England. It generally comes between late winter and early spring, when dirt pathways from hiking trails to roads become muddied, rutted, and gloppy due to melting snow and rain.

Hiking often becomes unpleasant in the mud, and some dirt roads become challenging to travel before local road agents and crews apply their annual nips and tucks.

One school of thought calls for heading to hike in areas of southern New England where spring gets an early jump on drying up trails, and trails are also at a lower elevation. Winters can be milder than up north too.

Another camp calls for sticking to low-elevation trails everywhere.

Then there is Vermont's Green Mountain Club, the nonprofit organization that maintains the Long Trail system that includes the state-long footpath and its side trails.

The GMC reminds outdoor enthusiasts that mud-season hikers can trample fragile alpine terrain and exacerbate soil erosion, particularly at higher elevations where mud season trails are wet and squishy. The GMC, the Green Mountain National Forest, and the Vermont Department of Forests, Parks and Recreation advocate being responsible on the state's hiking trails during mud season up to Memorial Day weekend. They suggest lower-elevation trails, dirt roads, and recreation paths for early spring rambling. Plus, the state closes hiking trails on two of Vermont's highest peaks—Mount Mansfield and Camel's Hump—from mid-April to Memorial Day.

So choose mud-season hikes accordingly.

Summer hiking

Summer is time for the swarm—both people and insects. Many hikes, particularly on weekends and holidays, will be done in the company of others. Mosquitoes, black flies, and other insects are out as well. Be prepared with the proper repellent. It may help to avoid trails with boggy, wet areas.

Summer also means hazy, hot, and humid. Start hikes early on, drink lots of water, and be sure to wear sun protection, from lotions to hats and glasses.

Hiking in the fall

Hikers shouldn't miss fall's annual New England spectacle of color. The reds, yellows, and oranges of trees like maple, birch, and beech are ablaze. Place them against a brilliant blue sky and sprinkle in a touch of early snow at higher elevations to make for a splendid day in the outdoors.

But fall's brisk temperatures and air often filled with the smell of homey woodstoves also means hunters are out in season with firearms and bows.

Hikers should take a cue from the blaze orange–wearing hunters and add bright orange clothing to their fall hiking ensemble. The color is easy to spot. Vests, hats, and jackets all make it so that hikers—and hunters—can be seen through the trees.

Generally, these items don't cost that much and also offer peace of mind to those venturing into the woods. Also, it's a good idea to not wear colors like white that can resemble the quick flash of a deer tail.

Of course, there are those hikers who avoid going into the forest in autumn at all costs. It's always a choice. But—and it varies throughout New England—there are various lands where hunting is banned. There are states that also ban or limit hunting on Sunday (Connecticut, Massachusetts, and Maine).

Hikers concerned about being in the woods with hunters should also be aware of vehicles parked at trailheads and along roads, which signal there are hunters about. Also, hunters are often aware that hikers frequent certain areas and decide to do their hunting elsewhere. Remember, licensed hunters have taken a hunter-safety course. Taught in those classes is to be absolutely certain about your quarry and also what's beyond it.

Hunters also tend not to hunt at high elevations. The game they seek usually stay at lower elevations, so that's where hunters will be.

Hunting season varies across the region, with states having various regulations (or not) in terms of wearing blaze orange. For example, hikers in Rhode Island's State Management Areas are required to wear 200 square inches of solid daylight fluorescent orange during specific time periods.

So make the decision that's best for you.

Cold-weather hiking

As the temperatures plummet, thoughts for many turn to snow sports and sliding down slopes. Far too many people put hiking on the shelf. Don't. Hiking is a year-round adventure.

Every season employs the same mantra—be prepared. Cold-weather hiking has its own lofty rewards of spectacular landscapes, fewer fellow hikers on the trails, and no bugs. Extra preparation is involved, and expect to carry a heavier pack. As a four-season hiker, I've come across and experienced some pointers to make the experience more enjoyable and safe. Here are some things I've learned.

- Scale it back. Climbing a tall, stark mountain above treeline is an incredible undertaking, but so is hiking up a smaller peak or hill with vistas that can include the patchwork of farm, field, and forest. Instead of making the top the goal, choose another natural landmark like a pond. At lower elevations, welcoming ponds that invite summer swimming are often transformed by the cold into frozen deserts of white worthy of a look from shore or exploration on foot, only if conditions make it safe.
- Scale it back even more. Shorter days greet cold-weather hikers. Packing a flashlight is a must for any hiker, no matter the season. Be sure to include extra batteries. For those not accustomed to hiking after dark (it takes getting used to), go on shorter hikes to beat the clock mentally for impending darkness. That said, being well-equipped and going on a full-moon winter hike is amazing.
- Pay attention to your water bottle. The key is to prevent the water you rely on for hydration from freezing. One way to keep it warm and snug is putting it in an insulated carrier that covers the entire bottle. These can attach to a belt or pack for easy access. Consider taking some boiled water with you on that hike to enjoy its balmy qualities. Some hikers carry well-closed water bottles (warm ones too) on the inside of their jackets.
- Layers, layers, layers. The base layer is the one that wicks away the moisture. Build on that with garments that are made of wicking material like fleece. Don't overheat. That can lead to hypothermia. Garments and shells with underarm zippers are excellent ways to keep air circulating. Don't start out with a bulky parka. It's almost guaranteed to come off during the first labored stretch of trail. Save that for later. Don't be afraid to shed or add layers during the hike. Some hikers, knowing they'll warm up as the hike progresses, start out warm but light of layers.
- Carry more than one hat. You lose valuable body heat through your head, so keeping it covered is a way to stay warm. But perspiration knows no season and it's pretty easy to overheat even when the forest is covered in snow. Having one hat for while in motion and another warmer one for rest periods works wonders. An all-encompassing balaclava is appreciated on single-digit days. A neck gaiter worn on top of the head often provides relief for a hiker

in motion as perspiration rolls in, but it doesn't score many fashion points.

- Carry goggles. Toss those ski goggles in the pack. With greater surface area than sunglasses, they also offer greater protection and warmth. If it snows, you'll be glad you have them.
- Keep feet happy. Wear light, layered socks closest to your skin before putting on the warm ones. Carry along a light traction system for underfoot. If you hit icy spots, you'll feel like a mountain goat after putting it on.
- Unsure? Go on a guided hike. Novices looking to try winter hiking for the first time should consider going on a group hike with an outing club. Look for an introductory hike with short mileage. Seasoned leaders should help you get used to the extra gear and explain the nuances of exploring the dazzling landscape.

Stormy weather

New England's weather is legendary, and many devastating storms have blown through the region, resulting in the loss of life and property, and alteration of the landscape.

Though history is loaded with records of tragic hurricanes and such dating back to the seventeenth century and earlier, the region has seen quite a few memorable events recorded just under 100 years ago.

Perhaps the most well-known historic storm was the New England Hurricane of 1938 that is credited with killing more than 600 people. It is considered the region's worst of modern times and registered a peak gust of 186 miles per hour at the Blue Hill Observatory outside Boston before the anemometer broke.

Though not as well documented as hurricanes, the Ice Storm of 1998 played havoc with northern New England, northern New York, and southeastern Canada in early January of that year. The storm is reported to have caused more than $3 billion in damage. Nearly 40 people were killed. People lost power for weeks, and many roads were impassable for quite some time.

Fast-forward to August 28, 2011, when Tropical Storm Irene arrived in New England. Officials in places like the White Mountain National Forest (WMNF) in New Hampshire and Baxter State Park in Maine actually closed the woods to hikers during what is considered peak season.

According to the WMNF, the storm brought torrential rain that carried woody debris and sediment, rolled boulders downstream, carved out wider banks, and "jumped" stream banks to find new routes—often rushing down adjacent roads or trails, which caused extensive erosion. The debris caught up in that high water created jams and clogged culverts, and backed up behind bridges, causing bridges to fail, rivers to divert, and flooding in areas that are normally high and dry.

The rain caused extensive erosion. Roads and trails seemed to have just washed away, leaving behind gaping holes in the path. Erosion in rock staircases along trails loosened stones and created instability for hikers. Trail tread and road prisms slumped, and sinkholes appeared. Bridge abutments were exposed and undermined, leaving potentially unstable and unsafe crossings. Whole sections of roads and trails just gave way to the massive flow of water.

In 2012, Hurricane Sandy hit the New York and New Jersey areas hard, but it also touched southern New England, tearing up the Rhode Island and Connecticut coastlines while also dropping torrential rain inland and farther north.

Keep in mind that storms impact the hiking trails people trek on.

UNCONVENTIONAL YET PRACTICAL HIKING TIPS

Aside from hiking safely and smartly, there are also ways to make hiking easier, more comfortable, and prudent. Hints and tips come with the territory. Here are some unconventional yet practical suggestions:

- Wrap long pieces of duct tape around your hiking poles (that is, if you use aluminum trekking poles). Duct tape, that indispensable adhesive, comes in handy in the woods for quick fixes and to avoid hot spots on your feet becoming blisters. There are those who carry a roll of duct tape with them, but then there are the weight and room issues that come with that. Affixing the tape to hiking poles means it's around if you need it. Speaking of poles, though collapsible ones are wonderful, there's nothing like using your ski poles. Pick some up cheap at a yard sale.
- Throw small snacks with long shelf lives in a zippered compartment of your backpack and forget about them. The surplus food may come in handy down the road, and sometimes it's nice to surprise yourself with something you may have forgotten you had. Of course, once you find that food, be sure to check the expiration date.
- Grab samples when you can. Attend trade shows, hiking events, or competitions? Keep an eye out for samples that easily fit into your backpack. Sunscreen, deodorant, insect repellant, and more come in small packages, making them perfect for hiking. So do lotions from hotel rooms.
- Use large plastic trash bags as a liner. Often a trash bag inside a backpack is another layer of protection against rain. It's also a good idea to put sleeping bags in them during those overnights. Keep an extra one on hand too to use as a quick raincoat (pop your head and arms out) so you don't have to dig out that poncho that's been sitting unused in your pack for years.
- Inspect your first aid and emergency kits more than you think. Nothing is forever. Many gauzes that contain alcohol and hand wipes can dry out over time. Check those batteries too.
- Flavor that water. There's nothing like a cool, refreshing sip of water from a water bottle during a sweaty hike, but adding some flavor is a welcome respite at times. That goes even more for water that's treated with tablets during a hike, even with a second set of tablets claiming to mask the taste of the first. Add some zing. It'll perk you up.
- Trim those toenails before a hike. Seriously. You'll be glad you did, especially when traveling downhill.
- Consider pre-hike ibuprofen. Hikers of a certain age may appreciate a little anticipation along the trail. Well-timed ibuprofen can be of help for those descents and rock scrambles.
- Take extra shoelaces. Put them in your pack. Forget about them. One day those boot laces are going to break and you'll be glad you have a spare.
- Carry a bandanna. This swath of cloth is tremendously versatile. Use it as a towel or washcloth. Make it a cooling headband. It's a handkerchief, protection from sun, and even a strainer. Sometimes all during one trip!
- Linger longer. Though a hike isn't finished until returning to the trailhead, spend more time at those places that make hiking worthwhile—summits,

scenic ledges, waterfalls, rushing streams, etc. Refresh your feet by kicking off the boots and stripping those socks. Have a snack or lunch and enjoy the alfresco spot you've worked to reach.

- Start early. The early bird gets the solitude (and close parking at popular trailheads). There's something to be said for getting a start not long after sunrise. Of course, if you're up there early, that means you're probably heading down when most people are hiking up. Be ready to answer a lot of questions about the views and the often asked, "How much longer to the top?"
- Be supportive of children. It's nice to see kids out on the trails, especially those who actually want to be. Talk to them. Answer their questions. Encourage them. They're hiking's future and if they're on the trails, they're not on the couch exercising their thumbs.
- Turn off your cell phone unless you absolutely need to use it. No one who has busted their hump to get to the glorious summit away from life's routine wants to hear your insipid, self-absorbed conversation about where you are. Then again, turn on that smartphone to take photos, video, etc.
- If you're hiking in winter, turn your water bottle upside down in your pack. Water freezes from the top down. Think frozen pond or lake. This way, an inverted bottle means the top closest to your mouth will be ice-free. Really. Just be sure the top is screwed on securely.
- Have post-hike goodies. Your vehicle acts as a rolling closet and refrigerator at times. Use it for an après-hike treat. Keeping a wet washcloth on hand in a closed plastic bag works wonders for wiping away the grit and grime. Having

a spare set of clothes to change into is a plus. So is having additional footwear to air out those tired puppies. Keep some liquid refreshment in a cooler in your vehicle. Keep it cold with ice packs or by freezing an iced tea or the like in a plastic quart container, leaving about 2 inches for it to expand. The beverage will not only keep everything else cool but can also be consumed after it melts.

TRAIL CREWS

While hiking, consider the paths underfoot. Those trails are planned, constructed, and maintained. Dedicated paid and volunteer trail crews from clubs, organizations, agencies, stewards, and landowners are outside in all sorts of weather conditions rehabilitating, relocating, and building trails.

Trail crews field all sorts of tools and often camp a few miles from their ongoing project, carrying their gear, food, and water to and from the site during their backcountry commutes.

The work is hard, physical, and rewarding, with long and dirty days regardless of heat, rain, cold, and annoying insects. They put in stone steps, construct and repair bridges, install culverts for drainage, prevent erosion, maintain the lean-tos, repair signs, and much more.

Trail-crew jobs are often sought by college students for the summer, but there are also opportunities for volunteers to enroll in various programs for multi-day work experiences. Many hikers use National Trails Day to give back to the pursuit they love.

So if you see a trail crew, be sure to tell them thanks for their good work.

TICKS AND OTHER INSECTS

Ticks, those pesky arachnids, love the places hikers go. In particular, they enjoy brushy fields and wooded areas. They sustain themselves with blood from their hosts.

There are some precautions to take when hiking during the warm months when ticks are active. The Centers for Disease Control and Prevention suggests sticking to the center of the trails and away from high grasses. Using insect repellent with DEET on skin or Permethrin on clothing, boots, pants, socks, and even tents helps too.

After hiking, do a full-body check, in particular checking under arms, around the waist, inside the belly button, behind the knees, between the legs, around the waist, and in the hair. A buddy system is good. Wearing light clothing is also helpful in spotting ticks. Bathing or showering soon after hiking aids in finding ticks too.

Don't forget to check gear. Tumbling clothes in a dryer on high heat for about an hour kills ticks.

And if hiking with pets, check them too.

Ticks aren't the only insects that antagonize hikers. There are plenty of others, like mosquitoes, black flies, bees, and more. Allergy sufferers and others might consider long pants, hats, and repellent to ward off unpleasant encounters.

FRIENDLY AND NON-FRIENDLY PLANTS

Traipsing about on the trails leads hikers through a myriad of wildflowers and plants worthy of guides of their own. In season, there are the three-petaled trilliums, white-flowered bunchberries, rare alpine dwarf cinquefoil, and more. But some are more common than others, and they are not always friendly.

Take poison ivy, which can cause injury and irritation to those who touch it. Often found with three oval leaflets, the plant also has small white berries that are poisonous. Stinging nettle is another pest, covered with thin hairs that can cause pain and a rash when touched. Be aware, and if unsure about a plant, don't touch it.

But there are plenty of wonders too, like the lovely and delicate lady slipper, often found in boggy and pine-heavy areas. The long leafless stalk ends with a long flower, often pink or white.

Of course, there are the fantastic and fabulous rulers of the forest—ferns. Whether in shade or sun, ferns can be downright enchanting; enjoy trekking by them.

LOW-IMPACT HIKING

The member-driven Leave No Trace Center for Outdoor Ethics teaches people how to enjoy the outdoors responsibly. Their Seven Principles are words to live by while on the trails.

1. Plan Ahead and Prepare. Suggestions here include knowing weather, potential hazards, and who to contact for emergencies. Travel in small groups if possible.
2. Travel and Camp on Durable Surfaces. Basically, stick to the trail and only use established campsites.
3. Dispose of Waste Properly. If you pack it in, pack it out.
4. Leave What You Find. Don't take souvenirs like rocks and plants.
5. Minimize Campfire Impacts. Keep fires small and only use fire rings, etc.
6. Respect Wildlife. Leave them alone and don't feed them. Also control your pet if hiking together.
7. Be Considerate of Other Visitors. Be kind, keep your voice low, and yield to other trail users.

HIKING FEES

The days of free hiking are coming to an end. Expect to pay some sort of entrance fee for a state park in season or for some sort of recreation or parking pass in places like the White Mountain National Forest. Many state parks only charge fees during prime time. It's a good idea to carry some small bills for those entrance charges.

LONG-DISTANCE TRAILS

New England is home to a number of long-distance hiking trails. The most popular are the Appalachian Trail and Vermont's Long Trail.

The Appalachian Trail

New England hikers might be familiar with a storied footpath that extends from Maine to Georgia. The white-blazed, approximately 2,180-mile trail between Georgia's Springer Mountain and Maine's Mount Katahdin is one of the longest blazed footpaths in the world.

Commonly called the AT, it winds through 14 states and attracts between 2 and 3 million hikers a year, including some 2,000 who try to walk the entire length in a single journey.

The pathway is a national scenic trail under federal protection and overseen by the nonprofit Appalachian Trail Conservancy. Many clubs maintain the trail, largely through the help of thousands of volunteers who contribute more than 200,000 hours a year.

With the exception of Rhode Island, the AT winds through five New England states. Maine contains the most, with 281 miles, while Vermont is second at 150. New Hampshire hosts some 117 miles of the AT, while Massachusetts is home to about 90 miles. About 51 miles are in Connecticut.

Some of the AT's roughest terrain passes through New Hampshire and Maine, with hurdles like mountain weather coupled with steep and often slippery terrain loaded with rocks and roots. The northern terminus of the AT—Mount Katahdin—is one of the highlights, as is the piece that passes over Mount Washington in New Hampshire. Maine is considered to have some of the most remote terrain, where backpackers can spend days deep in the woods without crossing any roads or being able to restock their supplies. Vermont's Long Trail, a footpath that extends from top to bottom along the Green Mountain State, also incorporates the AT.

Southern New England sections are often attractive to hikers in Boston and New York City, as the drive to the trailheads is relatively undemanding. The trail passes through the Berkshires of western Massachusetts and also through many stony river valleys. Though not as strenuous as its northern counterpart, the trail still offers challenging sections in the Bay State and Connecticut's northwestern corner.

While hiking in New England, it's possible to come across people walking the entire AT in a continuous journey. These are called "thru-hikers." They often have wonderful tales to tell, but also, especially when they reach New England, develop a certain aroma that comes from being months on the trail.

There are hikers who tackle segments of the entire trail over many years. They're called "section-hikers." Then there are "flip-floppers," who thru-hike the whole AT in sporadic pieces, largely due to inclement weather, terrain, crowds, and other matters.

The Appalachian Trail Conservancy (ATC) says 1 in 4 hikers attempting a thru-hike complete the journey. Most thru-hikers take to the trail in spring, beginning in Georgia, and finish in Maine some six months later.

Thru-hikers tend to burn about 6,000 calories a day, and are grateful to have a meal other than ramen noodles. Strangers along the way who help thru-hikers with food, lodging, and transportation are often called "trail angels." Thru-hikers leave their real names behind and adopt nicknames during the trek.

Along the way hikers might spot moose, the largest animal on the trail, generally from Massachusetts north. White-tailed deer are found along almost the whole way. Black bears have been noted too. But chipmunks, rabbits, squirrels, and other small animals are more common.

The AT is rooted in New England thanks to Harvard-educated Benton MacKaye, a Massachusetts regional planner and forester. In 1921, he published an article in the *Journal of the American Institute of Architects* lauding a continuous wilderness trail so people living in the city could recreate and get back to nature. MacKaye wrote that the Appalachian range—mountains that stretch from Alabama to Canada's province of New Brunswick—along the Eastern Seaboard are located among the "most densely populated portions of the United States." He continued, "The skyline along the top of the main divides and ridges of the Appalachians would overlook a mighty part of the nation's activities. The rugged lands of this skyline would form a camping base strategic in the country's work and play."

The idea had wings and was quickly welcomed by the outdoor community. Some 16 years later, the full trail was completed August 14, 1937. But MacKaye didn't do this single-handedly. There were a couple of other crucial players. The first was Connecticut's Judge Arthur Perkins. He helped found the Appalachian Trail Conference (now the Appalachian Trail Conservancy) in 1925 and later became its acting chairman. Perkins was succeeded by Myron H. Avery of Maine, who stayed on for seven terms.

Time marched on and in October 1968, the AT became a national scenic trail under the National Trails System Act. The National Park Service delegated the Appalachian Trail Conference to manage the entire trail in 1984.

On August 14, 2012, the 75th anniversary of the trail's completion was celebrated.

The ATC headquarters is located in Harpers Ferry, West Virginia. The mailing address is 799 Washington Street, PO Box 807, Harpers Ferry, WV 25425-0807. Phone is 304-535-6331. E-mail is info@appalachiantrail.org. The website is www.appalachiantrail.org.

The Long Trail

The Long Trail in Vermont is a 273-mile footpath following the major ridgeline of the Green Mountains from the Massachusetts border in the south to Canada to the north. The white-blazed pathway is called Vermont's "footpath in the wilderness" and is older than the Appalachian Trail.

The trail—on both private and public lands—through the heart of Vermont extends over the state's highest peaks and comes together with the AT for some 100 miles in the southern portion of the region. The two trails coincide from the Massachusetts border to Killington, where the AT then splits for New Hampshire and Maine.

The pathway is considered the oldest long-distance trail in the country and was constructed by the Green Mountain Club between 1910 and 1930 over and along rough mountains, muddy bogs, hardwood forests, unspoiled streams, and sparkling ponds. Along the way are about 70 primitive shelters. There are also more than 200 miles of blue-blazed side trails.

The trail was formulated by GMC founder James P. Taylor, the principal at Vermont Academy, where he created a mountain club that was later renamed the Green Mountain Club in 1909.

According to the GMC, he told some 23 people about his idea at a March 11, 1910,

Hikers may find themselves coming across black bears in the woods.

meeting in Burlington, and work soon began on Mount Mansfield and Camel's Hump. In just 10 years, more than 200 miles of trails were built.

In 1921—before the trail was finished—the club published the 55-page *Long Trail Guidebook*, which cost 55 cents.

It had some suggestions that appear dated and even humorous now. For example, women were told not to wear skirts, but rather riding breeches.

"No person should attempt to tramp The Trail without a light axe, and a good compass," the book advised. "Even women should take at least a belt-hatchet; fuel must be replaced as used with good fuel and not easily obtained rotten wood or none at all."

Other tips included: "A large bandanna neckerchief is useful as protection against sunburn and almost essential in fly time (June 1 to July 15). Canvas gloves give protection to tender hands while chopping or cooking, and weigh little. Flannel shirts should have pockets, and collar and long sleeves are essential in fly-time."

For two men out on the trail for two weeks, it was suggested they carry 10 pounds of flour, 5 pounds of bacon, an ounce of cinnamon, 1 can of instant cocoa, 4 pounds of cornmeal, a half ounce of pepper, a loaf of bread, and 9 pounds of sugar, along with raisins, chocolate, cheese, rice, butter, cans of salmon, and more. Modern backpackers have nothing to complain about!

When the trail was finished in 1930, the club held a party and lit flares on summits along the spine of the Green Mountains.

A hiker completing the entire trail is called an End-to-Ender. More than 3,000 hikers have done it, with an average time between 26 and 30 days. Late summer and early fall are good times to go to avoid the masses, nuisance insects, and heat, but many only have time during summer's peak periods.

Sound like fun? Contact the Green Mountain Club, 4711 Waterbury-Stowe Road, Waterbury, VT 05677. Phone is 802-244-7037; e-mail is gmc@greenmountain club.org; website is www.greenmountain club.org.

ANIMALS

You may not see them, but animals see you. You are also likely to hear them before you see them.

Black Bear

The stocky and powerful black bear may appear large to a hiker on the trail, but it is the smallest North American bear. An adult male is called a boar, while females are sows. With a glossy black coat with some brown and a tan muzzle, black bears have front feet that are smaller than the back and walk on the soles of their feet, just like us. Some bears sport a blaze, a small white patch on their chest. They have five toes with claws on each foot.

Boars, which can weigh a couple hundred pounds, are larger than sows. Sows have cubs that become yearlings.

Black bears breed in summer, which causes males to travel through the forest in search of a mate. They are not monogamous, and males may propagate more than once.

The young are born in a den in winter, typically January or February, and in litters of between one and four. The cubs stay with the female through the next winter and then go on their own that spring.

Bears like large wooded areas with an assortment of wetlands, thick vegetation, and an array of food sources from berries to beechnuts.

When natural food is scarce in the forest, they seek other sources, like garbage. That's where hikers come in. Never feed a bear, and keep a clean site if camping.

Black bears, like all wild animals, are unpredictable. If you see a bear, view it from a distance. Let the bear know you're there by talking, singing, or clapping. Get too close and the bear may do something of a bluff charge that starts with a slap on the ground or a chomping of the teeth to get you farther away. If that happens, maintain eye contact, talk to the bear in a low, calm voice, and slowly back away. Don't run or turn your back. A bear can outrun and outclimb you. If attacked, fight back.

If you see a cub, mom may be about. Get out of the neighborhood.

Hikers may also find themselves camping in bear country. To protect against an encounter, keep a clean campsite, don't put food scraps in a campfire, and keep food in a closed vehicle or hang it in a bag at least 10 feet off the ground and away from any limbs that may support a bear.

Moose

Moose are impressive. The king of New England forests, an adult male can weigh upward of a thousand pounds. The nearsighted mammal relies instead on hearing and smell. With long slender legs, they are able to jump over obstacles such as downed trees in the woods. With their sharp incisors, they're able to strip bark from trees and also eat leaves, buds, and twigs. They also forage in wetlands for sodium-rich aquatic plants, particularly in spring and summer.

Bulls (males) and cows (females) have different-colored coats that vary from tan to a black-brown. Males have something of a black or dark brown face, while females are light brown. A white patch under the tail is the sign of a female. They both have a flap of skin under their necks called a bell, which is larger on bulls than cows.

Moose enjoy aquatic vegetation.

Bulls have antlers, which they shed every year. Antlers start to bud in spring and are fully grown by the end of summer, when the velvet is shed by scraping against trees.

Moose rut, or breed, in the fall. That's when bulls can go head-to-head in sparring matches to win over a prospective cow.

After about eight months, cows give birth to calves, sometimes in pairs. They grow quickly and stay with the female for about a year.

Keep lots of space between you and any moose you might spot while hiking. They're quicker than you might think, and of course, the cows are protective of their young. A bull male in rut is extremely erratic.

Though seeing a moose on the trail can be exciting, there are also chances of seeing moose along the road while driving to a trailhead. In New Hampshire there are even BRAKE FOR MOOSE signs in certain moose-dense locations. It's estimated that nearly 250 moose are killed on Granite State roads. They can do serious injury to the motorist, the vehicle, and themselves. Most collisions happen at dawn or dusk, so be alert. Try not to drive more than 55 miles per hour. Scan the roadways. Don't expect moose to stop when they see you. If necessary, stop the car and wait.

Moose are big, but they're hard to see at night. Most moose collisions happen between April and November. But moose also like salt used in winter road management, so be aware.

White-tailed deer

White-tailed deer are probably the most angelic and graceful animals that hikers may spot from the trails in New England. Easily spooked, they prance and dance in their escape from intruders, with their white tails the last thing you'll see as they seek cover.

They also swim and run well, with speeds approaching 40 miles per hour.

Often seen at dawn and dusk, deer like to frequent the edge of forest and field, eating grasses in spring and summer, acorns and apples in fall, and buds and twigs in winter.

The males (bucks) are the ones with the antlers. Females (does) generally don't have them but there are exceptions. The antlers are shed annually, they begin to grow in April or May. Like moose antlers, they are covered in that soft, sensitive tissue called velvet. Deer scrape the velvet off in anticipation of the rut.

Deer collisions are also a concern for hikers en route to the trailhead. Scan the roads, be alert at dusk and dawn, and don't speed.

Chipmunks

They are pudgy, lively, and quick, but chipmunks are more than city-park dwellers. They're out in the forest, digging burrows to live in, complete with chambers and tunnels. The little mammals feed on nuts, insects, seeds, berries, and more.

But chipmunks are also sentries in the forest. You may hear them before you see them because they have already spotted you. When that happens, they unleash a shrill chirp that sounds something like a bird. The vocalization is also used by females as a mating call.

Rhode Island

Introducing Rhode Island

Rhode Island may be the smallest state in the nation, and its highest point at Jerimoth Hill is a scant 812 feet above sea level, but it does have a wide array of trails for hikers and others ensconced in the joys of outdoor recreation. Rhode Island is the Ocean State, but hikes here are in the wooded and rolling western side of the state, away from the rocky coast. To be sure, if mountains are the goal, it's best to look north and west to the five other New England states.

Rhode Island offers relatively easy hikes. The acres along the Connecticut and Massachusetts borders have a wealth of state parks, bird sanctuaries, and forest management areas. The state hosts two stellar public land areas. In the northwest is the George Washington Management Area and in the southwest is Arcadia Management Area. Both hold a surprising number of trails and woods roads for exploring.

Another plus for the tiny state is its mild winters, particularly compared to other states in the region. While skiers and snowshoers take to the wintry slopes and trails in other states, hikers can continue to walk the woods in winter. But also be cognizant in late fall and early winter during hunting season that blaze orange is required in some areas.

1

Walkabout Trail

Difficulty: Easy to Moderate

Time: 1 to 5 hours, depending on distance

Distance (round trip): 2, 6, or 8 miles

Elevation gain: 200 feet

Trails: Walkabout Trail

Map: USGS Thompson, CT

Trailhead GPS coordinates: N41° 55.42' W71° 45.46'

You have to love those Aussies. There's a powerful tradition dating back to the indigenous Aboriginal culture where people would go on a focused journey to make connections with the land, their spiritual side, and ancestors. They called this concept "walkabout."

Fast-forward to the modern age and walkabout has come to mean taking a holiday, or vacation in North American parlance, and leaving the pressures of daily life behind. Many young Australians might take a break after high school or college and go on an extended journey, calling it a walkabout. Those North Americans of a certain age might equate it with backpacking through Europe after college graduation.

Thank the Australians for Rhode Island's Walkabout Trail. In 1965, a crew of more than 300 Australian sailors were waiting for more than a month for their ship, the HMAS *Perth*, to be ready for their trip home. The Division of Forestry was developing the nearly 3,500-acre George Washington Management Area in the state's northwest corner on the Connecticut border, teeming with waterfowl, gray squirrels, rabbits, deer, and other mammals. The Aussies, with time on their hands, were looking for something to do. The state then asked them to help build trails in the forest. The Aussies agreed, and the Walkabout Trail, a testament to Down Under tradition and eager idle hands, was born.

The easy-to-follow Walkabout Trail is a wonderful way to ease into hiking, with its three loop options of 2, 6, and 8 miles in length. The terrain is relatively flat but rocky

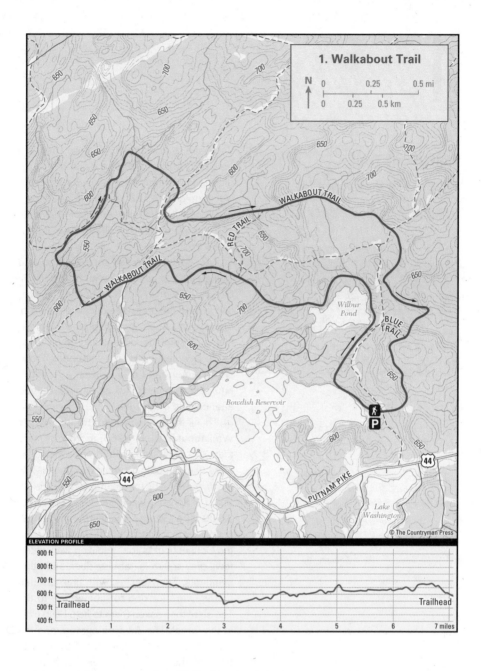

1. Walkabout Trail

ELEVATION PROFILE

at times, and there are some small hills. Plus, depending on the season, there can be wet and muddy sections.

But there is much to see along the way of the interconnected routes through wetlands with bridges, scattered boulders, busy wildlife, hemlock, stands of birch, marshy areas, possible beaver activity, and Bowdish

Reservoir, where those Aussie navy men did some swimming following their toiling in the woods.

Though the loop is largely used by hikers, expect to share it at times with trail runners and mountain bikers too. In winter, snowshoers and cross-country skiers ply the trails.

Portions of the trail are part of the state's North-South Trail, a 75-mile trail that spans the state between Charlestown on the coast to Burrillville by the Massachusetts border. The trail showcases the bucolic nature of Rhode Island through its forests, hills, beaches, and farms.

The trailhead is in the George Washington Memorial Camping Area, a 100-acre enclave with the sandy beach at Bowdish Reservoir that makes for fine swimming, boating, and fishing.

Bluntly, all you need to do is pick a distance and follow the color. Blue is 2 miles, red is 6 miles, and orange is 8 miles. The beauty is that you can plan for orange and bail out at red or blue if you don't have it in you.

HOW TO GET THERE

From the Connecticut border, travel I-395 to Exit 97 and drive about 7 miles on Route 44 traveling west. Turn left at sign for camping area and continue in a short distance to the park office.

From Providence, it's about 25 miles. Take Route 6 west to Route 295 going north to Route 44 heading west. Travel about 13.5 miles to the campground entrance on the right.

The trailhead is in the George Washington Memorial Camping Area (part of the George Washington Management Area), 2185 Putnam Pike, Chepachet, RI 02814; phone, seasonal: 401-568-6700 (camping), 401-568-2085 (management area); web: www.riparks.com. Fees.

Australians constructed Rhode Island's Walkabout Trail.

THE TRAIL

The loops begin by a large boulder with a plaque that tells briefly the Aussies' trail tale: THE WALKABOUT TRAIL NAMED AND CONSTRUCTED BY THE PERSONNEL OF HER MAJESTY'S AUSTRALIAN SHIP PERTH DURING "OPERATION BLACK SWAN" JUNE 1965.

The loop (8 miles as described here), done in a clockwise direction, dances along the eastern shore of the reservoir with trail markings blazed in all three colors. The trail eventually moves away from the glistening waters through some pines and mountain laurel, and at about .6 mile, those wishing to make the 2-mile circuit will stay on the blue-marked trail to the right, which goes to a picnic area and passes by camping. Continue to follow the red and orange markers as the trail slopes down to the edges of Wilbur Pond with its perch, trout, and bass. Scout for possible beaver activity along the pond.

The path leaves some wet areas for higher and oft drier ground, narrowing at times. At about 3.5 miles, near the top of a hill, the red trail materializes for those wanting to make the 6-mile circuit. Stay on the

The Walkabout Trail skirts the shores of Bowdish Reservoir.

orange trail as it begins a pleasant jaunt with several dirt-road crossings, bridges, hemlock, and mountain laurel in season.

The trail crosses the Center Trail, passes by a gate, and widens before heading over a bridge midway through the hike by the Pulaski Memorial State Forest. Follow along the stream before ambling upward and eventually hugging the shore of a swampy pond. The trail leaves the pond, heading up, and reconnects with the red trail for a short climb. Then it dips down to an often wet area, passage made easier by logs. Soon enough, the bands of colors are joined together as blue enters for a merry march of about a mile back to the trailhead.

2

George B. Parker Woodland

Difficulty: Moderate (Strenuous for some)

Time: 4 hours

Distance (round trip): 7 miles

Elevation gain: 200 feet

Trails: Paul Cook Memorial Trail, Foster Trail, Milton A. Gowdey Memorial Trail

Map: USGS Coventry, RI

Trailhead GPS coordinates:
N41° 43.02' W71° 41.89'

Cairns are an integral part of the hiking experience. The piles of intricately balanced stones are used for navigation along the trails, particularly in the mountains. Generally used in places where there are no trees, cairns help hikers travel through rain, snow, fog, and cloud.

But the stones are also magical, often works of art in their sizes, shapes, and order. One such place to find an enclave of weathered cairns is among the old-growth forest, brooks, hills, natural and manmade notable landmarks, fields, and countless birds of the 860-acre George B. Parker Woodland in Coventry. The Audubon of Rhode Island property is easy to get around, with its well-signed orange, blue, and yellow trails (some former carriage roads) over the oxbow-like 7 miles of trails. There are some rules that come with hiking the property, so heed them for the good of everyone. No dogs or horses are allowed. There's no picnicking. Don't take the rocks or plants. No hunting is allowed, so during Rhode Island's days of mandatory blaze orange in certain public places, this is a good spot to bring the family, snap photos, watch birds, learn a bit about the natural world and early settlers, and burn calories.

Hikers can certainly do less than the 7 miles of the entire network, and hike in either direction. This hike follows the trails clockwise (saving those crafty cairns for last), but creativity seems to be alive and well in the woods here, so mix it up if it suits you.

And don't think these are all easy trails. There are hills and some uneven terrain underfoot.

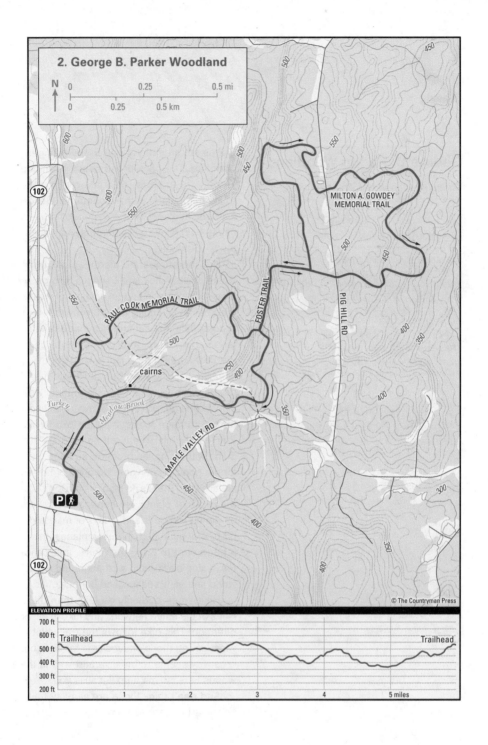

2. George B. Parker Woodland

N

0   0.25   0.5 mi

0   0.25   0.5 km

MILTON A. GOWDEY
MEMORIAL TRAIL

PAUL COOK MEMORIAL TRAIL

FOSTER TRAIL

PIG HILL RD

cairns

Turkey Meadow Brook

MAPLE VALLEY RD

102

102

600

550

500

450

550

500

450

500

550

500

450

450

500

400

350

350

400

400

400

450

500

400

350

300

350

400

© The Countryman Press

ELEVATION PROFILE

700 ft
600 ft Trailhead   Trailhead
500 ft
400 ft
300 ft
200 ft

1   2   3   4   5 miles

HOW TO GET THERE

From Providence, travel on I-95 south to Exit 5B and travel Route 102 going north for about 10 miles. Make a right going east on Maple Valley Road (look for Waterman Hill Road on the left). Travel about 0.1 mile and turn left by sign for the property. If that lot is full or the gate is closed, there is another parking area farther in, about 0.3 mile.

The George B. Parker Woodland property, 1670 Maple Valley Road, Coventry, RI 02827; phone: 401-295-8283; web: www .asri.org. The property is open year-round.

THE TRAIL

The ramble begins by an informational kiosk and fence. Follow the orange blazes north into the forest (keeping an eye out for a bird box on the left) where a signboard with a map waits. Continue on the trail as a stone wall comes into view. Walk by ferns and over a boardwalk. Eventually, cross over a wooden bridge spanning the Turkey Meadow Brook. Then come to a junction with the blue-marked Paul Cook Memorial Trail at about 0.5 mile. Turn left and enjoy the civilized stroll with stone walls adding to the regal atmosphere. The trail crosses the narrow Biscuit Hill Road at about 1 mile with its farmhouse foundation dating back to the mid-eighteenth century.

The trail ascends and descends some as it goes along rocky outcroppings, crosses a road, and finds its way to the intersection at about 2 miles with yellow-blazed Foster Trail. (For those hikers who feel they can't make it, this is a bailout point by turning right on Foster, and then following Biscuit Hill Road to the Paul Cook Memorial Trail and back to the nature center for about a 3-mile loop).

Stone cairns tower along a section of trail in the George B. Parker Woodland.

A boardwalk provides the way through the George B. Parker Woodland.

Continue the clockwise circuit by turning left on the rocky Foster Trail as it follows Pine Swamp Brook, soon crossing over it on a footbridge where it begins a climb to the blue-blazed Milton A. Gowdey Memorial Trail at some 2.5 miles.

The trail eases a bit and eventually catches up again to Pine Swamp Brook before rounding a bend and coming upon another old farm site with foundation and stone walls. Descend to Pig Hill Road at 3.5 miles, cross it, and in about 0.5 mile come upon the first of two stone quarry sites before crossing Pig Hill Road again. At 5 miles, bear left on the yellow-blazed Foster Trail again and follow it less than 0.5 mile before bearing left on the blue-blazed Paul Cook Memorial Trail again. The trail descends, crosses Biscuit Hill Road, and then follows along Turkey Meadow Brook before coming upon the cairns at over 6 miles into the journey. Tall, short, funky. Why are they there? The origins are iffy. Could be the Narragansett people, the Celts, or early colonial farmers. To early farmers, stones were a pain because they had to be removed before the fields could be plowed. But crafty as they were, the farmers used those stones to build rock walls.

Enjoy them and then continue on to the junction with the orange-blazed trail at 6.4 miles, turn left, and follow it to the parking area to complete the circuit.

3

Stepstone Falls

Difficulty: Easy

Time: 2 hours

Distance (round trip): 3.4 miles

Elevation gain: 150 feet

Trails: Ben Utter Trail, River Trail

Map: USGS Hope Valley, RI

Trailhead GPS coordinates:
N41° 35.88' W71° 44.76'

In a state with a high point of only 812 feet at small Jerimoth Hill, it shouldn't come as a surprise that its highest waterfall plunges a scant 3 feet. But Stepstone Falls in West Greenwich does just that.

The falls are by no means massive. Instead they are a pleasant diversion, a wide little cascade in the Falls River with its ledges in the peaceful woods. But the tiny falls are part of a much bigger place, one of the most popular recreation areas in Rhode Island—Arcadia Management Area. The nearly 14,000 protected acres in the western part of the state along the Connecticut border is the Ocean State's largest recreation area. The outdoor playground in West Greenwich, Hopkinton, Exeter, and Richmond is a place to hike, mountain bike, fish, boat, and ride horses. So be aware that others will be playing as well. Not only are there hiking trails, but lots of dirt and gravel roads too. The area is also open to hunting, so plan accordingly during the late fall.

Though it's possible to visit the falls without hiking, the trip along the Ben Utter Trail is a delightful woods ramble. The trail is named after a man largely known for promoting hiking in flat Rhode Island. By day George Benjamin Utter was a newspaperman, editor of a daily paper that served Rhode Island and Connecticut. But he loved the outdoors and hiking. According to the Appalachian Mountain Club, he was a member of the original trail committee of the Narragansett chapter of the AMC and was a staunch supporter of not only trails but also their maintenance and blazing. Utter helped develop AMC trails

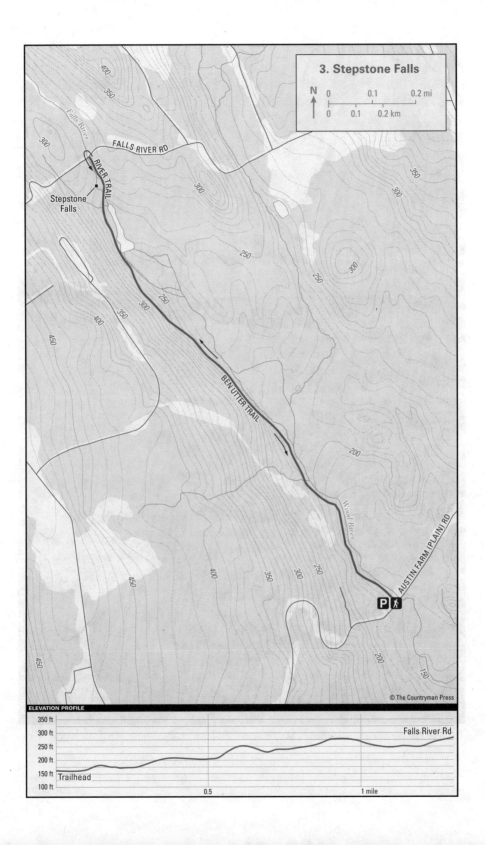

3. Stepstone Falls

N

| 0 | | 0.1 | | 0.2 mi |
| 0 | | 0.1 | 0.2 km | |

Falls River

400

350

300

FALLS RIVER RD

RIVER TRAIL

Stepstone
Falls

300

250

300

350

300

350

250

250

300

250

200

BEN UTTER TRAIL

Wood River

450

400

350

300

250

200

450

400

350

300

250

200

AUSTIN FARM (PLAIN) RD

P 🚶

450

200

150

© The Countryman Press

ELEVATION PROFILE

350 ft			Falls River Rd
300 ft			
250 ft			
200 ft			
150 ft			
100 ft	Trailhead	0.5	1 mile

The trail follows along the peaceful Falls River.

Stepstone Falls are Rhode Island's highest waterfall.

in South County and was also instrumental in organizing Rhode Island Camps (Beach Pond Camps) for underprivileged kids.

HOW TO GET THERE

At the junction of Routes 165 and 3 in Exeter, travel west on Route 165 for about 5.5 miles and turn right on Escoheag Hill Road. In about 1 mile, turn right on dirt Austin Farm Road and go about 2 miles to a small parking area by a bridge over the Falls River. Austin Farm Road is a seasonal road.

The trails are in the Arcadia Management Area. Arcadia Management Area Headquarters, 260 Arcadia Road, Hope Valley, RI 02823; phone: 401-539-2356; web: www .riparks.com.

THE TRAIL

Bring a picnic on this one and start by following the yellow-blazed trail from the parking area as it runs through something of a wooden fence and then along the west bank of the Falls River with its myriad of cascades.

The river flows into the Woods River, known for its fly-fishing opportunities for trout. The trail also happens to be part of Rhode Island's North-South Trail, a 75-mile trail (blazed in blue) that runs the length of the state from the Atlantic Ocean to the Massachusetts border.

Under the hardwoods and white pines, the narrow trail passes over a wooden bridge and eventually leads by the remains of an old gristmill and sawmill.

At about 1.3 miles, the Ben Utter Trail turns left to go through a camping area. Though it's possible to stay on the trail and reach the falls that way, bear right on the white-blazed River Trail, cross over the bridge, and make your way to Stepstone Falls. The roar of the falls makes them appear larger than they are. But that depends on how much rain has fallen.

The trail does continue on to Falls River Road. Best bet is to find a spot to relax, enjoy the serenity, and return along the same route.

4

Mount Tom Trail and Cliffs

Difficulty: Moderate	
Time: 2 hours	
Distance (round trip): 4.2 miles	
Elevation gain: 400 feet	
Trails: Mount Tom Trail	
Map: USGS Hope Valley, RI	
Trailhead GPS coordinates: N41° 34.38' W71° 43.30'	

Mount Tom and its cliffs are known as places to get a step above it all in Rhode Island. A scant 430 feet high, Mount Tom has a wooded summit. But there are ledge views at its cliffs that are bigger than itself. On a lighter note, there are those who like to have fun calling Mount Tom the state's only mountain. Of course, that is open for debate. Mountain or hill, the sometimes craggy and steep Mount Tom Trail is another favored romp in the Arcadia Management Area. Remember when traveling through the area during portions of fall and winter, being outfitted with blaze orange (consider a light vest) during hunting season is required. So plan accordingly.

The cliffs are the highlight of the hike. It's okay to turn around after visiting them and not continue on to the Mount Tom summit, which is little more than a place to say you've climbed the highest mountain in Rhode Island (but it's definitely not the highest point in the state. That's Jerimoth Hill at 812 feet).

Mount Tom doesn't just attract hikers. It is also home to rock climbers scaling its crags and slabs. They come to try their skill on climbs called Firewall, Main Wall, Halloween, and Overlook Roof.

HOW TO GET THERE

From I-95 and Exit 5A, travel east on Route 102 for about a mile before turning right on Route 3. Drive about 1.5 miles to a blinking traffic light and turn right on Route 165 (also called Ten Rod Road). Travel about 3.5 miles to Rhode Island Department of Environmental Management (RIDEM) parking

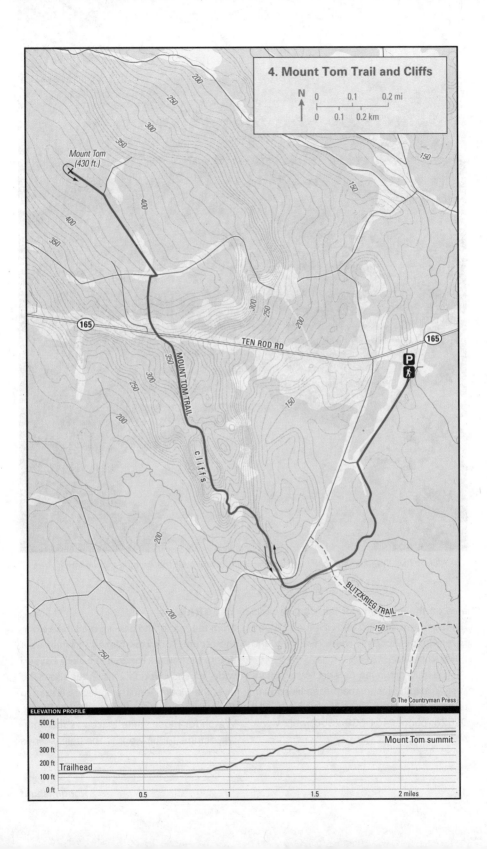

4. Mount Tom Trail and Cliffs

N

| 0 | 0.1 | 0.2 mi |
| 0 | 0.1 | 0.2 km |

200
250
300
350
400
400
350
Mount Tom
(430 ft.)
150
150
150
300
250
200

(165)   (165)

TEN ROD RD

P

350
MOUNT TOM TRAIL
300
250
200

c l i f f s

150

200

200

200

250

BLITZKRIEG TRAIL

150

250

© The Countryman Press

ELEVATION PROFILE

500 ft				
400 ft				Mount Tom summit
300 ft				
200 ft				
100 ft	Trailhead			
0 ft				
	0.5	1	1.5	2 miles

The Mount Tom Trail leads to cliffs and ledges with a view over the Arcadia Management Area.

area on the left. Look for the sign: Arcadia Management Area, Check Station, Wood River Canoe Access. There is a toilet and covered pavilion.

The trails are in the Arcadia Management Area. Arcadia Management Area Headquarters, 260 Arcadia Road, Hope Valley, RI 02823; phone: 401-539-2356; web: www.riparks.com.

THE TRAIL

From the rear of the parking area, hike along the Mount Tom Trail blazed in white as it enters the forest. The trail is initially flat and wide, an easy woods walk. After about 0.6 mile, the Mount Tom Trail crosses Blitzkrieg Trail, a dirt road, by flowing Parris Brook. Watch for those white blazes as the pathway returns to the woods. The trail ascends

The Mount Tom Trail follows Parris Brook for a spell.

comfortably and reaches the paved Mount Tom Road at about 0.9 mile and again returns to the forest. The road is a bridge over Parris Brook. You may want to linger for a bit.

The easy stuff is over, but it doesn't get terribly hard. The trail heads uphill and in a few minutes you start to reach the ledges and then cliffs on a ridge aptly named Mount Tom Cliffs with its far-reaching views above Arcadia.

Take a bit of time to poke around on the granite with its muted wooded vistas.

Pressing on, the trail begins its descent and eventually reaches Route 165 nearly 2 miles into the hike. After being in the woods, the road can be a bit startling. Be cautious when crossing and look for the white blazes on the other side as the trail becomes a tad rocky, but it soon reaches the tree-covered summit with its intersection of trail and woods road.

Say a word of congratulations to yourself and return the way you came, perhaps lingering a bit longer on Mount Tom Cliffs the second time there.

5

Breakheart Pond Loop

Difficulty: Moderate

Time: 3½ hours

Distance (round trip): 6.3 miles

Elevation gain: 240 feet

Trails: John B. Hudson Trail, Breakheart Trail, Shelter Trail

Map: USGS Hope Valley, RI

Trailhead GPS coordinates: N41° 35.27' W71° 42.55'

Oblong-shaped Breakheart Pond, with its seasonal lily pads, and diminutive 370-foot-high Penny Hill are two of the natural landmarks found along the rolling and unwinding terrain that comprises the well-utilized circuit in the Arcadia Management Area that bears the small pond's name.

Though one might be tempted to swim in the 33-acre pond, it's not allowed. Fishermen often ply its shores, which also contain a boat ramp. Certainly hikers looking for an easy stroll can just make the trip to the pond and back, but the longer odyssey is a nice romp, particularly during the less sweltering days of summer's high heat and humidity.

Penny Hill, though nothing more than a blip compared to large New England mountains, is largely ensconced by trees that mute the views. But those vistas are better in winter, and ledges along the way afford glimpses into Arcadia's forested domain.

As with other hikes in the area, there is a trail that is named after an Ocean State trailblazer—this one is John B. Hudson. He was also an early pioneer in Rhode Island hiking and a member of the Narragansett chapter of the Appalachian Mountain Club.

Be sure to stick to the route on this hike. There are often crisscrossing trails and roads. Having fun is good, but paying attention is required.

HOW TO GET THERE

From I-95 and Exit 5A, travel south on Route 102 for about a mile and turn right on Route 3. Drive some 1.5 miles to a light and turn right onto Ten Rod Road (also Route 165).

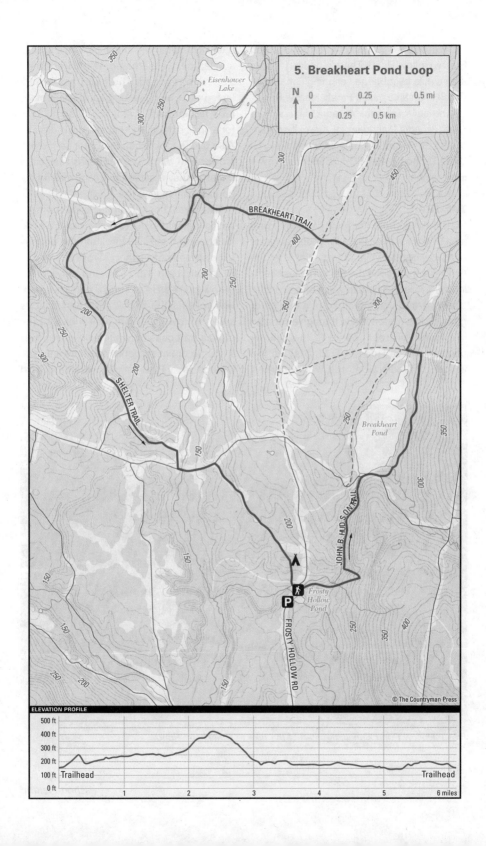

5. Breakheart Pond Loop

N

| 0 | 0.25 | 0.5 mi |
| 0 | 0.25 | 0.5 km |

Eisenhower Lake

BREAKHEART TRAIL

SHELTER TRAIL

Breakheart Pond

JOHN B. HUDSON TRAIL

Frosty Hollow Pond

P

FROSTY HOLLOW RD

© The Countryman Press

ELEVATION PROFILE

500 ft						
400 ft						
300 ft						
200 ft						
100 ft	Trailhead					Trailhead
0 ft						
	1	2	3	4	5	6 miles

Go west about 2.8 miles and turn right on Frosty Hollow Road. There's parking in less than a mile by a bridge spanning Breakheart Brook in an area called Frosty Hollow Pond.

The trails are in the Arcadia Management Area. Arcadia Management Area Headquarters, 260 Arcadia Road, Hope Valley, RI 02823; phone: 401-539-2356; web: www.riparks.com.

THE TRAIL
Start the hike from the Frosty Hollow Pond area (there's a dock there for young anglers) by following the white blazes east from the parking area beyond the gate and soon turning left by a set of double white blazes on the Shelter Trail. In about a third of a mile, after going by lots of stones and through a canopy-like tunnel of trees, come to the yellow-blazed John B. Hudson Trail. Stay on the yellow-marked trail as the white-marked

pathway is often wet and muddy. In less than a mile, the southern shores of Breakheart Pond are reached. The pond has broad-leafed trees along its edge and some pines a bit farther back. Enjoy the peacefulness for a spell if there isn't much activity around. Also take a look around and notice the fish ladder and dam. The ladder gives fish a boost as they resettle upstream, making it a popular fishing joint too.

The Breakheart Trail sticks to the right and follows along the east shore of the pond for about 0.5 mile. Before long the pond is but a shimmering memory. Cross Breakheart Brook at about 1.5 miles and stay on the yellow-blazed Breakheart Trail. The pathway follows the brook and then dances away, following under some lovely pine groves on occasion while also going over a couple of small brooks that flow into the Woods River—the sinister-sounding Acid

Frosty Hollow Pond signals the start of the hike to Breakheart Pond.

Serene Breakheart Pond is in Rhode Island's Arcadia Management Area.

Factory Brook and more benign Phillips Brook.

Though the white blazes of the Shelter Trail will come at an intersection near Penny Hill, stay on the Breakheart Trail for a spell and climb the hill's ledgy shoulder for that birds-eye view about 4.5 miles into the hike. Instead of continuing on, return down the hill on the Breakheart Trail and leave it for the Shelter Trail and pass what's left of an old camp. The trail eventually becomes one with Austin Farm Road (go left) temporarily before the white blazes go right from field into forest again. A small camping area is passed at about 6 miles and then it's about 0.3 mile back to the parking lot.

Introducing Connecticut

Connecticut—particularly the eastern side of it—often seems a place to pass through on an interstate while traveling to hike the bigger peaks in northern New England or zipping to a more urban experience in New York. There's a sense of sprawl and malls, thick population densities, and something of a frenetic rush woven into the lifestyle.

But there is much to take in upon exiting the speeding interstate for lazy country lanes going east and west through charming towns with smart greens and classic white-steepled churches, and acres of state forests and parks. The western side of Connecticut, particularly the northwestern corner of the Litchfield Hills, is prime hiking real estate as the Appalachian Trail winds its way through the Nutmeg State, passing over its highest peak, named Bear Mountain. It is a draw for hikers, towering above the Housatonic and Farmington Rivers.

That's not to say eastern Connecticut doesn't have anything to offer. It too has state parks, many off-the-beaten paths that allow for an easy escape in the woods and hills.

6

Mount Tom State Park Tower

Difficulty: Easy	
Time: 1 hour	
Distance (round trip): 1 mile	
Elevation gain: 400 feet	
Trails: Tower Trail	
Map: USGS New Preston, CT	
Trailhead GPS coordinates: N41° 41.72' W73° 16.81'	

About a mile with views that make you smile. That quickly sums up tiny Mount Tom in Litchfield's Mount Tom State Park. The small mountain contains a 34-foot-high tower that looks like a castle. One of the oldest state parks in Connecticut, dating back to 1915, the 232-acre protected area contains the spring-fed Mount Tom Pond, beach, and facilities, which turn the short hike into a refreshing outing complete with swim (thus taking the sting out of the seasonal entrance fee).

The family-friendly jaunt is a leg-stretcher for most hikers, while a first big little hill for others. Kids may find it an enjoyable challenge to the castle, while the occasional hiker might find a tad of the trail on the steep side. But it's a very popular and playful place with lots of creatures scurrying about the oaks, and birds enjoying the uplifting thermals overhead. Frankly it's a good place to introduce someone (or some family) to hiking.

The park is located in the northwest section of Connecticut known as the Litchfield Hills. The foothills of the Berkshires, with New York in the west and Massachusetts to the south, are an area of rolling hills, broad forests, bucolic villages, and the meandering Housatonic River.

Mount Tom—and there are many other Mount Toms in New England, including in Vermont, Massachusetts, and Rhode Island—stands a scant 1,291 feet high, but that's still taller than its Bay State counterpart some 125 feet lower. Talk about bragging rights.

Apparently the stone tower tucked in the

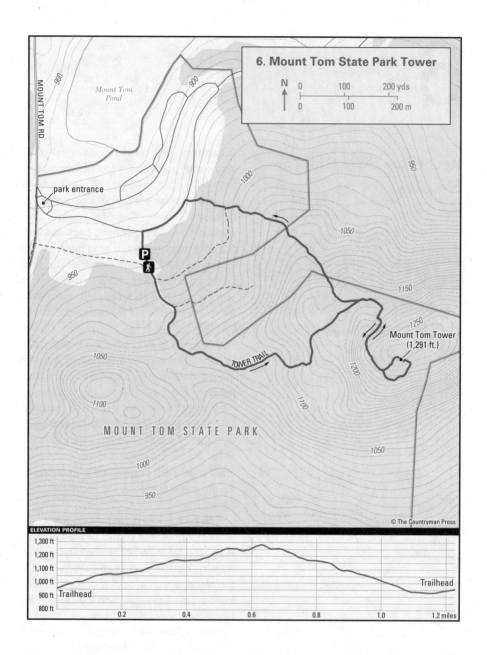

6. Mount Tom State Park Tower

N
0   100   200 yds
0   100   200 m

Mount Tom Pond

MOUNT TOM RD

900

900

950

park entrance

1000

1050

950

1150

1050

1250

Mount Tom Tower
(1,291 ft.)

TOWER TRAIL

1200

1100

1100

MOUNT TOM STATE PARK

1050

1000

950

© The Countryman Press

ELEVATION PROFILE

1,300 ft
1,200 ft
1,100 ft
1,000 ft
900 ft
800 ft

Trailhead

Trailhead

0.2   0.4   0.6   0.8   1.0   1.2 miles

state's northwest corner was preceded by a wooden one. This tower was built in 1921 with teams of horses hauling all the necessary supplies to the summit. Some four years later, a phone was installed. Now, it's a place to see a startling panorama of Litchfield and its surrounding counties and beyond, depending on the day.

HOW TO GET THERE

From Litchfield and the junction of Routes 202 and 63, travel west on Route 202 for about 6.3 miles. Turn left on Old Town Road for Mount Tom State Park and drive to the gatehouse. Once in the park, drive about 0.2 mile to Hillside Picnic Area and Tower Trail.

The trail is in Mount Tom State Park, Route 202, Litchfield, CT 06759; phone: 860-567-8870 (Memorial Day to Labor Day), 860-868-2592 (September to May); web: www.ct.gov/dep. Fees.

THE TRAIL

The counterclockwise loop starts from the parking area and follows the yellow-blazed Tower Trail. Though it's a simple hike, there is much to be culled from the geology along the way.

Stay with the yellow blazes and bear right as another trail soon branches off and the way winds by an area that looks like it's seen lots of erosion. Many of the rocks on the trail are made of blackish hornblende with streaks of white quartz. Some of the rocks sparkle nicely. That's because they're made of gneiss.

Gaze down upon Mount Tom Pond from the tower on Mount Tom.

The tower atop Mount Tom lifts hikers above the trees.

Soon there's another split with the trail, but just stick to the yellow, bearing left, and soon, left again. Along the way are many boulders that were left behind by glaciers as they melted. Some of the boulders (glacial erratics) have white rectangular specks of feldspar. Keep an eye out for weird shapes, like jumbles of rock piles and trees that have grown in, over, and around the rocks.

The trail curves right as it passes a large rock formation and begins the final stretch to the summit and the tower. There are some side trails by the summit that afford views.

But now it's time to climb the flights of stairs in the tower some 34 feet to be 1,325 feet above sea level. Be sure to take it easy for the last stretch onto the observation platform, as bumped heads can happen.

Once outside the tower, be cognizant of where the tower ends, particularly if you've got children with you.

The view is really outstanding. Look down to Mount Tom Pond. To the north is the state's highest peak, Bear Mountain, followed by peaks in Massachusetts like Mount Everett and Mount Race.

After ogling the countryside, descend the tower and follow the trail back to the section where it curved, this time bearing right for the way down. Just watch your footing as you descend, especially if the leaves are falling or it's wet.

The trail passes by a foundation and old stone chimney, all that remains of a Scouting camp from the 1900s. Then a picnic area comes into view, a signal for a return to pavement. Turn left on the park road to go back to the car, completing the kingly walk.

7

Devil's Hopyard State Park

Difficulty: Easy to Moderate (for some)

Time: 2 hours

Distance (round trip): 2.6 miles

Elevation gain: 300 feet

Trails: Vista Trail

Map: USGS Hamburg, CT

Trailhead GPS coordinates:
N41° 29.05' W72° 20.52'

Though the name might sound ominous, off-the-beaten-path Devil's Hopyard State Park in East Haddam is an exemplary locale for a family jaunt spanning the generations. With seasonal camping, picnic tables, a covered bridge, a scenic waterfall, and some 15 miles of color-coded trails, the 860-acre park formed in 1919 features the Vista Trail, which is generally an easy hike but does contain a stretch or two that might have un-seasoned hikers taking time along the way for a slight rest.

About the eastern Connecticut park's name: it's hard to pin down the exact ori-gin of it, though stories abound. One pop-ular tale tells of a local named Dibble who tended a garden filled with hops used for brewing beer. This plot came to be known as Dibble's Hopyard, but over time—remember the childhood game Telephone?—it became known as Devil's Hopyard.

Another account links the name with the potholes near Chapman Falls. The well-rounded holes in the stone were formed by downstream-moving rocks that were trapped in an eddy and starting spinning. The myste-rious markings perplexed early settlers, and their explanation was darker than a Dibble. They believed the devil passed through the falls and, angered by his tail getting wet, smoldered holes in the stone with his hooves.

The falls over the Scotland schist still stand today, plunging some 60 feet. The lovely cascades are created by the wild and scenic Eightmile River, a 150-mile-long watershed, and are one of the state's most popular. The falls once powered a couple

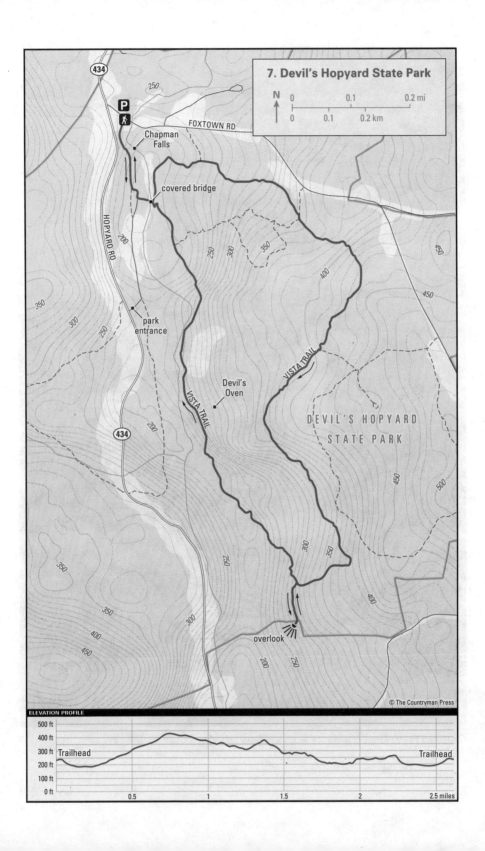

7. Devil's Hopyard State Park

N

| 0 | | 0.1 | | 0.2 mi |
| 0 | 0.1 | | 0.2 km | |

434

250

FOXTOWN RD

P

Chapman
Falls

covered bridge

HOPYARD RD

200

250

300

350

250

300

350

400

450

450

park
entrance

350

300

250

200

VISTA TRAIL

VISTA TRAIL

Devil's
Oven

DEVIL'S HOPYARD
STATE PARK

434

200

450

500

250

300

350

300

350

400

350

400

450

overlook

200

250

© The Countryman Press

ELEVATION PROFILE

500 ft				
400 ft				
300 ft	Trailhead			Trailhead
200 ft				
100 ft				
0 ft				
	0.5	1	1.5	2	2.5 miles

Chapman Falls plunge down rock ledges in Devil's Hopyard State Park.

of mills in the late 1800s. Though always picturesque, the waters really gush after a heavy rain and during spring runoff.

HOW TO GET THERE

From I-95 in Old Lyme, take Exit 70 and travel on Route 156 north for about 8.5 miles before turning right onto Route 82. Travel about 0.25 mile and turn left on Hopyard Road (Route 434) and go about 3.4 miles to right on Foxtown Road and parking area.

From I-395, take Exit 80 going west. Make at right on Route 82. Make a right on Hopyard Road and follow signs.

From Route 9, take Exit 7, make a left at the end of the ramp onto Route 82/154. Make a right at the first traffic light following Route 82 going east and follow signs.

The hike is in Devil's Hopyard State Park,

366 Hopyard Road, East Haddam, CT 06423; phone: 860-526-2336; web: www .ct.gov/deep/devilshopyard.

THE TRAIL

Start the hike by crossing Foxtown Road and traveling to the informational kiosk by Chapman Falls. Follow the board pathway by a stone tunnel underpass and bench. There's a spur trail on the left that goes down by the falls. Take it, and in no time be by the base of the falls with its roar, cool temps, and dancing spray glittering in the sun. When your time's up, return to the wide footpath and descend along the river to a picnic area and covered bridge. Cross the bridge to begin the orange-blazed Vista Trail, a loop of about 2.3 miles. Stick to the orange blazes to complete the loop.

Cross a covered bridge in Devil's Hopyard State Park.

After the bridge, turn left on the Vista Trail for the clockwise circuit. Follow the trail, which soon crosses over a stream. The rooty trail begins to climb, passing hemlock, oaks, and the occasional boulder. There's another stream crossing, this one done by rock-hopping, and shortly come to an intersection with a white-blazed trail at 0.4 mile in the circuit. Stay with the orange as the pathway ascends moderately through all sorts of hemlock, ferns, and rocks. In about 0.5 mile, stay left at the intersection and walk along the rolling terrain.

There's another intersection at 1.3 miles that affords the opportunity for a side trip to a ledge. Take it by turning left and hiking a few hundred feet. This is a good spot to rest and look upon the Eightmile River and the pastoral valley with its undulating hills and fields.

When it's time, return to the intersection and bear left as the trail begins a downward slope by rock outcroppings and comes closer to the river. At 1.7 miles, there's a chance to visit a small cave, the Devil's Oven. It's a short, steep jaunt to the hole by making a right turn and then returning to the orange blazes again.

The Vista Trail soon passes an intersection with a blue-blazed trail before returning to the covered bridge. Cross the bridge, turn right, pass the falls, and then head back to the parking area to complete the devilishly fun loop.

8

The Wolf Den at Mashamoquet Brook State Park

Difficulty: Moderate

Time: 2½ to 3 hours

Distance (round trip): 4 miles

Elevation gain: 300 feet

Trails: Blue, Blue Red

Map: USGS Danielson, CT

Trailhead GPS coordinates: N41° 51.09' W71° 58.13'

With unusual rock formations like the Wolf Den and Indian Chair, handsome manmade stone walls, a romp through an enchanting swamp, and a wealth of history, the easy-to-follow and well-marked Blue Trail circuit through Mashamoquet Brook State Park in Connecticut's bucolic Quiet Corner is a trip well worth making.

Outside of Storrs and within an easy drive of Hartford, the park's location is also ideal for those looking to take a break from a road trip, say between Boston and New York.

Connecticut's northeast corner is farm and field rural. There is an elegance inside the homes, inns, and shops here, while country casual is alive and well among the hills, streams, and woods. So wear your good hiking clothes for the exploration.

The wondrous Pomfret park is a genteel jewel with more than 1,000 acres for recreation, including opportunities for hiking, camping, picnicking, and fishing. The Nutmeg State's multiuse Airline Trail, a 50-mile trail that once served as the corridor for train travel between New York and Boston, is also nearby.

The park's location was once the dominion of Mohegan chief Uncas. Mashamoquet is a Native American term meaning "stream of good fishing." At one time, three state parks took up the acreage, but officials combined the original Mashamoquet, Wolf Den (protected by the Daughters of the American Revolution back in 1899), and Saptree Run into one bigger park.

The park's claim to fame is housing the Wolf Den, a cave right along the trail. During

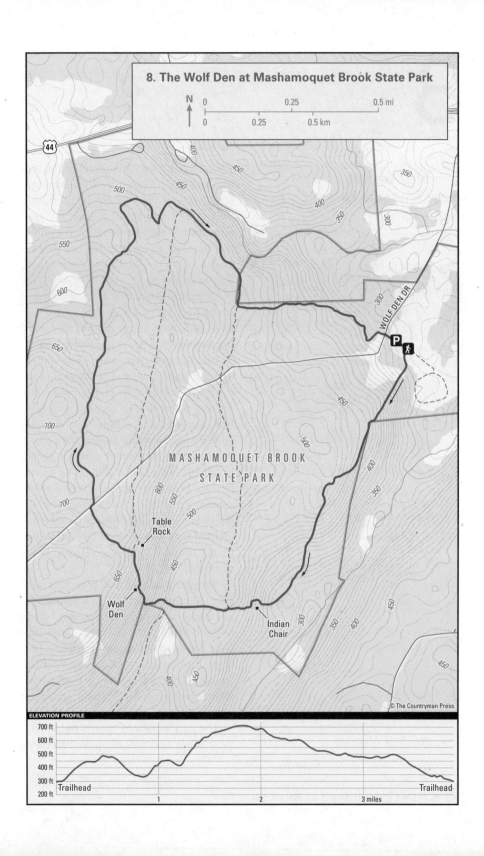

8. The Wolf Den at Mashamoquet Brook State Park

N

0   0.25   0.5 mi

0   0.25   0.5 km

44

WOLF DEN DR.

P

MASHAMOQUET BROOK
STATE PARK

Table
Rock

Wolf
Den

Indian
Chair

© The Countryman Press

ELEVATION PROFILE

700 ft
600 ft
500 ft
400 ft
300 ft
200 ft

Trailhead

Trailhead

1   2   3 miles

the early snow of a December night in 1742, settler Israel Putnam shot a wolf that had preyed upon local farm animals. Putnam later became a Revolutionary War icon as a major general in the Continental Army.

Near the den is also a natural stone formation called the Indian Chair, which overlooks a ledge. Table Rock, a huge slab, is another popular destination.

The hike also dispels the notion that eastern Connecticut is flat. Some hikers may find portions of the initial hilly mile and a half a tad difficult. But this is a forgiving hike, and though it can be done in either direction, go clockwise to get the tougher stuff out of the way first.

HOW TO GET THERE

From I-395, take Exit 93. Turn right on Route 101 traveling west for about 5 miles. Before the traffic lights, turn left on Wolf Den Drive. Travel about .75 mile and turn left to use the visitor parking lot by an office building on the right-hand side.

The hike is in Mashamoquet State Park, 147 Wolf Den Drive, Pomfret Center, CT 06259; phone: 860-928-6121; web: www .ct.gov/deep/cwp.

THE TRAIL

The journey begins from the parking area behind the office building, where signs point to the left. The way is initially grassy before another sign indicates it's time to head up into the woods.

Stone walls and rock formations are frequent companions during that initial mile and a half. There are many places to stop to take a look at the various rock piles and ledges with their quirky shapes. The trail does have some bite to it as it winds over the hilly terrain passing over bridges and through a swampy area bursting with various vegetation.

Scampering up a hillside, look for the

Mashamoquet Brook State Park contains a wealth of wonderful woods.

Indian Chair at about a mile. It's a fine spot for photographs (just watch the ledge). No doubt the kids will love having their pictures taken sitting in the stone throne. The way continues up to the Wolf Den in about 0.3 mile (the Blue Trail merges with the Red Trail to become the Blue Red Trail for a spell). Do note that in the 7-mile network of trails here, the red trails lead back to Wolf Den Drive and by traveling east can get back to the parking area for those who may want to cut the hike short.

The Wolf Den is another fun spot along the way. A cave-side plaque tells the story of Putnam and the wolf. In what must have been quite the headline for its time, the torch-

The Indian Chair is one of several fascinating rock formations found in Mashamoquet Brook State Park.

carrying Putnam, with a rope tied to his feet, entered the cave with his musket and "by the light of her angry eyes, shot and killed the marauder." He then "dragged forth the body of the last wolf in Connecticut." That last piece of information may not make Putnam much of a hero in animal activists' eyes.

Nonetheless, onward the path leads to another easily found landmark, Table Rock, a huge slab perfect for a rest, reflection, and nourishment.

Onward from Table Rock, the trail soon crosses Wolf Den roads and becomes a leisurely stroll of sorts down the hillside. Dally a bit by a field and take note of the lovely ferns in the woods as well. The trail soon leads over a bridge before coming to a junction where sticking to blue is the thing to do.

Eventually the way continues through more stone walls, integral reminders of the early settlers in a splendid slice of New England.

Cobble Mountain

Difficulty: Moderate to Strenuous

Time: 4 hours

Distance (round trip): 6.4 miles

Elevation gain: 700 feet

Trails: Macedonia Ridge Trail

Map: USGS Kent, CT

Trailhead GPS coordinates:
N41° 45.63' W73° 29.62'

A rock scramble, easygoing rambles, flowing brooks, ferns, seasonal wildflowers, and first-rate views make the loop over 1,365-foot Cobble Mountain an outing filled with diversity. Don't be fooled by this little mountain. There is a taxing rock scramble before gaining the glorious summit in the hefty hills of pretty Kent in northwest Connecticut by the New York border.

The mountain is located within the 2,300-acre Macedonia Brook State Park, with its views to the rolling Housatonic River Valley, Catskills, and Taconics.

The park had its beginnings in 1918 as a 1,552-acre gift to the state from Litchfield's White Memorial Foundation and expanded from there to now have miles of color-coded hiking trails for all levels of hikers. A seasonal camping area within the park means hikers can while away a weekend or more. The park is also of interest to rock lovers, with its various geologic features, minerals, and rock types. An ironworks in a gorge with an old furnace by the park entrance operated here, dating back to the late 1700s. The area also contained gristmills, saw and cider mills at some point.

The pleasantly rustic park with Macedonia Brook rambling through it has many dirt roads and a camping area, making it a place for a menu of activities. Birders like it too for its many migrating species passing through.

The park trails are noted by their blue, green, orange, white, and yellow blazes. There are also combinations of them. This counterclockwise adventure simply follows the blue-blazed Ridge Loop along the

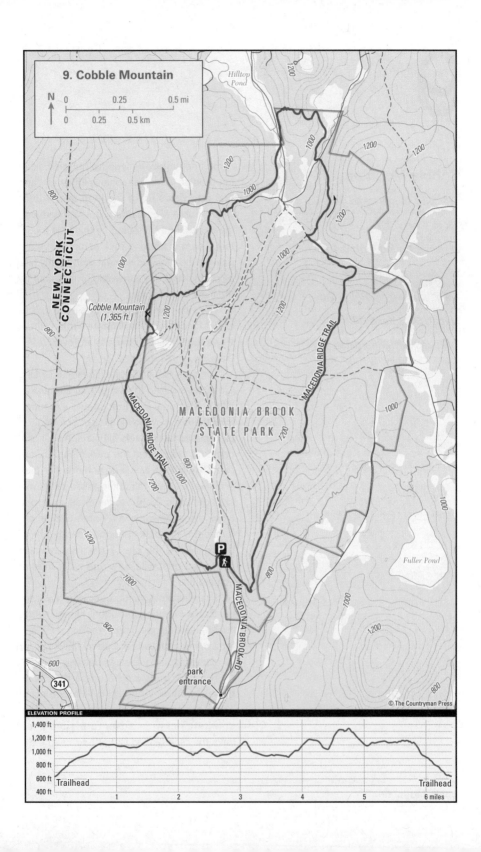

9. Cobble Mountain

N

0   0.25   0.5 mi

0   0.25   0.5 km

Hilltop Pond

NEW YORK
CONNECTICUT

Cobble Mountain
(1,365 ft.)

MACEDONIA RIDGE TRAIL

MACEDONIA RIDGE TRAIL

MACEDONIA BROOK
STATE PARK

Fuller Pond

MACEDONIA BROOK RD.

park
entrance

341

© The Countryman Press

ELEVATION PROFILE

1,400 ft
1,200 ft
1,000 ft
800 ft
600 ft
400 ft

Trailhead

Trailhead

1   2   3   4   5   6 miles

Rocky outcroppings on Cobble Mountain afford fine valley views.

Macedonia Ridge Trail. Stay with blue and the hike will be true. Because of the number of trails, there is room for bailing out along the way if necessary. Generally, the trails eventually lead to Macedonia Brook Road and other roads in the park.

This is a challenging circuit. For those looking for a more moderate undertaking, simply take the Macedonia Ridge Trail clockwise from the parking area 1.6 miles to the top of Cobble Mountain and return.

HOW TO GET THERE

From Kent, travel on Route 341 going west from the intersection with Route 7 for about 1.8 miles. Make a right on Macedonia Brook Road and follow it about 1.5 miles to the parking area by a bridge over the brook. There are places to park on both sides of the

bridge. One has picnic tables, the other has a toilet and picnic tables.

The trail is in Macedonia Brook State Park, 159 Macedonia Brook Road, Kent, CT 06757; phone: 860-927-3238; web: www .ct.gov/dep. The park is open from 8 A.M. to sunset.

THE TRAIL

For the loop, cross the road by the bridge and enter the woods on the blue-blazed trail, as it's time to begin an unfaltering climb up the east ridge by big gneiss boulders. At about the 0.9 mile mark, a yellow-blazed trail enters—stay on blue—and the woods become a mixture of oak, birch, and maple. The trail shortly comes upon a green-blazed pathway—stay on blue (green too)—and passes through a breach in a stone wall as

Hilltop Pond is a serene spot.

it flattens. Soon, stay left on blue and come to a tributary at 2 miles by an old roadway. The trail follows the old path under oak trees and by a rushing brook. The blue-blazed trail descends to the brook and crosses it on rocks before a stone wall comes into play. At 2.4 miles, the trail crosses Keller Road and flowing Macedonia Brook. At the road, go left, go over the bridge, and turn right to stay on the blue-blazed trail. The pathway leaves the brook and starts to ascend some through the ferns before dipping down and up as the trail winds by Hilltop Pond with its grassy area by a dam and crosses Weber Road at 3.2 miles, the midway point in the hike.

Stay on the blue-blazed trail as it follows an old Civilian Conservation Corps roadway with its rocks and wall. The trail meets Chippewalla Road in about 0.4 mile before

heading upslope and going into a series of zigs and zags up the ridge with its mountain laurel. A green-blazed trail is reached at 4.3 miles. Then cross into a little ravine and over a brook before reaching a steep ledge. Now it's time to make that scrambling ascent to the summit, which is slippery when wet.

During the ascent over the lichen-dotted rocks, the views keep improving.

From the summit, gaze out to New York in the west, south, and north. Break out the sandwiches.

When it's time, head down, soon crossing the white-blazed and steep Cobble Mountain Trail. The south side of Cobble contains some rolling pitches by outcrops with its valley vista and a flowing stream as the trail leads back to where it all started after negotiating a series of switchbacks and fine wooded span.

10

Bear Mountain

Difficulty: Strenuous

Time: 4 to 5 hours

Distance (round trip): 6.7 miles

Elevation gain: 1,560 feet

Trails: Undermountain Trail, Paradise Lane Trail, Appalachian Trail

Map: USGS Salisbury, Bashbish (MA, CT, NY)

Trailhead GPS coordinates: N42° 1.73' W73° 25.73'

Well-trodden Bear Mountain in Salisbury is Connecticut's highest peak. Tucked in the northwest corner by the Massachusetts border, the summit is crowned with a stone tower dating back to 1885. From the top, views stretch across Connecticut, Massachusetts, and New York onto rolling mountains, sweeping valleys, and glistening waterways.

Rugged 2,316-foot Bear Mountain, the eminent peak in the southern Taconics, is something of an oddity. It is the Nutmeg State's highest mountain, but not its highest point. That honor goes to a spot at 2,380 feet above sea level located on the south shoulder of 2,453-foot Mount Frissell, which is actually situated in Massachusetts. Go figure. The hike here also briefly touches into Bay State space.

But Bear's both a popular and pretty place with blueberries in season, fascinating vistas, and the tower that serves as a glorious stage above the natural splendor. Plus, the mountain's not that far from the upmarket town of Salisbury with its post-hike options for ample nourishment.

There is also a backcountry camping area along the way at Paradise Lane camping area with a few spots that afford an opportunity to turn this into an overnight, which can be a boon to those early-morning or nocturnal hikers craving some summit solitude time, particularly on prime-time weekends.

This is one of those hikes where proponents can make arguments about which way to do the challenging circuit. There are those who prefer ascending steeps and

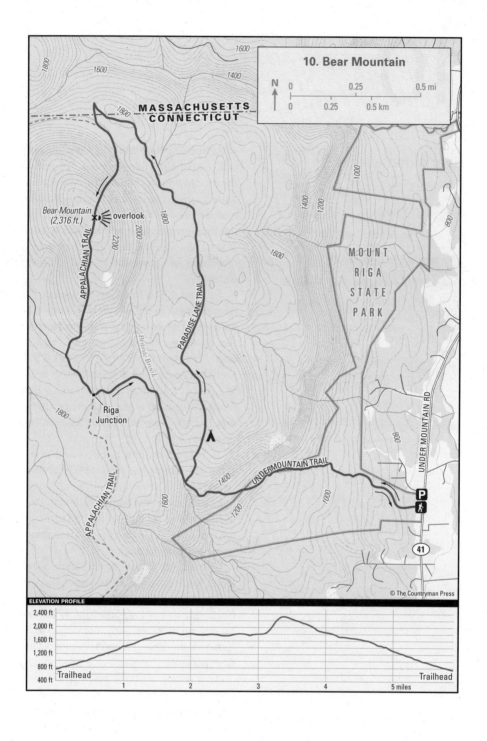

10. Bear Mountain

N

0   0.25   0.5 mi

0   0.25   0.5 km

1800
1600
1400
1600

MASSACHUSETTS
CONNECTICUT

1800
1000

Bear Mountain
(2,316 ft.)   overlook

1400
1200
800

APPALACHIAN TRAIL

2200
2000
1800

PARADISE LANE TRAIL

1600

M O U N T

R I G A

S T A T E

P A R K

Brassie Brook

1800

Riga
Junction

UNDER MOUNTAIN RD

800

APPALACHIAN TRAIL

1400

UNDERMOUNTAIN TRAIL

1600
1200
1000

P

41

© The Countryman Press

ELEVATION PROFILE

2,400 ft						
2,000 ft						
1,600 ft						
1,200 ft						
800 ft						
400 ft	Trailhead					Trailhead

1   2   3   4   5 miles

other descending them. This loop ascends the steep section on the north side of the mountain and goes counterclockwise from the parking area with its privy and informational kiosk. Often there are brochures at the kiosk detailing the Connecticut section of the Appalachian Trail, the legendary Georgia to Maine footpath. The literature provides information about area camping, stores, gear, and restaurants.

HOW TO GET THERE

In Salisbury and the junction of Routes 41 and 44, travel north on Route 41 for about 3.5 miles to the parking area on the left. Look for the blue sign for the Undermountain Trail. On busy days, hikers park along the roadway, so be cautious.

THE TRAIL

Start on the blue-blazed Undermountain Trail, which leads through something of a tree tunnel and begins at a modest grade. The trail passes through the mixed northern hardwood forest of the 276-acre Mount Riga State Park before it comes to Brassie Brook in less than a mile and then some stone steps up to the junction with the blue-blazed Paradise Lane Trail at 1.1 miles.

For the next 2 miles, Paradise Lane is the route, as it starts with a brief climb and then leads to a side trail that offers group camping. The trail eases a bit after that going through a series of wetlands that can have melodious croaking creatures. A hemlock grove with white pines is the sign for entering Massachusetts before reaching the junction with the white-blazed AT. So don't be surprised if you run into thru-hikers, those people hiking the entire AT.

The hemlocks are in a place called the Lorenz Grove, named for trail steward Edward Lorenz and recognizing him for his work with the Connecticut chapter of the Appalachian

Mountain Club. The grove has a nice look at Bear Mountain too.

Then it's time to climb. The AT segment before reaching the summit is the most arduous of the journey. Turn left on the AT, navigate a col, pass unmarked Northwest Road, and then prepare for the taxing 0.3 mile or so steep stretch over rocks that can be slippery when wet. The sweet reward comes soon on Bear Mountain's ledgy summit with its broad vistas and stone tower. Climb on up. In the east sit the glistening Twin Lakes—Washington and Washinee Lakes. To the

Bear Mountain is a rugged piece of Connecticut.

Portions of the Appalachian Trail run through Connecticut and along Bear Mountain.

north in Massachusetts are 2,365-foot Mount Race and 2,302-foot Mount Everett. Mount Frissell stands in the west with 2,311-foot Mount Grisley nearby in the southwest.

Also on the summit is the plaque that mistakenly calls Bear the highest summit in Connecticut. That happened in 1885. However, the whole state hadn't been surveyed yet, and it was later found the highest point in the state was on Frissell's south slope.

Continue south on the AT from the summit with its moderately steep sections. The trail does ease some and passes along several scenic viewpoints, eventually coming into colorful mountain laurel, Connecticut's state flower, by the t-junction known as Riga Junction. Leave the AT for the Undermountain Trail as it descends from Riga Ridge, crosses Brassie Brook, and finds the junction with the Paradise Lane Trail. Return to the parking area on the Undermountain Trail for the last leg of the loop.

Massachusetts

Introducing Massachusetts

Massachusetts is the king of southern New England hiking. Though the mountains don't reach the elevation of its neighbors to the north, there are a myriad of challenges, scenic offerings, and plenty of woods to roam. The Bay State has a surprising array of trails, all within reasonable drives of the main population centers of Boston, Worcester, and their suburban surroundings.

That's the beauty of Massachusetts: the hikes aren't as remote as they are in sections of northern New England. The weather, though always a consideration, is less harsh (but formidable, as the Blizzard of 2012 choked southern New England for days).

Though the eastern section of the state has its opportunities for hikes along the sea, it is the mountains of central and western Massachusetts that draw hikers seeking peaks.

Mount Greylock is the state's beacon and highest point. It and other mountains in the Berkshires often contain views out to rolling hills and patchworks of forest and small towns. Central Massachusetts has its own jewels, with mountains like Wachusett and Watatic serving as natural stages for commanding outdoor performances.

The Bay State is also home to a section of the Appalachian Trail between Connecticut and New Hampshire that winds over the Berkshires, Holyoke Range, and rippling hills. Other long-distance trails lead hikers through the state: Midstate Trail, Metacomet-Monadnock Trail, Robert Frost Trail, etc.

11

Monument Mountain

Difficulty: Easy to Moderate
Time: 2 hours
Distance (round trip): 2.8 miles
Elevation gain: 720 feet
Trails: Hickey Trail, Squaw Peak Trail, Indian Monument Trail.
Map: USGS Great Barrington, MA
Trailhead GPS coordinates: N42° 14.59' W73° 20.12'

Be among the 20,000 people annually who walk in the footsteps of some of New England's incredible literary heroes. *Moby Dick* author Herman Melville and Nathaniel Hawthorne, who penned *The Scarlet Letter*, both spent time on the summit of Monument Mountain's 1,642-foot Squaw Peak, with outstanding vistas to Mount Greylock in the north and New York's Catskills to the west. The two embarked on a hike up the mountain in 1850 when a thunderstorm forced them to seek shelter in a cave. The story goes that during their stay there, Melville was inspired to write *Moby Dick*, which he dedicated to Hawthorne.

The mountain, comprised mostly of pale quartzite, stands to the east of the Housatonic River outside the Berkshire town of Great Barrington. The popular peak embedded in a 503-acre plot is preserved by The Trustees of Reservations, a large 100,000-member land conservation group that oversees some 100 parcels of land in Massachusetts, totaling nearly 25,000 acres.

According to the group, thank poet William Cullen Bryant for the mountain's name. During his time in Great Barrington from 1815 to 1825, Bryant wrote a poem called "Monument Mountain" about a Mohican maiden, her prohibited love, and her leaping to her death from the cliffs.

A trio of trails in the preserve offer several loop opportunities. The circuits are no more than 3 miles. This loop isn't particularly difficult but does have some steepness (stone steps help sometimes) that places it above a leisurely stroll. Plus, the hike does

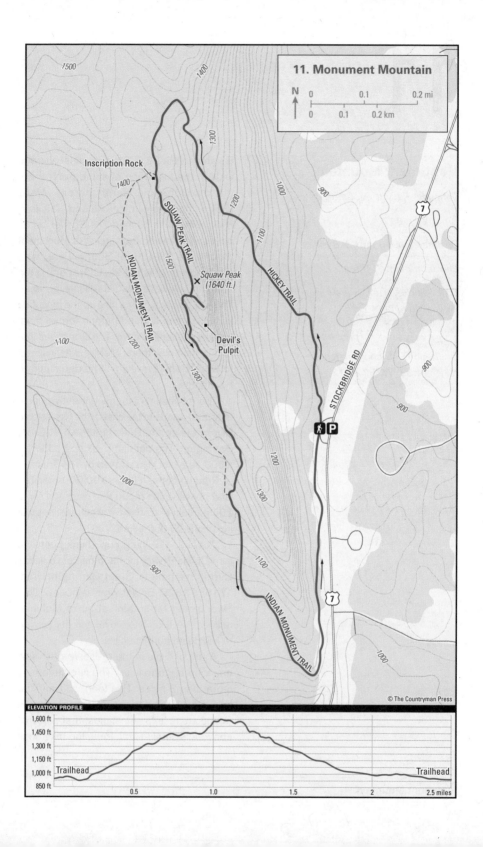

11. Monument Mountain

N

| 0 | 0.1 | 0.2 mi |
| 0 | 0.1 | 0.2 km |

1500

1400

1300

1000

900

Inscription Rock

1400

1200

SQUAW PEAK TRAIL

1100

HICKEY TRAIL

INDIAN MONUMENT TRAIL

1500

× Squaw Peak
(1640 ft.)

Devil's
Pulpit

1100

1200

1300

900

STOCKBRIDGE RD

7

P

900

900

1200

1000

1300

900

1100

INDIAN MONUMENT TRAIL

7

1000

© The Countryman Press

ELEVATION PROFILE

1,600 ft					
1,450 ft					
1,300 ft					
1,150 ft					
1,000 ft	Trailhead				Trailhead
850 ft					

0.5   1.0   1.5   2   2.5 miles

go along some cliff areas. So, remember slippery when wet on this one. The trails are well marked and maintained on this Berkshire hike.

For those looking for an easier way up the mountain, consider instead taking the Indian Monument Trail up and down to Inscription Rock for a gentle 3-mile ascent along a onetime carriage road on the mountain's west side.

HOW TO GET THERE

From the center of Great Barrington, follow Route 7 north for about 4 miles to the entrance on the left.

Under the auspices of The Trustees of Reservations, hiking is available year-round, from sunrise to sunset.

The Berkshire Regional Office is Mission House, PO Box 762, Stockbridge, MA, 01262; phone: 413-298-3239; web: www .thetrustees.org.

THE TRAIL

The circuit begins on the initially level Hickey Trail as it leads north into a forest of pine, maple, ferns, and more. The trail passes by a jumbled boulder field before entering into a wondrous grove along a stream (sometimes dry). Cross the log bridge and ascend the trail, soon reaching a junction of the Hickey, Squaw Peak, and Indian Monument Trails at 0.8 miles.

Continue on the 0.7-mile-long Squaw Peak Trail, first noting Inscription Rock located on the north end of the trail. The handsomely inscribed smooth rock tells of how a woman named Rosalie Butler left the land to the Trustees in 1899.

The Squaw Peak Trail proceeds south, steepens some but has some rock steps, and grows narrower as it affords a look at the Housatonic River Valley. The summit is soon reached, with its ledges and lichen.

A red eft scurries along the woods floor of Monument Mountain.

The white rocks, birds overhead, and precarious cliffs make for a stunning mountaintop with an enchanting skyline that has many vantage points. The South Taconic Range holds court in the southwest while the town of Stockbridge is close in the north with Greylock in the distance.

Stay with the Squaw Peak Trail as it follows the ridge downward going south, shortly coming to a spur path well worth taking to the ominous-sounding Devil's Pulpit. The overlook towers over sharp cliffs of quartzite and a vista that includes the ski trails of Butternut and Monument Mountain Regional High School.

The Hickey Trail winds through a splendid hemlock grove on Monument Mountain.

Retrace your steps to the Squaw Peak Trail and follow it as it descends steadily to the junction with the Indian Monument Trail at about 1.5 miles.

Complete the loop by turning left on the Indian Monument Trail as it leads through the hardwoods, widens, and becomes a nice wooded stroll that comes close to Route 7 before venturing back to the picnic tables, informational kiosk, and roadside parking.

12

Northfield Mountain

Difficulty: Moderate

Time: 2 hours

Distance (round trip): 3.1 miles

Elevation gain: 690 feet

Trails: 10th Mountain Trail, Rose Ledge Trail, Lower Ledge Trail

Map: USGS Northfield, MA

Trailhead GPS coordinates: N42° 36.65' W72° 28.26'

Northfield Mountain is a marriage between outdoor recreation and power. Buried in the bowels of the mountain is a giant pumped storage hydroelectric station that shuttles water between the Connecticut River and a mountaintop reservoir operated by FirstLight Power Resources. A licensing agreement with the federal government calls for the utility to produce a myriad of outdoor recreation and environmental opportunities and programs.

The result is a year-round playground with some 25 miles of hiking trails, including those reaching the mountain's 1,100-foot top and sub-summit ledges. Hikers and mountain bikers trek through forests, valleys, and fields. Rock climbers enjoy scaling and rappelling down the popular gneiss Rose Ledge area with climbs for all abilities. Classic routes include Solar Flare, Tennessee Flake, and Beginners Corner. Camping is offered in season while the visitor center contains interpretive displays and maps. Picnicking is also available. Be sure to check out the yurt outside the visitor center too.

A bit unusual, it's also possible to go on a river cruise from the facility. The *Quinnetukut II* riverboat departs the Riverview Picnic area in season for a 12-mile 90-minute cruise down the Connecticut River.

Not only do hikers and the like call Northfield Mountain their home, but the trails also host high-school competitions. Every November hundreds of student athletes come to run the trails during the Western Massachusetts High School Cross Country

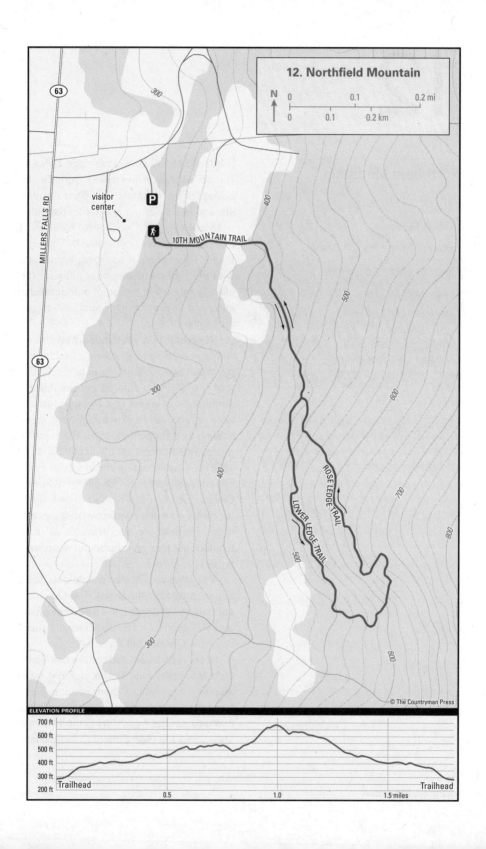

12. Northfield Mountain

N

| 0 | | 0.1 | | 0.2 mi |

| 0 | 0.1 | 0.2 km |

63

MILLERS FALLS RD

visitor center

P

10TH MOUNTAIN TRAIL

63

300

400

500

600

700

800

ROSE LEDGE TRAIL

LOWER LEDGE TRAIL

300

400

500

600

© The Countryman Press

ELEVATION PROFILE

| 700 ft |
| 600 ft |
| 500 ft |
| 400 ft |
| 300 ft |
| 200 ft |

Trailhead

Trailhead

0.5

1.0

1.5 miles

The trail system at Northfield Mountain is well-signed.

JAN BASCH

Running Championships, giving the facility a festive flair. There are also the state championships that follow the regional competition.

In winter, trails are groomed for cross-country skiing while snowshoers take to the snowy pathways.

A trip isn't complete without stopping into the visitor center with its displays and programs. There are also various outdoor programs that often include hikes throughout the year.

Hikers will find both grassy ways for easy walking and narrow footpaths over rugged terrain. The routes are clearly marked, and there are several maps along the way to aid in figuring out exactly where you are.

Before going, note the visitor center is closed Monday and Tuesday in summer. There is a trail status board by the entrance road that updates users with current conditions. Most trail work is done during the summer and fall. For those who enjoy orienteering, there are maps available for purchase in the visitor center. You can generally hike anywhere on the mountain except in the fenced-off areas.

This moderate trek is a loop over Rose Ledge, but there is an option for extending the trip by 1.8 miles and making the trip to the summit. It's a hike for all seasons, peaking with fall color and offering a touch of solitude in winter. Eighty-foot-high Rose Ledges towers above the Connecticut River Valley. On the way, pass through a diversity of trees like birch, hemlock, maple, and oak.

HOW TO GET THERE

From Route 2 in Erving, travel 2 miles north on Route 63 to the main entrance on the right.

The trails are under the auspices of the Northfield Mountain Recreation and

Trail options are many at Northfield Mountain.   JAN BASCH

Environmental Center, 99 Millers Falls Road (Route 63), Northfield, MA; phone: 413-659-3714 or 800-859-2960; web: www.firstlightpower.com.

THE TRAIL

Begin from the visitor center by following the leisurely blue-marked 10th Division Trail through the field, staying with it as it enters the forest (signs for Rose Ledge) and begins to go up the hill, eventually crossing under the power lines. At 0.4 mile, turn right on the orange-blazed Rose Ledge Trail with its roots. The trail crosses both the Hemlock Hill and Jug End Trails and a couple of streams, winding through the hemlock and by mountain laurel. Beyond the second stream at 0.6 mile, turn right on the Lower Ledge Trail, as it soon opens to valley views. The trail then pops back into the forest and soon goes by an area that was once an active 19th century stone quarry.

At 1.2 miles the trail bears right and crosses Rock Oak Ramble before passing under Rose Ledges, millions of years old. The trail comes to another junction at 1.6 miles. Turn left along the Upper Rose Ledge Trail (a right takes you to the summit some 0.9 mile away). Linger on the ledges. Take in the views to the west. Just be cognizant of where you are and where terra firma ends.

The trail descends and once again crosses Rock Oak Ramble at 2.1 miles, forking left at the intersection with the Lower Rose Ledge Trail for the forgiving downhill, turning left at the junction with the West Slope Trail and bearing right at 2.5 miles to retrace your steps across the Jug End and Hemlock Trails, and then following those blue-blazes back to the center.

13

Mount Tom State Reservation

Difficulty: Moderate to Strenuous

Time: 4 hours

Distance (round trip): 5.1 miles

Elevation gain: 650 feet

Trails: Metacomet-Monadnock (MM)
Trail, Quarry Trail, DOC Trail

Map: USGS Easthampton,
Mount Tom, MA

Trailhead GPS coordinates:
N42° 16.03' W72° 38.13'

Mount Tom rises above the Connecticut River majestically and contains a scenic ridge walk that makes it a prime point for Pioneer Valley hikers. The 1,202-foot mountain provides a sweeping panorama of the Connecticut River Valley, basalt cliffs called traprock, Berkshires, and more.

It must have been something back in the day, when visitors arrived by railroad to stay at the swanky Mount Tom Hotel at its traprock top. But only the foundations are there now; the hotel burned in 1929 (actually first in 1900, and it was then rebuilt). Today Mount Tom has antennas and all for modern-day communications. In fall, hawks migrate above it in their annual rite of travel.

Mount Tom anchors the Mount Tom Range, a ridge of five mountains in the 2,161-acre Mount Tom State Reservation. The preserve holds 22 miles of color-coded hiking trails, picnicking, cross-country skiing, a museum, and the Stone House visitor center, putting it squarely on the populace radar. Mount Tom is the tallest of the peaks in the range that encompasses 882-foot Mount Nonotuck, Goat Peak at 850 feet, 1,015-foot Whiting Peak, and Dead Top at 1,100 feet.

More than half of the tree species found in Hampshire County are found within the reservation. The mountain was also home to the Mount Tom ski area that operated from 1962 to 1998. The small ski area had a vertical drop of 680 feet and started with a double chair, T-bar, and rope tow to access its three slopes and one trail. Open for night skiing, it was also a summer attraction with alpine slide, water slide, and wave pool.

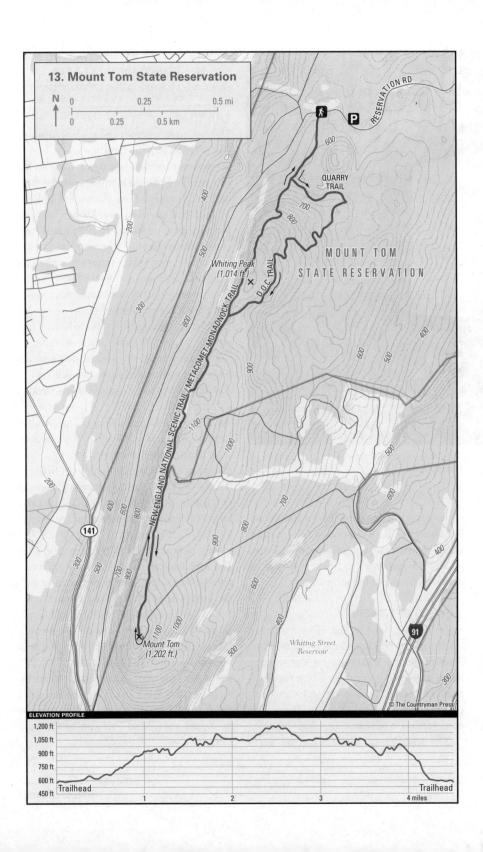

13. Mount Tom State Reservation

N

0 ——— 0.25 ——— 0.5 mi
0 ——— 0.25 ——— 0.5 km

RESERVATION RD

600

QUARRY
TRAIL

700

800

MOUNT TOM
STATE RESERVATION

Whiting Peak
(1,014 ft.)

D.O.C. TRAIL

NEW ENGLAND NATIONAL SCENIC TRAIL / METACOMET-MONADNOCK TRAIL

900

1100

1000

700

800

600

500

400

141

200

300

400

500

600

700

800

900

Mount Tom
(1,202 ft.)

1100

1000

500

400

Whiting Street
Reservoir

91

300

© The Countryman Press

ELEVATION PROFILE

1,200 ft
1,050 ft
900 ft
750 ft
600 ft
450 ft

Trailhead

Trailhead

1   2   3   4 miles

*The Metacomet-Monadnock Trail leads to
Mount Tom.*   JAN BASCH

Hiking is but one of the park's attractions. Be aware the park is popular with groups. There is also a lookout tower along the road well worth walking up. Stop in the visitor center for a look at the exhibits.

HOW TO GET THERE

From I-91, take Exit 18 (Easthampton /Holyoke), turn right, and travel 3.5 miles on Route 3 south. Turn right on Reservation Road and into Mount Tom State Reservation in 0.3 mile. Drive another 1.4 miles to parking on right by picnic tables. There is an entrance fee in season.

The trails are in the Mount Tom State Reservation, 125 Reservation Road, Holyoke, MA, 01040; phone: 413-534-1186; web: mass.gov/dcr/parks/central/mtom.htm.

THE TRAIL

The hike begins from the parking area on Reservation Road where the white-blazed Metacomet-Monadnock (MM) Trail, an approximately 114-mile footpath from the Connecticut border to New Hampshire's Mount Monadnock crossing over Mount Tom and the neighboring Holyoke Range at the Metacomet Ridge. The trail was pioneered by the late University of Massachusetts professor Walter M. Banfield in the late 1950s and is chiefly maintained by the Appalachian Mountain Club's Berkshire chapter.

Though it's possible to hike to Mount Tom strictly on the MM Trail, this banjo-shaped hike includes a couple of other trails near the beginning before sticking to the MM Trail.

Start on the MM Trail as it leads through a hemlock grove for 0.3 mile before turning left at the yellow-blazed Quarry Trail at a trail junction. The trail is a fairly level old woods road that passes a small pond and then climbs easily to the junction with the red-blazed DOC Trail and Keystone Extension at 0.6 mile. Turn right on the DOC Trail and begin to climb in earnest as the trail scales Whiting Peak through the hardwoods. The footing gets a little rocky before easing a bit. The trail also passes by some ledge areas with limited views before connecting with the white-blazed MM Trail at 1.5 miles.

Turn left on the MM Trail for the 1.3-mile ridge stretch to the Mount Tom summit above Easthampton, with its stunning look above western Massachusetts. The trail along the cliffy ridge increases in drama. By no means flat, there are dips and rises along the way, with several view points as the way continues over Dead Top with its towering cliffs.

The Mount Tom State Reservation offers countryside vistas.

Continue on to Mount Tom at 2.8 miles, with its somewhat crowded but splendidly craggy summit. Look around at everything from the antennas to the graffiti to the buildings. There's also the old stone platform from the railroad days.

When it's time to come down, return on the MM Trail for the 2.3-mile trek back to the trailhead. The way is on now-familiar ground, enjoying the vistas again back along Dead Top. Later on, this time stay straight on the MM Trail at the junction with the DOC Trail as the pathway leads over Whiting Peak with its valley vistas before the trail begins to descend rather quickly. It levels out, though, as it reaches that junction with the Quarry Trail again, and staying straight, leads back to the trailhead.

14

Mount Toby

Difficulty: Moderate	
Time: 2½ to 3 hours	
Distance (round trip): 3 miles	
Elevation gain: 900 feet	
Trails: Robert Frost Trail	
Map: USGS Williamsburg, MA	
Trailhead GPS coordinates: N42° 30.23' W72° 31.87'	

Mount Toby is a place to get schooled. The 1,239-foot top mountain with fire tower affords birds-eye views over the Connecticut River Valley. The mountain and neighboring Holyoke Range are prime spots in fall to look out with binoculars during raptor migration.

The tiny but husky peak also delights those who enjoy geology and botany, as unusual bedrock outcroppings of rough conglomerates called "puddingstones" are commonplace, while its hearty terrain contain a bevy of ferns and seasonal orchids.

But there's also something poetic about Mount Toby, as the 47-mile-long Robert Frost Trail passes over it as it crosses through 10 towns on state and private lands between South Hadley and Wendell. The trail was introduced in 1982 and is maintained by the Amherst Conservation Department, Amherst Area Trails Committee, Kestrel Land Trust, and others.

Frost, the peripatetic poet, often touches New England hikers through his work and quotations like "Two roads diverged in a wood and I, I took the one less traveled by, and that has made all the difference." Frost taught English at nearby Amherst College, as well as teaching in Vermont and New Hampshire. Wherever hikers in New England go, they likely will venture across a path walked by Frost.

Oval-shaped Mount Toby, with its 25-mile network of hiking and cross-country ski trails, is also a working outdoor laboratory. The University of Massachusetts at Amherst oversees the 755-acre Mount Toby Demonstration Forest as students use

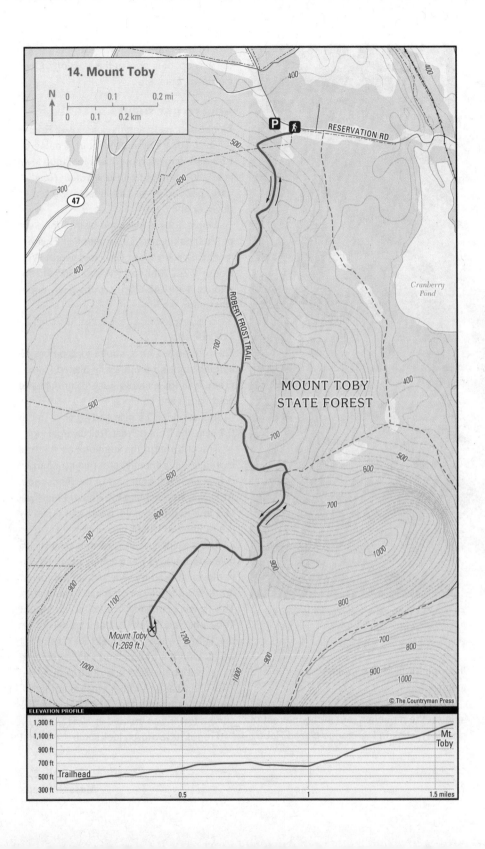

14. Mount Toby

N

0   0.1   0.2 mi

0   0.1   0.2 km

RESERVATION RD

400

500

300

47

600

400

ROBERT FROST TRAIL

700

Cranberry
Pond

MOUNT TOBY
STATE FOREST

400

500

700

600

500

700

800

600

700

1000

700

900

1000

800

Mount Toby
(1,269 ft.)

1100

1200

900

700

800

1000

1000

900

1000

© The Countryman Press

ELEVATION PROFILE

1,300 ft			Mt. Toby
1,100 ft			
900 ft			
700 ft			
500 ft	Trailhead		
300 ft	0.5	1	1.5 miles

Frost for an up-and-down experience. On the way up, bear right at the junctions. Coming down, bear left.

HOW TO GET THERE

From Sunderland and the junction of Routes 47 and 16, travel north about 4 miles on Route 47 (crossing over the Montague town line) and turn right on Reservation Road. A gate, parking area, and kiosk are 0.5 mile down on the right.

Mount Toby is managed by the University of Massachusetts Department of Environmental Conservation, 160 Holdsworth Way, Room 224, Amherst, MA, 01003-9285; phone: 413-545-2665; web: www.eco.umass.edu.

THE TRAIL

The hike begins on a woods road before diverging right on the brightly blazed Robert Frost Trail for a stable ascent through the hardwoods and conifers.

In just under 0.5 mile and again at about 0.7 mile, the Robert Frost Trail diverges right.

Travel through the hemlock as the trail increases in difficulty, steepening sharply. Power lines become part of the landscape. At 1 mile, bear right on the Robert Frost Trail and in about 0.25 mile, bear right again by the red-blazed Upper Link Trail.

There's a push to the grassy summit at 1.5 miles. Get above the trees by climbing the fire tower (called the Sunderland fire tower) for a 360-degree panorama in three states. The tower is not the first to grace Mount Toby, once considered a potential ski area in the 1930s by the Springfield Ski Club. First was a wooden tree platform, followed by a tower put up in 1923 and destroyed by the 1938 hurricane. Another was constructed, and it succumbed to the 1950 hurricane. The current tower was erected in 1951.

From it, have a lovely look south to Amherst

Pileated woodpeckers have gone to work on a tree leading to Mount Toby.

the area for field and forestry research and teaching.

There are a number of loop options available on the mountain, but in the interest of simplicity, stick to the orange-blazed Robert

Mount Toby rises above Cranberry Pond.

and the Holyoke Range. The north yields clear day vistas to Mount Snow and Mount Ascutney in Vermont and New Hampshire's Mount Monadnock. The Connecticut River flows below. Look west for the Berkshires and Greylock while Wachusett and the Quabbin Reservoir hold court in the east.

Return to the trailhead along the same trails.

And if there's time before you go, drive the 0.5 mile beyond the gate on Reservation Road for a gander at Cranberry Pond, a glacial kettle pond with Mount Toby on the horizon. You'll be glad you did.

15

Mount Watatic

Difficulty: Moderate	
Time: 2 hours	
Distance (round trip): 3 miles	
Elevation gain: 600 feet	
Trails: Midstate/Wapack Trail, State Line Trail	
Map: USGS Ashburnham, MA	
Trailhead GPS coordinates: N42° 41.80' W71° 54.27'	

Tiny 1,832-foot-high Mount Watatic in central Massachusetts near the New Hampshire border is a scenic crossroads. The rounded peak in Ashburnham is the northern end of the 92-mile Midstate Trail that goes through the Bay State between Rhode Island and the Granite State and the southern terminus of the 21-mile Wapack Trail along the Wapack Range to North Pack Monadnock in New Hampshire.

The mountain's bald top, outcroppings, and wooded slopes are protected as part of the Mount Watatic Reservation, which includes bordering lands like the Ashburnham State Forest and Watatic Mountain Wildlife Sanctuary. Though the mountain is more of a hill to some hikers, there are extensive views from the summit, as far away as Boston on a clear day, that make the trek to the top well worth it. It's another little peak with big rewards.

Not only are hikers drawn to the little mountain, skiers once schussed its slopes. The small area that started with a rope tow operated for about 50 years until the mid-1980s. An ad from the winter of 1969 to 1970 trumpeted the 550-foot vertical drop on five novice and intermediate trails and slopes. Skiers used a pair of T-bars and rope tows to access the northwest exposed paths some 60 miles from Boston. Lift tickets were $5 on weekends for adults. The ski area had night skiing too.

HOW TO GET THERE

Trailhead parking is on the north side of Route 119 in Ashburnham, about 1.4 miles west

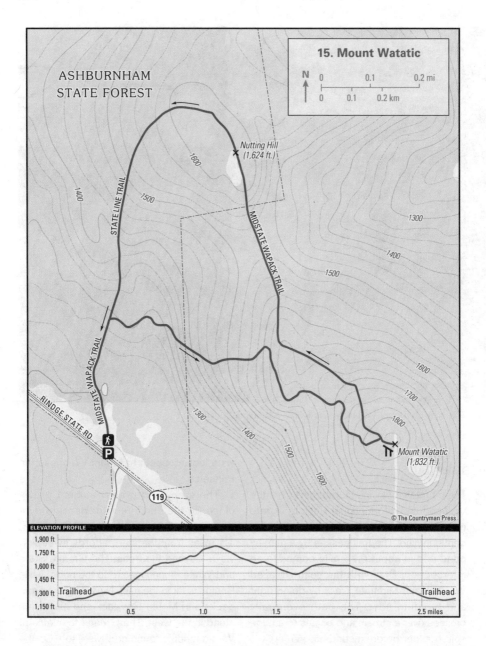

15. Mount Watatic

ASHBURNHAM STATE FOREST

Nutting Hill (1,624 ft.)

STATE LINE TRAIL

MIDSTATE WAPACK TRAIL

MIDSTATE WAPACK TRAIL

RINDGE STATE RD

119

Mount Watatic (1,832 ft.)

© The Countryman Press

N

| 0 | 0.1 | 0.2 mi |
| 0 | 0.1 | 0.2 km |

ELEVATION PROFILE

1,900 ft
1,750 ft
1,600 ft
1,450 ft
1,300 ft Trailhead
1,150 ft

0.5   1.0   1.5   2   2.5 miles

Trailhead

of the junction with Routes 119 and 101. If coming from New Hampshire, it's about 1.7 miles from the border on Route 119.

There is more information about the Wapack Trail from the Friends of the Wapack Trail, PO Box 115, West Peterborough, NH 03468; web: www.wapack.org.

More information about the Midstate Trail is available from the Midstate Trail Committee, www.midstatetrail.org.

The hike up Mount Watatic starts with a nice woods walk.

THE TRAIL

The counterclockwise loop begins from the trailhead and informational kiosk by a gate on a wide old woods road with a welcoming gentle incline. The trail passes by a marshy pond and in about 0.25 mile comes to an intersection. Stay with the yellow-blazed Wapack and Midstate Trails by going right and heading east. The path eventually crosses over a stream and comes to a huge split boulder before meandering steeply at times over the sometimes rocky and rooty footpath through the shaded hemlock and by stone walls. As the route approaches the summit, there are views northwest to Mount Monadnock in New Hampshire and then a vista looking south to Mount Wachusett in Princeton.

The stony and grassy summit grows closer in the conifers after passing by a ramshackle wooden shelter. The summit, 1.1 miles from the start, affords sweeping views beyond the trees. The Granite State and White Mountains are to the north, while Boston is far in the east. New York's Adirondacks and Mount Greylock and its towers stand in the west. The Green Mountains of Vermont ripple to the northwest too. On the summit are remains of an old fire tower and an inscribed rock giving the elevation and how the mountain is protected by the people of Ashby, Ashburnham, and the Commonwealth of Massachusetts.

A marshy pond makes for a fine place for reflection while hiking to Mount Watatic.

There is also another vantage point from a side trail that leads to East Watatic at 1,801 feet, which is well worth taking for its sweeping vistas too.

Nutting Hill, at 1,624 feet, is the next stop, about 0.75 mile away. Continue on the Wapack and Midstate Trails on an old road and bear left through the woods of spruce and hemlock by a stone wall. The trail eases, dips into a col, and climbs the rocky way to Nutting Hill at 2 miles and its views, including a look back at Mount Watatic.

Make the descent and come to a junction at 2.1 miles that tells of distances for both the Midstate and Wapack Trails. Turn left for MA 119, and then in a few hundred yards, another marker comes into play for the way home along the blue-blazed State Line Trail and old woods road for a nice final stretch.

16

Pine Cobble

Difficulty: Moderate

Time: 2 hours

Distance (round trip): 3.2 miles

Elevation gain: 1,000 feet

Trails: Pine Cobble Trail

Map: USGS North Adams, MA

Trailhead GPS coordinates:
N42° 42.99' W73° 11.11'

Nestled in the hilly northeastern corner of Massachusetts squeezed between New York and not far from the orderly Williams College campus in Williamstown, the hike up 1,894-foot Pine Cobble offers a splendid birds-eye view of the rambling Hoosic River Valley. The well-worn Pine Cobble Trail is maintained by The Williams Outing Club, founded in 1915, and the nonprofit Williamstown Rural Lands Foundation. With nearly 800 members, the WOC is known as the largest student group at the college. The WRLF's mission is to preserve the bucolic nature of Williamstown.

The blue-blazed trail leads to a fine summit with vistas into three states and links up to other regional footpaths—the Appalachian Trail and Vermont's state-long, end-to-end Long Trail. Though many hikers might associate the word "cobble" with picturesque urban lanes, according to the outing club, these cobbles are the substantial ledgy quartzite bedrock found on the low-lying mountain.

This hike through pine and oak draws not only the local students but also families and children, whether visiting the Berkshires or on campus. Younger hikers might find the trek more of a challenge as there are some rocky sections to navigate. Bring lunch on this one, and munch on the summit.

HOW TO GET THERE

From Williamstown and the junctions of Routes 7 and 2, drive east on Main Street about 0.6 mile, turn left on Cole Avenue, and drive about 0.8 mile, soon crossing the

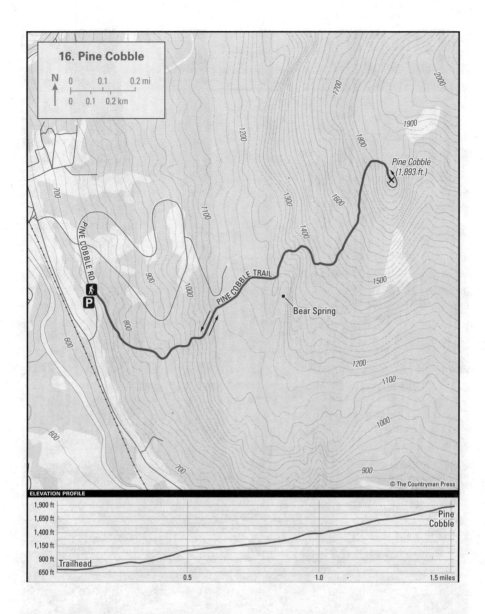

16. Pine Cobble

N
0   0.1   0.2 mi
0   0.1   0.2 km

Pine Cobble
(1,893 ft.)

PINE COBBLE RD

PINE COBBLE TRAIL

Bear Spring

© The Countryman Press

ELEVATION PROFILE

1,900 ft
1,650 ft
1,400 ft
1,150 ft
900 ft   Trailhead
650 ft

Pine Cobble

0.5   1.0   1.5 miles

Hoosic River and train tracks. Turn right on North Hoosac Road and travel about 0.4 mile before making a left on Pine Cobble Road. The parking area is up on the hill some 0.2 mile on the left. The trailhead is across the road. Heed signs not to park on the roadway, as it in near a residential area.

More information is found through Williamstown Rural Lands Foundation, 671 Cold Spring Road, Williamstown, MA 01267; phone: 413-458-2494; web: www.wrlf.org.

Even more information is found through The Williams Outing Club, 39 Chapin Hall

The well-used trail up Pine Cobble attracts a myriad of hikers.

The Pine Cobble Trail is maintained by the Williams Outing Club.

Drive, Williamstown, MA 01267; phone: 413-597-2317; web: woc.williams.edu.

THE TRAIL

The 1.6-mile hike to the top begins on a level note by crossing the road and heading into the oak forest on an unhurried ascent. The forest also contains white pine and pitch pine. In about a half mile, the trail eases before reaching a spur trail at the midway mark. That pathway drops a few hundred feet down to Bear Spring on the south side of the mountain, which tends to attract the local inhabitants like rabbits, deer, and scurrying chipmunks.

The trail continues its moderate pace before leveling off a bit about a mile into the journey and shortly passing by a border with the 3,000-acre Clarksburg State Forest and meandering through a couple of jumbled boulder areas. Soon the trail flattens for a spell. It is here in spring the Massachusetts state flower, the trailing arbutus with is wide, oval leaves and white or pink flowers, tends to bloom.

The last push to the top is steep and at about 1.5 miles a jumble of paths venture right, leading to various vantage points atop Pine Cobble, while a link trail goes to the AT a half mile away. In the east is the town of North Adams and Williamstown to the south within the Hoosic River Valley. Also in the south is Mount Greylock with its communications towers and war memorial. In the west, the Taconic Range holds court.

Return along the same trail.

17

Wachusett Mountain

Difficulty: Moderate	
Time: 3 hours	
Distance (round trip): 3.2 miles	
Elevation gain: 930 feet	
Trails: Balance Rock Trail, Old Indian Trail	
Map: Sterling, Fitchburg, MA	
Trailhead GPS coordinates: N42° 30.19' W71° 53.25'	

Wachusett is every man's—and woman's—mountain. A popular central Massachusetts landmark within an hour or so of Boston, the 2,006-foot mountain in Princeton is the highest Bay State peak east of the Berkshires. Located in the 3,000-acre Wachusett Mountain State Reservation, the summit yields outstanding views on clear days all the way to the Boston skyline in the east and the lovely Berkshires in the west. Let's not forget New Hampshire's Mount Monadnock in the north too.

With about 17 miles of hiking trails, there are many ways to explore the mountain with its streams, fields, meadows, and forests. The mountain is a monadnock (basically a peak that rises from a surrounding flat area). There's also plenty of evidence of glacial activity, particularly on the northeastern side by Balanced Rock, two huge boulders piled on top of each other.

Wachusett is a Native American word. There are those who believe it means "mountain place" while others say "the great hill." Henry David Thoreau called it "the observatory of Massachusetts." They're all good.

The woods are also home to the biggest old-growth forest east of the Connecticut River in Massachusetts, with trees more than 350 years old. Bird-watchers enjoy watching the hawks playing above in the thermals.

About 4 miles of the yellow-blazed Mid-State Trail, the 92-mile trail between Ashburnham and the Rhode Island border, runs through the reservation and reaches its high point.

The mountain also contains a seasonal

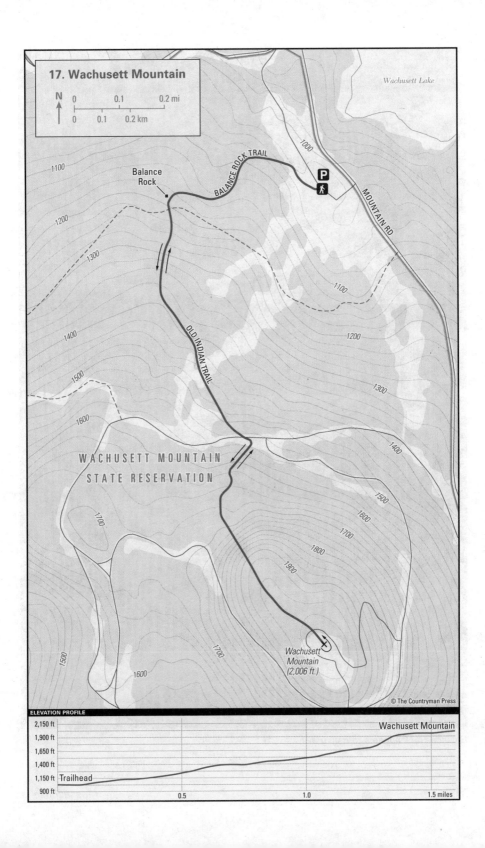

17. Wachusett Mountain

N

| 0 | | 0.1 | | 0.2 mi |
| 0 | 0.1 | | 0.2 km | |

Wachusett Lake

1000

1100

Balance
Rock

BALANCE ROCK TRAIL

P

MOUNTAIN RD

1200

1300

1100

1400

1200

1500

1300

OLD INDIAN TRAIL

1600

WACHUSETT MOUNTAIN
STATE RESERVATION

1400

1500

1700

1600

1700

1800

1900

1500

1700

1600

*Wachusett
Mountain
(2,006 ft.)*

© The Countryman Press

ELEVATION PROFILE

			Wachusett Mountain
2,150 ft			
1,900 ft			
1,650 ft			
1,400 ft			
1,150 ft	Trailhead		
900 ft			
	0.5	1.0	1.5 miles

Balance Rock appears to defy gravity.

JAN BASCH

summit road and the John Hitchcock Visitor Center with its worthy exhibits (and warmth on a cold day). Not only does it serve hikers, but in winter skiers and snowboarders fly down the 22 trails on the north side of the mountain. The first ski trails on Wachusett were cut by the Civilian Conservation Corps in the late 1930s, while the first chairlift, a T-bar, was installed in 1960.

The reservation trails are also used by snowshoers, cross-country skiers, and equestrians. Cyclists see the summit road as a challenge; there's an annual hill climb.

Wachusett has a strong tourism connection. Its first summit hotel was constructed in the late 1800s and there was even a mountaintop bowling alley. A new summit hotel was built in 1907 with a billiard room. Electricity made its way to the peak in 1925, but the hotel eventually closed and burned in December 1970.

Wachusett isn't a difficult mountain to climb, but there is some elevation change here. Hike it in early spring and watch the spring skiers. Hawks typically soar above in spring and fall. Have a glorious relatively warm early winter day before the snow arrives? Hike Wachusett.

HOW TO GET THERE

In Westminster, take Exit 25 off Route 2. Turn right to travel south on Route 140. Drive about 2.2 miles and turn right on Mile Hill Road. Travel about 0.5 mile and turn right on Bolton Road, then left into a ski-area parking lot about 0.2 mile later. Look for the tan maintenance building on the right. The trailhead is there.

The trails are in Wachusett Mountain State Reservation, 345 Mountain Road, PO Box 248, Princeton, MA 01541; phone: 978-464-2987; web: www.mass.gov/dcr/parks /central/wach.htm. Fee to access parking along the summit road in season.

A foggy Wachusett summit obscures the vistas.
JAN BASCH

THE TRAIL

The yellow-blazed Balance Rock Trail (part of the Mid-State Trail) leaves the ski-area lodge parking area by the trailhead on a dirt road before a quick bend as it enters the woods and soon reaches Balance Rock at 0.4 mile. The rocks seem to defy gravity a bit. Maybe 20 feet high, it looks like they're stacked on top of each other.

Continue past Balance Rock to the dirt Balance Rock Road and walk up the dirt road about 150 feet to the 1.2-mile-long Old Indian Trail (a portion is part of the Mid-State Trail) as it ascends with more of a bite through the pine and hardwood forest, shortly crossing the junction with the Semuhenna Trail. Stay with the Old Indian Trail as its blazes turn blue. The pathway crosses ski trails and passes under a ski lift, eventually coming to the summit road. Walk down the road maybe 50 yards and continue on the other side, crossing a brook bed and ascending to a junction with the West Side Trail. Zigzag some over a rocky section before leveling off to reach the summit with its towers.

At the summit, take in the almost-360-degree panorama that on a clear day means seeing Boston's buildings in the east and the Worcester skyline in the south. The lake to the north at the mountain's base is Wachusett Lake, while farther on is the stony top of Mount Monadnock in the Granite State. Gaze to the east of Monadnock to spot Mount Watatic in Massachusetts edged by the New Hampshire border.

When you've had your fill of the mountain place on top, make your way back down the great hill to the trailhead along the same pathways.

18

Alander Mountain

Difficulty: Moderate to Strenuous
Time: 3½ to 4 hours
Distance (round trip): 5 miles
Elevation gain: 840 feet
Trails: Alander Mountain Trail
Map: USGS Bash Bish Falls, MA
Trailhead GPS coordinates: N42° 5.17' W73° 27.73'

The extreme southwestern corner of Massachusetts is home to low-lying Alander Mountain with its extensive three-state views and twin summits. One of the best vantage points in the Berkshires, the 2,250-foot-high mountain in Mount Washington State Forest towers above the glorious hills, farms, mountains, and forests of the southern Berkshires, New York (about a mile away), and Connecticut (some 6 miles to the south).

The 4,169-acre Mount Washington State Forest provides about 30 miles of hiking trails over some hardy terrain while also serving up wilderness camping (no amenities). Alander Mountain is home to a small rustic cabin in the saddle between the twin summits that fills up fast, especially on weekends. It's first-come first-serve and sleeps six. The trash policy is simple—if you lug it in, then lug it out. The trail also leads to one of those primitive camping areas.

Don't be nonchalant about a trek to a sub-2500-foot peak. The way to Alander's top along the blue-blazed Alander Mountain Trail is often rocky and muddy (depending on the season). In times of heavy rainfall, the streams in the hardwood forest swell easily and mightily. But there are also ferns in summer and mountain laurel in spring, plus scrub oak and seasonal blueberries. The forest has been regrown, clear-cut in the late eighteenth century to make fuel for local iron forges.

HOW TO GET THERE

In South Egremont at the junction of Routes 41 and 23, drive south on Route 41 for about

The trail passes through a meadow with a pond en route to Alander Mountain.

0.1 mile and turn right on Mount Washington Road, which later becomes East Street. Travel about 9 miles to Mount Washington State Forest on the right. The forest is open year-round, sunrise to sunset.

The trail is in Mount Washington State Forest, RD 3 East Street, Mount Washington, MA 01258; phone: 413-528-0330; web: www.mass.gov/dcr/parks/western/mwas .htm.

THE TRAIL

The initially wide Alander Mountain Trail leaves from behind headquarters with its picnic tables and informational kiosk, heading west across a field and into the woods. The pathway rises gradually, passing under some nice hemlock that offers shade before crossing by a stone wall and then a meadow where first glimpses of the mountain can be seen. Soon the trail reaches Lee Pond Brook and crosses over the rushing waters on a bridge.

At about 0.6 mile, the Charcoal Pit Trail enters left. Stay with the Alander Mountain Trail as it dips down to run alongside Lee Pond Brook for a spell.

At about 0.8 mile, the Ashley Brook Trail branches left. Again, stay on the Alander Mountain Trail as it comes to a bridge over

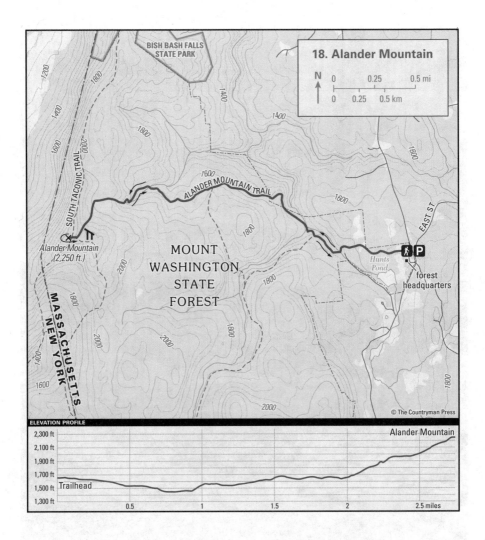

Ashley Brook. It's a nice spot to linger and take in the sun. Plus, it's near the confluence of Lee Pond and Ashley Hill Brooks. When the water's high, it's a roaring place.

The trail rises gently along an old woods road and by some aged stone walls. At 1.5 miles, the trails reaches a spur that leads to a primitive camping area.

The pathway narrows some as it parallels a stream and reaches the base of rocky ledges that increase in steepness. Relief is soon at hand. Once the trail flattens, shy of the summit and more than 2 miles into the hike, it reaches that cabin.

After the cabin, the trail bends to the right. The cover of trees is replaced by open sky. There is ledgy footing underneath and then there is the wonderful west summit and ridge of Alander Mountain.

A stunning platform, New York State's Catskills frame the horizon in the west, forming a ridge beyond the rural and forested

A bridge spans Lee Pond Brook to Alander Mountain.

landscape. Mount Greylock reigns to the north, while the Adirondacks and Albany are in the northwest. Nearby Mount Everett stands to the east. In the south, look back on Mount Frissell, the mountain in Massachusetts with a shoulder in Connecticut.

Alander Mountain is in a region called the Taconic Plateau where Massachusetts, New York, and Connecticut meet. Actually, the west side of the mountain is in New York, and the east in Massachusetts. The summit is also a place to gaze upon more hiking opportunities. The white-blazed South Taconic Trail is a north-south 15.7-mile-long pathway along the western side of the Taconics. Following it south for a spell along the ridge yields more stunning panoramas. A few miles to the north, the South Taconic Trail leads to Bash Bish Falls State Park (perhaps it's better to drive once down from the trailhead) and one of the Bay State's finest waterfalls.

But in the end, there's nothing wrong with returning to the trailhead along the Alander Mountain Trail after visiting a staggering small summit.

19

Mount Everett and Mount Race

Difficulty: Strenuous	
Time: 5 hours	
Distance (round trip): 7.2 miles	
Elevation gain: 2,200 feet	
Trails: Race Brook Trail, Appalachian Trail	
Map: USGS Bash Bish Falls, MA	
Trailhead GPS coordinates: N42° 5.36' W73° 24.68'	

Tackle two of the Bay State's tallest mountains while taking in Massachusetts, Connecticut, and New York vistas from the Appalachian Trail.

This outstanding and challenging T-shaped hike summits 2,624-foot Mount Everett and 2,365-foot Mount Race in a single journey within the 1,356-acre Mount Everett State Reservation (encompassed by the Mount Washington State Forest).

Both summits offer outstanding vistas, though the look from Race is less encumbered. Do both, or just do one.

Called the "Dome" by locals, Everett is the prominent Berkshire peak known for its summit of short pitch pine and scrub oak, fine views from ledges, and the site of a former fire tower dismantled in 2003. The way also passes splendid Race Brook Falls, an exceptional spot during the spring melt. Race also contains those stunted trees. Both mountains are known as being windswept places, so plan accordingly.

As if hiking both peaks isn't challenging enough, determined hikers can add another 2.6 miles to this trek for a total of 9.8 miles by continuing to and from tranquil Guilder Pond, with its spring blooms of azalea and mountain laurel. Also note a seasonal road provides easy access to Guilder Pond and Everett's summit as well.

For those who want to turn this into an overnight, there is a small primitive area called Race Brook Falls Campsite shy of the Dome's summit.

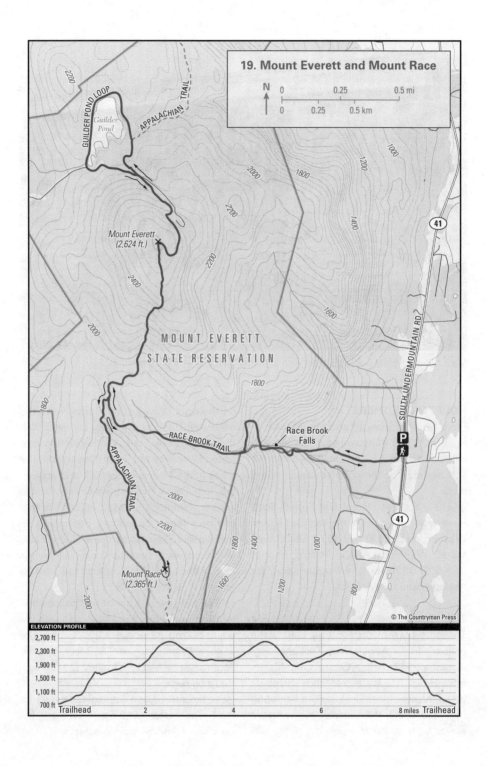

19. Mount Everett and Mount Race

N
0   0.25   0.5 mi
0   0.25   0.5 km

GUILDER POND LOOP

Guilder
Pond

APPALACHIAN TRAIL

2200

2200

2000

1800

1200

1000

2000

2200

1400

Mount Everett
(2,624 ft.)

2400

1600

2000

M O U N T   E V E R E T T
S T A T E   R E S E R V A T I O N

1800

1800

SOUTH UNDERMOUNTAIN RD

41

RACE BROOK TRAIL

Race Brook
Falls

P

APPALACHIAN TRAIL

2000

2000

1800

1400

1000

800

2200

41

1600

1200

Mount Race
(2,365 ft.)

2000

© The Countryman Press

ELEVATION PROFILE

2,700 ft
2,300 ft
1,900 ft
1,500 ft
1,100 ft
700 ft

Trailhead   2   4   6   8 miles Trailhead

Mount Everett hosts a stone shelter with a nearby bench shy of its summit.

HOW TO GET THERE

From South Egremont and the junction of Routes 23 and 41, travel south for about 5 miles on Route 41 to a small parking area and trailhead on the right-hand side of the road.

The trails are in the Mount Everett State Reservation. Contact is the same as Mount Washington State Forest, RD 3 East Street, Mount Washington, MA 01258; phone: 413-528-0330; web: www.mass.gov/dcr/parks/western/meve.htm.

THE TRAIL

The blue-blazed Race Brook Trail is the pathway to the Appalachian Trail, the long-distance trail between Georgia and Maine. Race Brook Trail is steep at times and starts by an informational kiosk before venturing by a field. Under the hemlock, the trail soon serves up a choice as a side trail to the falls on the right provides an alternative to the main way. That trail eventually connects with the Race Brook Trail. Another option it to ascend one way and on the return take the other route. For now, bear left and stay on the Race Brook Trail as the path has a stable ascent, eventually crossing tributaries that can be a trickle or gushing, depending on the season. Take a breather at Upper Falls, where the water tumbles down a large rock face. At about 0.5 mile, a side trail leads a short way to Middle Falls.

The path eases up a bit and passes that tent site just below the intersection with the white-blazed AT about 1.9 miles into the journey. Mount Race, at 2,365 feet, is to the south and reached in 1.1 miles. Don't worry. You'll be back.

At the intersection, turn right at the AT for the Everett summit at 2.5 miles. It's only flat for a short time before the steep and rocky

Guilder Pond is nestled on the shoulder of Mount Everett.

ascent to the top. Note the trees shrinking in size as you gain elevation and views with looks out to Race Mountain.

On the summit, the iron Mount Washington Tower is no more. Named for the town in Massachusetts where it stood, it dated back to 1915. The original tower was 30 feet high, and the three states that command the horizon also contributed to its operation and upkeep during its heyday. The state of Massachusetts staffed the tower until 1972.

From the summit, there are views from ledges to the northeast and south. Greylock is to the north while the south and west are packed with mountains like Alander, Frissell, and Connecticut's Bear Mountain. Stick around to take in the sun, vistas, and lunch before embarking on the next section to Mount Race.

For those hikers feeling motivated, it's a 2.6-mile out-and-back journey north along the AT to beautiful Guilder Pond, its picnic area, and loop trail around the shores. This option begins by descending the AT where soon a spur trail leads to a clearing with a bench and stone shelter affording fine views.

But for this hike, return down from the Everett summit to the col junction with the Race Brook Trail, this time staying on the white-blazed AT to Race. The trail displays typical behavior as a link between two peaks, dipping down while the trees increase in size before the swell rises again and trees become dwarfed as the AT leads to a rock scramble and the summit, with 360-degree views.

Much of the same real estate is encountered at Race's ledgy summit as on Everett, but you see more of it with Alander and the Catskills to the west and Greylock to the north. Of course, there is one mountain you couldn't see from Everett that you can from Race, and that's the Dome next door.

Lounge about for a bit or venture a tad farther south on the AT for more dramatic views before climbing down Race to the col junction with the Race Brook Trail, turning right on the blue-blazed trail and hiking down the steeps to the falls, enjoying it one more time but from a different perspective.

20

Mount Greylock

Difficulty: Strenuous

Time: 5 to 6 hours

Distance (round trip): 8 miles

Elevation gain: 2,390 feet

Trails: Hopper Trail, Appalachian Trail

Map: USGS Williamstown, MA

Trailhead GPS coordinates:
N42° 39.33' W73° 12.31'

At 3,491 feet, Mount Greylock is not only the highest peak in Massachusetts but also in southern New England. Plus, it's also a large mountain, running more than 10 miles in length from north to south. Nestled in the Bay State's rolling northwest corner, the Taconic Ranges stand to the west while the Hoosac Range calls the east home. To the north, the Hoosic River Valley is laid out in the foreground, followed by Vermont's rippling Green Mountains. The mountain touches some six towns too.

Located in the 12,500-acre Mount Greylock State Reservation, there are more than 70 miles of trails for hiking, cross-country skiing, mountain biking, snowshoeing, and snowmobiling. The Appalachian Trail graces the reservation. Primitive camping, like at Sperry Campground or at the five lean-to shelters, provide a remote experience for backpackers while birders enjoy the wildflowers and butterflies as well. Hunters also use the area, so blaze orange in season works.

Throw in a summit road with a war memorial at its top and an appreciated seasonal lodge. Road bikers use the road as a challenge; there's even an annual bicycle race to Greylock's top. Downhill skiing also has its place on Greylock. The storied Thunderbolt Ski Trail graces the eastern slope. Cut in 1934, the trail was the site of the first Massachusetts State Downhill Championship race. Today, it's a classic backcountry run worthy of bragging rights.

Mount Greylock State Reservation was the Bay State's first wilderness park,

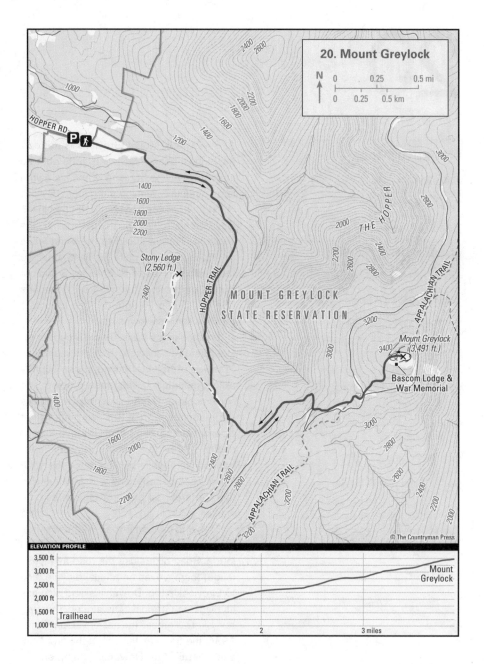

20. Mount Greylock

N
0   0.25   0.5 mi
0   0.25   0.5 km

HOPPER RD

Stony Ledge
(2,560 ft.)

HOPPER TRAIL

THE HOPPER

APPALACHIAN TRAIL

MOUNT GREYLOCK
STATE RESERVATION

Mount Greylock
(3,491 ft.)

Bascom Lodge &
War Memorial

APPALACHIAN TRAIL

© The Countryman Press

ELEVATION PROFILE

3,500 ft
3,000 ft
2,500 ft
2,000 ft
1,500 ft Trailhead
1,000 ft

Mount
Greylock

1   2   3 miles

established in 1898 with some 400 acres. The paved road—there are two ways up (from Lanesborough and North Adams)—was first constructed in 1906, and in 1996 the parkway was named a state-designated scenic byway. The summit is on the National Register of Historic Places.

The 93-foot-high memorial, with its spiral

The Massachusetts Veterans War Memorial Tower graces the summit of Mount Greylock.

looking north. Finally, a western gaze yields the Hudson River Valley, Taconics, Albany, and Berlin Mountain.

The rustic wood-and-stone Bascom Lodge is named after John Bascom, a former Williams College professor and champion for protecting the mountain and its surroundings. It was constructed between 1932 and 1938 and has a welcoming stone fireplace.

So, you're right in thinking Greylock is a busy place. It's one of those hikes where you can get a burger at the top. But it's also beautiful. Think midweek, non-holiday on this one, as peak periods draw masses of all types.

Choosing a route up Greylock is no easy task, but using the Hopper and Appalachian Trails serves up a popular and rewarding hike up and down Greylock through the Hopper, a glacially carved cirque through the thick forest and by gushing brooks in season.

HOW TO GET THERE

From Williamstown, drive south on Route 43 about 2.5 miles and make a left on Hopper Road. Travel some 1.3 miles and bear left on Hopper Road, going to the trailhead at Haley Farm (a working cattle farm) some .8 mile down.

The trails are in Mount Greylock State Reservation, 30 Rockwell Road, Lanesborough, MA 01237; phone: 413-499-4262; web: www.mass.gov/dcr/parks/mt Greylock/. There is a visitor center open seasonally.

THE TRAIL

The hike begins on a gentle farm road. At 0.2 mile, turn right on the Hopper Trail. Initially the trail is somewhat uniform, but it doesn't take long for the trail to enter the Hopper on Greylock's west side and start the steep climb through the unspoiled ravine. There's

staircase and windows, is open seasonally and affords wondrous views. The smart-looking tower was built in 1932 and marks the highest point in Massachusetts. Plaques help visitors identify the landscape. To the south is Cheshire, the Berkshires, Onota Lake, Pittsfield, and New York's Catskills. Mounts Monandock and Wachusett, the Hoosic River Valley, and Adams are in the east. New York's Adirondacks, Vermont's Green Mountains, and the towns of North Adams and Williamstown are found while

The clouds open up a brief window for a view of the countryside below Mount Greylock.

some relief as the trail catches up to Sperry Road and the campground at 2.4 miles. There are some options at this point for those wanting to extend the outing. The road (to the right) leads to Stony Ledge some 0.8 mile away, with its splendid look down over the Hopper.

But for this journey, turn left and stay on the road for another 0.2 mile (for a total of 2.6 miles) as it leads by the campground entrance and another side trip, this one 0.8 mile to March Cataract Falls, which plunge some 30 feet down the mountain's western slope. The Hopper Trail pushes into the forest on the left and continues upward to an intersection with the Overlook Trail, itself a fine striking alternative for the return trip, for those who want to shake things up.

Stay on the Hopper Trail. The trail parallels Rockwell Road, preparing hikers for their immersion with humanity on the summit. The Hopper Trail ends at the junction with the white-blazed Appalachian Trail at about 3.5 miles. It's about 0.5 mile up to the summit from here, first passing a tranquil pond and crossing the paved road.

Take your time on top. When you've had enough, head down the same way.

Introducing New Hampshire

Put simply, New Hampshire's White Mountains hold the best hiking in New England. There are countless adjectives to describe the highest mountains in the region: rugged, wondrous, majestic, awe-inspiring, deadly, severe, humbling.

They are all of that and more.

The highest peak in the northeast, Mount Washington, holds court in New Hampshire, surrounded by its Presidential Range brethren. The Franconia Range to the west has its incredible ridge trek. Not ready for those? Stick to the foothills for looks about the lakes.

Some 800,000 acres of the White Mountain National Forest unveil an impressive and protective wrap through the central and northern parts of the state. It is a giant playground and proving ground loaded with some 1,200 miles of trails, mountains, streams, rivers, lakes, bogs, and wilderness—true wilderness—where motors and wheels are banned.

Though hiking is well linked to the Whites, so is tourism. The region is loaded with scenic byways and state parks that offer visitors a chance to explore not only the trails but also the towns and villages. The Kancamagus Highway is a winding connection between Conway and Lincoln. Route 302 through Crawford Notch between Bartlett and Twin Mountain is loaded with waterfalls, history, and in winter, ice climbers easily seen from the road. Backroads are many. Even I-93 through Franconia Notch State Park is a pleasing roadway most taken to enter a land rich with an alpine landscape waiting for hikers.

21

West Rattlesnake

Difficulty: Easy	
Time: 1 hour	
Distance (round trip): 1.8 miles	
Elevation gain: 450 feet	
Trails: Old Bridle Path	
Map: USGS Squam Mountains, NH	
Trailhead GPS coordinates: N43° 47.33' W71° 32.91'	

West Rattlesnake along the Old Bridle Path is the hike that gets you hooked on hiking.

Why?

The commanding views from the sunny ledges on the low-lying mountain topping out at 1,245 feet overlooking the nooks and crannies of Squam Lake are among the best in the region, if not the state. The gradual incline along the well-worn trail through the woodlands is about as uncomplicated as it gets. It's less than a mile to the top. Plus, the much-heralded lake itself is famous, the setting for the 1981 classic Academy Award–winning film *On Golden Pond*, about an aging couple spending the summer at their lake cottage.

But this is also a hike that many children will remember as the first one they did on their own power. Plus, as a hike in the southernmost foothills of the White Mountains, it is one that is hospitable in the early and late seasons, as trails to the north may be in the grip of cold and snow.

So, the hike is very popular, particularly with picnicking families. As such, if solitude is sought, midweek and off-peak are the mantras.

The path is maintained by the Squam Lakes Association, which also oversees some 50 miles of trails in the area while offering remote camping on islands in the lake.

Squam Lake is a shimmering liquid jewel. The vast 6,765-acre lake is loaded with coves, inlets, and islands. A Lakes Region water playground for paddlers and motor boaters, the grand lake also contains island

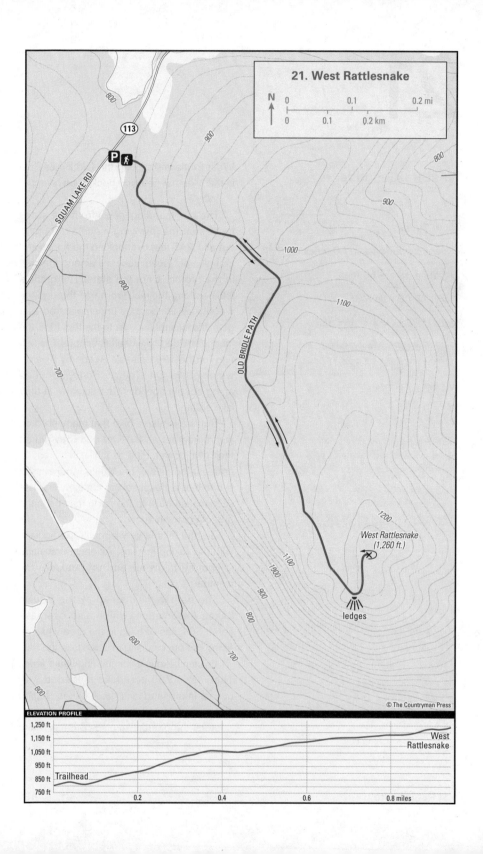

21. West Rattlesnake

N 0   0.1   0.2 mi
   0   0.1   0.2 km

113

SQUAM LAKE RD

P

800

900

800

900

1000

1100

OLD BRIDLE PATH

1200

*West Rattlesnake
(1,260 ft.)*

ledges

1100
1000
900
800
700
600
600

700

800

© The Countryman Press

ELEVATION PROFILE

1,250 ft
1,150 ft
1,050 ft
950 ft
850 ft
750 ft

Trailhead

West
Rattlesnake

0.2   0.4   0.6   0.8 miles

camping and a notable loon population. Bald eagles have also nested on Squam Lake. So bring the binoculars for those south and west views.

HOW TO GET THERE

From I-93, take Exit 24 and drive south on US Route 3 about 4.5 miles to Holderness and turn left on NH 113. The trailhead is about 6 miles down the road, with trailhead parking on the left. The trail is on the right.

The trail is maintained by the Squam Lakes Association, 534 Route 3, Holderness, NH 03245; phone: 603-968-7335; web: www.squamlakes.org.

THE TRAIL

The trail, an old cart road, is welcoming through the oak, beech, and pine forest as it ascends the northwest side of the mountain. There are long and wide stone and log steps to navigate. As the trail ascends to the edgy outcroppings, red pine becomes commonplace. The forest thins.

Maybe three-quarters of the way up, there is a spot to rest on the right side by a few boulders, including a flat one.

Soon thereafter, a spur path diverges right to a scenic outlook that has some overgrown vegetation. The view is just a taste of things to come.

Just before reaching the summit, a spur path leads to a helmet-shaped rock that seems almost cave-like.

Near the top is a junction for a number of trails, so be sure to return along the Old Bridle Path. There are also log steps to climb before reaching the stunning ledges.

From the top, and the open ledges, look some 500 feet below upon the lake's many coves and islands. The state's largest lake, Winnipesaukee, is out in the distance along with the Belknap Range and Mount Belknap at 2,834 feet with its fire tower. To the west,

The Old Bridle Path up West Rattlesnake is easy and well-maintained.

the flat ridge of Mount Webster, part of the Squam Range, is spotted.

If possible, stop and listen as the waters below echo the rhythms of lake life, from boats to docks to homes.

The summit is preserved and part of the University of New Hampshire's Armstrong Natural Area. A sign states the area should "be left undisturbed in its natural state for scientific, educational and inspirational purposes."

According to a brochure created by the New Hampshire Natural Heritage Bureau,

From the ledges of West Rattlesnake the view is outstanding.

the summit and its ledges are "rich red oak rocky woods."

The flat slabs of rock at the summit are ideal spots for a lunch and a wonderful place to gather inspiration.

Keep an eye out for children, making sure they don't venture too close to the edges. Take in the views. Enjoy the company and surroundings on a wonderful perch before returning the same way you came.

22

Mount Willard

Difficulty: Easy to Moderate

Time: 2 hours

Distance (round trip): 3.2 miles

Elevation gain: 900 feet

Trails: Avalon Trail, Mount Willard Trail

Map: USGS Crawford Notch, NH

Trailhead GPS coordinates:
N44° 13.07' W71° 24.69'

There is one word that comes to mind when describing Mount Willard—wow.

The fabulous panorama from the rocky ledges overlooking rugged Crawford Notch, said to have been discovered by Lancaster hunter Timothy Nash during a 1771 moose hunt, is one of the best views for the effort in the White Mountains. Stand above a huge U-shaped valley carved by glaciers. Look for Mount Chocorua's rocky summit cone in the south. See the scars from rockslides on 4,285-foot Mount Willey next door.

And during summer's radiance, scour about the outcrop for blueberries in season.

The way up to Mount Willard's 2,865-foot summit is fairly elementary, but some could find the hike on the harder side of easy. Seasoned hikers may see it as a bit of a friendly jaunt, while those just discovering hiking may sweat a bit more than they thought.

Either way, the investment in time and energy yields staggering rewards for all generations of outdoor lovers.

The block-like mountain is in a popular outdoor recreational hub: Crawford Notch. The Appalachian Mountain Club's Highland Lodge is next to the trailhead, and the Mount Washington Hotel, with its ski trails and plush accommodations, is nearby. Keen-eyed kids might spot the trunk on Elephant Head rock across the road by the entrance to Crawford Notch State Park by a couple of roadside cascades—Silver and Flume.

The park is a splendid and rugged 5,775-acre playground loaded with trails, those waterfalls, wildlife spotting, and wonderful alpine views. The park is open year-round to

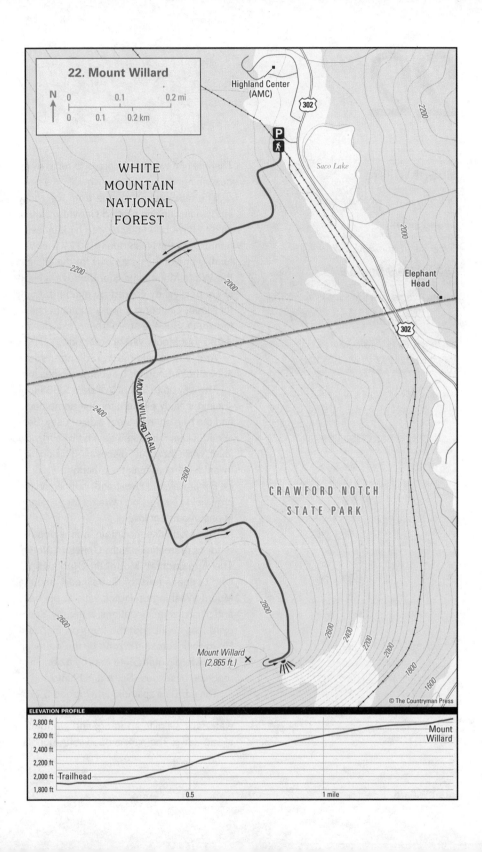

22. Mount Willard

N

0   0.1   0.2 mi
0   0.1   0.2 km

Highland Center
(AMC)

302

Saco Lake

WHITE
MOUNTAIN
NATIONAL
FOREST

2200

2200

2000

2000

Elephant
Head

302

MOUNT WILLARD TRAIL

2400

2400

2600

2600

CRAWFORD NOTCH

STATE PARK

3000

2800

2600

2400

2200

2000

1800

1600

Mount Willard
(2,865 ft.)

© The Countryman Press

ELEVATION PROFILE

2,800 ft	
2,600 ft	Mount Willard
2,400 ft	
2,200 ft	
2,000 ft	
1,800 ft Trailhead	

0.5   1 mile

Mount Willard makes quite an impression from Route 302 in Crawford Notch.

recreation, but there is seasonal camping in the Dry River Campground along Route 302 several miles east of the trailhead.

Also a few miles east of the trailhead is the seasonal Willey House. The location is the site of an August 1826 landslide that claimed nine lives. The house was once an inn and family residence. An oddity of the slide is that the house still stands, yet around it were strewn boulders and other detritus.

Also across the way from the trailhead is tiny Saco Lake, the source of the Saco River, which flows to the Atlantic Ocean through Maine. The notch is also home to the Conway Scenic Railroad and the track-side station is a familiar landmark alongside the AMC's Macomber Family Information Center.

Though more bustling in summer and fall, the neighborhood doesn't hibernate in winter, as ice climbers venture up the frozen pitches by the roadside and beyond. Mount Willard also makes an excellent introduction to winter hiking for those who want to get outside when the bugs are at bay.

HOW TO GET THERE

From I-93, take Exit 35, then Route 3 north to Twin Mountain and Route 302 east about 10 miles to Crawford Notch. From Glen, take Route 302 west about 21 miles to Crawford Notch. Trailhead parking is near an information center and Crawford Depot next to the Appalachian Mountain Club's Highland Center.

The route passes through Crawford Notch State Park, 2057 US Route 302, Harts Location, NH 03812; phone: 603-374-2272; web: nhstateparks.org.

THE TRAIL

Begin the out-and-back hike by carefully crossing the train tracks and heading into the quiet of the woods on the Avalon Trail for

The ledges of Mount Willard afford a look at a glorious landscape no matter the season.

about a tenth of a mile. Take a left by a kiosk (an information board) on the blue-blazed Mount Willard Trail to the sun-drenched ledges that are just below the peak's actual summit, about a mile and a half away.

The pathway blazes through the hardwood and birch forest along a brook, eventually coming to a basin at the bottom of a small waterfall. That's Centennial Pool, and it's cold.

The trail is forgiving as it follows a former wide carriage road, which at one point was the way for guests to go to the Crawford House, a hotel lost in a 1977 fire. As the way leads into the state park, the trail narrows, and boughs from evergreens act as sentries. Grommets will be able to continue on their way, while adults may have some ducking to do before bursting out onto the glorious ledges. There are no rails for protection on the splendid outcrop. Don't venture close to the edge.

Many players take part in the magnificence of the Willard view. At times, the ledge is visited by plump jays who stay steady for the camera. Below, Route 302 slithers like a serpent while the train tracks cut their way through the mountainside. The notch has seen many rockslides over the years, the most famous in 1826 following torrential rains that caused an avalanche, killing the Willey family. The ledgy scars can still be seen on the right-hand side (the west) of Mount Willey.

To the left, in the east, Mounts Webster, Jackson, Pierce, and Eisenhower stand mightily. If the weather's right, look for Mount Washington in the distance before exiting one of the Whites' most picturesque stages and returning the same way.

23

Welch-Dickey Loop

Difficulty: Moderate	
Time: 3 hours	
Distance (round trip): 4.4 miles	
Elevation gain: 1,800 feet	
Trails: Welch-Dickey Loop Trail	
Map: USGS Waterville Valley, NH	
Trailhead GPS coordinates: N43° 54.27' W71° 35.32'	

Double the mountains, double the fun. The 4.4-mile circuit over the top of a pair of sub-3,000 footers is high on the popularity list of White Mountain hikes. Quite simply, the views are superb, the blueberries are sweet, the plant life is educational, and the ledges provide that alpine feeling well below treeline. The granite slabs and bedrock make exceptional viewpoints, but again, they are slippery when wet. This is a popular family outing, and parents need to pay attention to their children.

Welch Mountain is the smaller of the pair, at 2,605 feet. But it's the winner on this one, with its eagle-eye vantage point down to the Mad River Valley and across to Sandwich Mountain and more. Dickey is no slouch at 2,734 feet, with its open ledges and rock slabs.

Keep watch for jack pine on Welch Mountain. Though readily found in the boreal forests of Canada, it's not very common in New Hampshire. Look for the inch-long needles in bundles of two. There's also fragrant Labrador tea, with its white flowers, to be found along the way.

The hike is easily accessible from I-93 and is near the Waterville Valley Resort, which means you won't be alone during peak hiking season. The trail is also noted for being among the first in the White Mountains to be clear of snow. Those hikers seeking less humanity might consider an off-season or midweek experience.

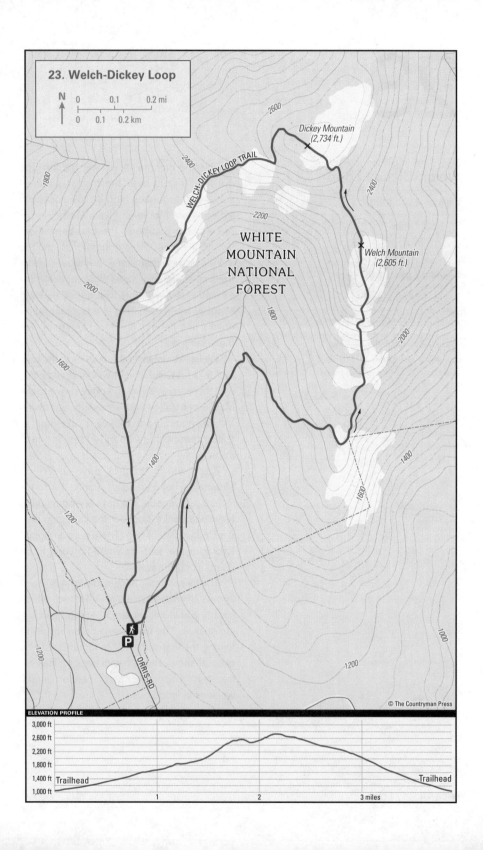

23. Welch-Dickey Loop

N

| 0 | 0.1 | 0.2 mi |
| 0 | 0.1 | 0.2 km |

2600

Dickey Mountain
(2,734 ft.)

2400

WELCH-DICKEY LOOP TRAIL

1800

2400

2200

WHITE
MOUNTAIN
NATIONAL
FOREST

× Welch Mountain
(2,605 ft.)

2000

1800

2000

1600

1400

1400

1200

1600

1000

1200

© The Countryman Press

ORRIS RD.

P

1200

ELEVATION PROFILE

| 3,000 ft |
| 2,600 ft |
| 2,200 ft |
| 1,800 ft |
| 1,400 ft | Trailhead |
| 1,000 ft |

Trailhead

1   2   3 miles

HOW TO GET THERE

Leave I-93 on Exit 28 and travel east toward Waterville Valley on NH 49 for about 5.6 miles. Turn left on Upper Mad River Road. In about a half mile, turn right onto Orris Road by a sign for the trail. Travel about 0.6 mile and turn right on a dirt road to the trailhead.

A White Mountain National Forest Service Recreation Pass is required for parking at the trailhead.

The hike is in the White Mountain National Forest. White Mountain National Forest Headquarters, 71 White Mountain Drive, Campton, NH 03223; phone: 603-536-6100; web: www.fs.usda.gov/white mountain.

THE TRAIL

Nearly immediately into the hike, a decision must be made. The moderate trail leads to both mountains and subsequently over both peaks. This hike is described counterclockwise. Why? It's about 1.3 miles to the scenic panorama, so if you run out of gas—or the kids are antsy—it's an easy out and back down to the parking area. Plus, this also means hiking up a steep portion of Welch's south ridge, much better than gingerly going down it.

The right branch leads to a pleasant stream—readily crossed—and then follows the bank for about a half mile on a gentle ascent before making a right and rising to the first of the open summit ledges.

A sign warns hikers they are entering a regeneration area. Using rocks to cordon off the mosses, lichens, and herbaceous plants in this high-traffic area gives them a chance to spring back to life. The ledges take on the feel of a rock garden. Blueberries appear in summer. The mountain vistas are year-round.

The Welch-Dickey Loop is one of the most popular hikes near Waterville Valley.

Rock-hopping skills help navigate streams on the Welch-Dickey Loop.

To the east, gaze across the valley to hulking 3,980-foot Sandwich Mountain in the Sandwich Range. Also out there is 4,000-plus-foot Tripyramid, with its jagged peaks.

The trail then proceeds steeply, with some scrambling to be done up to the ledges atop Welch, first passing some of those jack pines and some stunted birches.

The Welch summit, with its splendid panorama, is reached at 2 miles. For those who don't like dealing with much humanity, try this one off-peak. In the eastern sky, the slides of Tripyramid can be spotted. Mount Moosilauke is to the west. There's Waterville Valley, and to the south, the ripples of central New Hampshire. Of course, there is also Dickey, next spot on the loop.

The trail descends quickly into the col between the mountains among the spruce, moss, and blueberries before climbing steadily again to the wooded summit of Dickey at about 2.4 miles, with its open ledges and vistas to the Sandwich Range and the triangulated Franconia peaks of Lafayette, Lincoln, and Flume.

Views are many from the rocky ledges of Dickey on the descent. Cairns and blazes mark the way along the dwarf evergreens. The spruce forest has lots of ferns, and wildflowers tend to bloom in spring.

The ledge experience isn't over with yet. About 3.2 miles into the loop, there is an impressive outlook with an equally impressive drop-off. Take a last look at Welch before entering back into the forest, with its maple and beech trees. As the trail descends somewhat steeply, it's back to hardwoods. The open vistas are gone, replaced with the limbs and leaves of the forest. The trail eventually joins an old logging road and makes its way along a small ravine before returning to the parking area.

24

Boulder Loop

Difficulty: Easy to Moderate

Time: 2 hours

Distance (round trip): 3.1 miles

Elevation gain: 950 feet

Trails: Boulder Loop Trail

Map: USGS North Conway West, NH

Trailhead GPS coordinates:
N44° 0.29' W71° 14.32'

Worthy cliffs, protruding ledges, a covered bridge, the flowing Swift River, and a touch of history meld together to make the Boulder Loop Trail on the edge of the Moat Range a small mountain classic.

The nearly thousand feet of elevation gain yields glorious White Mountain National Forest views of peaks like Chocorua and Passaconaway. The trail sees lots of use, particularly in autumn's glory and summer's heat, and in 2007 and 2009 received cosmetic improvements like rock steps and waterbars that help prevent erosion.

The trail to the ledges at 1,750 feet is in an interesting neck of the woods. There are many huge boulders or glacial erratics left behind from the tremendous ice sheet that once covered the area thousands of years ago. The glacier ice melted and sort of sandblasted the terrain. The rocks are fun for careful exploration and perhaps a bit of bouldering. But they are also home to lichen, a plant that's basically a combination of a fungus and algae. The plants emit an acid which seeps through the rock, crumbling it down in one of the first steps in producing soil.

The pathway also leads through a couple of forest types: the broad-leaf deciduous forest and the evergreens, known as conifers.

The trailhead is generally reached by traveling the popular and winding Kancamagus Highway (Route 112) that meanders more than 30 miles between Conway and Lincoln. The scenic byway leads to the photo-worthy Albany Covered Bridge built in 1859 and renovated in 1970. The bridge crosses the rambling and rocky Swift River. There are

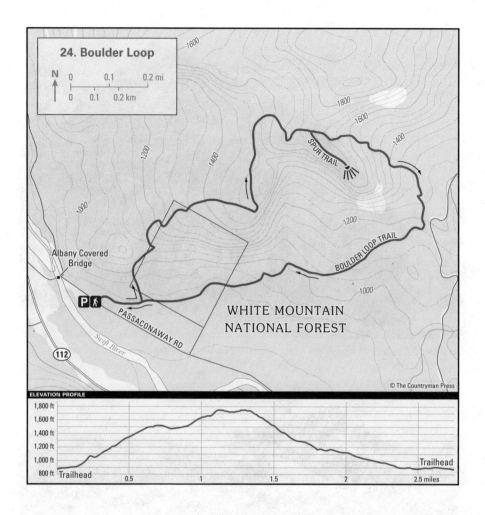

24. Boulder Loop

N
0   0.1   0.2 mi
0   0.1   0.2 km

SPUR TRAIL

BOULDER LOOP TRAIL

Albany Covered Bridge

PASSACONAWAY RD

Swift River

112

WHITE MOUNTAIN
NATIONAL FOREST

© The Countryman Press

ELEVATION PROFILE

1,800 ft
1,600 ft
1,400 ft
1,200 ft
1,000 ft
800 ft   Trailhead

Trailhead

0.5   1   1.5   2   2.5 miles

restrooms on both sides of the river, and historical placards. Take a few minutes to read about the bridge, constructed to allow vehicles "a load of hay high and a load of hay wide" to pass. Benches by a tiny pier offer spots for rest and reflection. The US Forest Service's Covered Bridge Campground is across the road too.

HOW TO GET THERE

From the junction of Route 16 and the Kancamagus Highway (Route 112), travel west on the Kancamagus Highway for 6.5 miles and turn right on Dugway Road, cross the covered bridge, and turn right in to trailhead parking. The trail begins across the road.

A White Mountain National Forest Service Recreation Pass is required for parking.

The hike is in the White Mountain National Forest. White Mountain National Forest Headquarters, 71 White Mountain Drive, Campton, NH 03223; phone: 603-536-6100; web: www.fs.usda.gov/white mountain.

The Albany Covered Bridge is the gateway to the Boulder Loop Trail.

The ledges along the Boulder Loop Trail serve up wonderful views of the valley in all seasons.

THE TRAIL

This circuit is described in a clockwise direction.

The yellow-blazed trail through the maple, hemlock, red pine, oak, and ash leaves the north side of Dugway Road, quickly entering the woods and soon reaching a trail junction. Stay left and begin the ascent that soon reaches a vantage point to the rocky cone of Mount Chocorua, the Kanc, and the Swift. This is only a taste of what is to come.

There are also remnants of nature's wrath left behind along the trail. Uprooted trees and snapped tree crowns are the aftermath of serious storms, while stumps remain from timber sales in the 1940s.

At about 1.3 miles, a spur path leads to the first-class ledges with a birds-eye view of the lush Passaconaway Valley. Pay attention to the sheer cliffs' edges. The views encompass the south, east, and west. Rocky top Chocorua is familiar. The mountain's northern ridge is formed by the summits called Three Sisters. From the ledge, Middle Sister stands out at 3,354 feet and contains an old fire tower. Also on the horizon is the massive wooded and viewless crown of 4,043-foot Mount Passaconaway in the Sandwich Range.

After enjoying the ledges, return to the main trail and continue the loop by turning right. The ledges are left behind for an initial spiral drop through the woods before returning to relatively easier terrain. A small brook, a tributary of the Swift that flows into the nearby Saco River, is easily negotiated.

Too soon it seems, the circuit is completed when those large granite boulders come into sight again. They are a fitting start and finish to the Boulder Loop.

25

North and Middle Sugarloaf

Difficulty: Easy to Moderate

Time: 2½ hours

Distance (round trip): 3.2 miles

Elevation gain: 1,100 feet

Trails: Trestle Trail, Sugarloaf Trail

Map: USGS Twin Mountain, NH

Trailhead GPS coordinates:
N44° 15.28' W71° 30.24'

Sugarloaf Mountain is like Main Street, USA, in New England. There are so many of them. There's one in western Massachusetts, another in northern Vermont, and the pyramid-shaped one in Maine that hosts a ski area (plus the Pine Tree State has a smaller Sugarloaf near the New Hampshire border in Evans Notch). Even Rhode Island has one. Sort of. It's called Sugarloaf Hill.

New Hampshire is king of the Sugarloafs (or is that Sugarloaves?), with a backpack filled with them.

The Sugarloaf Mountains—that's the 2,539-foot Middle Sugarloaf, and North Sugarloaf at 2,310 feet—in the White Mountain National Forest are well worth the journey. Actually, there's a third Sugarloaf in the bunch, with South Sugarloaf chiming in at 3,024 feet. But it doesn't have any trails.

Middle and North are both bare, ledgy summits with the Presidential Range on the horizon. The T-shaped hike is loaded with features, from a flat walk along the Zealand River to the towering trailside glacial erratics. Wooden steps lead to the summit of Middle, while North is home to a long-abandoned quarry where smoky quartz used to be mined.

They are a couple of small mountains that serve up big views, towering above Twin Mountain with a trailhead located between Franconia and Crawford Notches. This is a good choice for a family hike and also for those who are young at heart. Either spot is ideal for lunch and lingering.

Get up and down Middle Sugarloaf with the help of a ladder.

HOW TO GET THERE

From the junction (traffic light) of US 3 and 302 in Twin Mountain, travel about 2 miles east on 302 and turn right on Zealand Road, also called Forest Road 16 (by the White Mountain National Forest Zealand campground; the road is closed in winter) and drive about a mile–past the two Sugarloaf Campgrounds–to the trailhead by the Zealand River bridge on the right.

A White Mountain National Forest Service Recreation Pass is required for parking.

The hike is in the White Mountain National Forest. White Mountain National Forest Headquarters, 71 White Mountain Drive, Campton, NH 03223; phone: 603-536-6100; web: www.fs.usda.gov/white mountain.

THE TRAIL

The hike begins by briefly walking the road and going over the bridge. The trail is on the right.

The Sugarloaf Trail coincides with the Trestle Trail for about the first 0.25 mile of the hike as it parallels the river and passes by an area that saw a washout from the storm of 2011. The two trails soon diverge, with the Trestle Trail continuing straight. Turn left on the Sugarloaf Trail as it rises with rock steps to cross an old logging road and snowmobile trail in the birch and fir forest. Fairly soon log bridges make it easier to navigate a muddy area, while following that there's a short flat section clearly done by those who maintain the trail.

Boulders are next on the journey, left behind by the glaciers that once ruled the region. There are many shapes and sizes: split, mossy, covered in lichen. Squeeze through or go around, making time to examine the landscape.

About 0.75 mile into the hike, the pathway steepens. But rock staircases and switchbacks help ease the effort.

Soon enough, the trail enters the gap between the two mountains and then reaches the col where the trail splits at 0.9 mile with signs to both peaks.

For North Sugarloaf, turn right and follow the yellow blazes to the summit, 0.3 mile away. The trail soon drops fairly sharply for

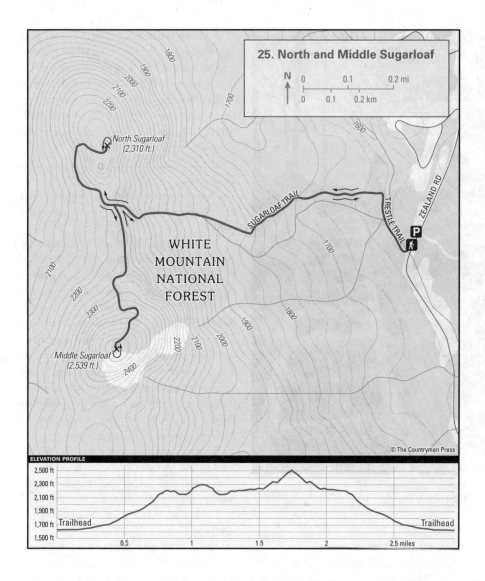

25. North and Middle Sugarloaf

North Sugarloaf
(2,310 ft.)

SUGARLOAF TRAIL

TRESTLE TRAIL

ZEALAND RD

WHITE
MOUNTAIN
NATIONAL
FOREST

Middle Sugarloaf
(2,539 ft.)

© The Countryman Press

ELEVATION PROFILE

2,500 ft
2,300 ft
2,100 ft
1,900 ft
1,700 ft — Trailhead — Trailhead
1,500 ft

0.5   1   1.5   2   2.5 miles

---

a spell before wrapping around the base of the ledges at an easier grade, though there are rocks and roots.

The first ledge tackled isn't the top, so continue following the yellow blazes as they curve on to the summit at 1.2 miles, where Mount Washington is easy to spot along with the Zealand Valley, Mount Hale, and Route 302. North has expansive views, but Middle is more enchanting.

Return the 0.3 mile to the col (1.5 miles) and then continue 0.4 mile to the Middle Sugarloaf summit at 2 miles after negotiating a series of slabs, a steep pitch or two, and a much-appreciated wooden ladder. Middle's summit is more open and offers more

New Hampshire

Find a rock and relax on Middle Sugarloaf.

extensive views to the Rosebrook Range (home to the Bretton Woods ski area), the village of Twin Mountain below, and more hulking landmarks like the Twins, among the state's tallest. There's also a look back at the ledges on North Sugarloaf.

There are also some nice boulders and ledges that make for outstanding photo opportunities. Be sure to be aware of the edges though.

The trailhead is reached by retracing the route to the saddle, turning right, and following the pathway back to the road. Some of the footing on the way down from Middle may prove irritating to some hikers. Just take it slow and easy.

26

Mount Chocorua

Difficulty: Moderate	
Time: 5 hours	
Distance (round trip): 7.6 miles	
Elevation gain: 2,250 feet	
Trails: Champney Falls Trail, Piper Trail	
Map: USGS Mount Chocorua, NH	
Trailhead GPS coordinates: N43° 59.40' W71° 17.97'	

Step up to Mount Chocorua. It is one of the White Mountains' most distinguished natural landmarks. From the large bare 3500-foot rocky cone-domed summit, the Granite State's glory rolls out below in a seemingly endless horizon of waves of mountains and shimmering waterways.

The mountain is extremely photogenic. If traveling to or from the Whites on Route 16, be sure to stop in the small parking area on Chocorua Lake Road north of Chocorua Village for a look at the peak on the eastern edge of the Sandwich Range, with a foreground of sparkling 220-acre Lake Chocorua.

Chocorua was an Abenaki Indian chief, and legend has it he leaped to his death off the mountaintop while putting a curse on the settlers he blamed for his son's accidental death. The mountain also once hosted the two-story Peak House, which was blown apart by high winds in 1915. Visitors paid 13 dollars per week to stay there during its heyday.

The mountain also was home to the Halfway House, a former logging camp. That hotel was one story higher than the Peak House. There was something of a toll there, as pedestrians had to pay a quarter each way.

The Chocorua Mountain Club built a cabin on the Peak House site in 1924. It succumbed to the elements when strong winds blew off the roof in 1932. The US Forest Service replaced that cabin with the Jim Liberty Cabin.

Chocorua, though not a 4,000 footer, is a first big mountain for many hikers. Its popularity is legendary, especially approaching

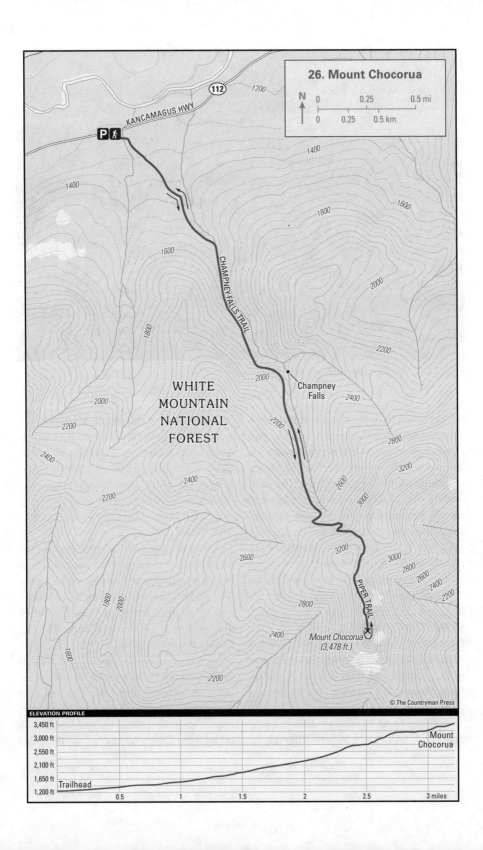

26. Mount Chocorua

N 0   0.25   0.5 mi
0   0.25   0.5 km

112

KANCAMAGUS HWY

1200

1400

1400

1600

1800

2000

1600

CHAMPNEY FALLS TRAIL

2000

2200

■ Champney
Falls

2400

WHITE
MOUNTAIN
NATIONAL
FOREST

2000

2200

2400

2200

2600

2200

2800

2600

3000

3200

3200

PIPER TRAIL

3000

2800

2600

2400

2200

1800

2000

1600

2400

2800

*Mount Chocorua
(3,478 ft.)*

2200

© The Countryman Press

ELEVATION PROFILE

3,450 ft
3,000 ft   Mount
2,550 ft   Chocorua
2,100 ft
1,650 ft
Trailhead
1,200 ft
         0.5   1   1.5   2   2.5   3 miles

Mount Chocorua's rocky spire is a popular place.

the mountain from the Kanc and the north. What is more, the trailhead is an easy find compared to many other trailheads for pathways up the mountain. Plus, it allows a visit to beautiful Champney Falls. The falls, and the trail, are named after nineteenth-century landscape painter Benjamin Champney. The acclaimed artist once sat in the middle of North Conway's Main Street to paint towering Mount Washington.

The landscape as seen from the slabs on the Chocorua summit is a work of art too.

HOW TO GET THERE

From Lincoln, take Route 112 (Kancamagus Highway) east about 20 miles. From Conway at the junction with Route 16, travel east on the Kancamagus 11.5 miles. The trailhead is on the south side.

A White Mountain National Forest Service Recreation Pass is required for parking.

The hike is in the White Mountain National Forest. White Mountain National Forest Headquarters, 71 White Mountain Drive, Campton, NH 03223; phone: 603-536-6100; web: www.fs.usda.gov/white mountain.

THE TRAIL

The hike begins from the trailhead on the Champney Falls Trail that crosses Twin Brook on a bridge before coming to a junction with the Bolles Trail on the right. Continuing on the Champney Falls Trail, it's a simple jaunt to Champney Brook. The trail follows the brook, eventually rising above it.

At 1.4 miles, a side trail parts to the left to Champney Falls, a trip well worth taking. The 70-foot cascades are a goal unto themselves for many hikers not wanting to make the summit trip. The trail loops back up with the Champney Falls Trail 0.3 miles

The views from Mount Chocorua take in the White Mountains and Lakes Region of New Hampshire.

up. Waterfalls are fickle. Depending on the amount of rain or snowmelt, the falls can be a trickle or remarkable and romantic curtains of rushing and refreshing water. Still, caution is advised near the sometimes slippery ledges.

The spur trail rejoins the main trail at 1.7 miles and soon affords looks to the east of a round rocky shoulder of Chocorua called Middle Sister. At 2.4 miles, the trail allows a better glimpse of the alpine landscape and winds to the right as a succession of switchbacks begin to the rocky ledges.

Soon it's time for a chain of trail junctions. At 3 miles, the Champney Falls Cutoff turns left. Turn right for Chocorua, and fairly soon stay right at the junction with the Middle Sister Trail. Enjoy the flats for a spell before navigating more rock and a look at Chocorua's cone.

The Champney Falls Trail ends at the intersection with the yellow-blazed Piper Trail. Follow it 0.6 mile to the summit through an evergreen gangway before scrambling over the rocks that can be slippery when wet. With each plateau, the views get better and more dramatic. Don't get too excited. Pay attention to the trail markings.

Don't expect to be alone on the summit. Whether it's a warm summer day or crisp day in autumn, the ledges are popular gathering places. From the summit, gaze upon the shimmering Lakes Region and White Mountains. There are commanding views to Chocorua Lake and Lake Winnipesaukee, the state's largest. Mount Washington is to the north while in the west are peaks like Tripyramid and Whiteface. Look for other natural sights like Cranmore's ski trails and Franconia Ridge.

Pick a spot and enjoy the views. Then return along the same trails.

27

North Moat

Difficulty: Strenuous

Time: 7 hours

Distance (round trip): 10 miles

Elevation gain: 2,750 feet

Trails: Moat Mountain Trail, Red Ridge Trail

Map: USGS North Conway West, NH

Trailhead GPS coordinates: N44° 4.48' W71° 9.84'

The Moat Mountains, or "The Moats" as locals call them, form a panoramic ridge west of North Conway. Often ignored by serious hikers focused on climbing New Hampshire's impressive 4,000-foot peaks, the three mountains themselves are worthy destinations serving up stunning White Mountain vistas in a neighborhood of low scrub brushes, odd rock formations, and stark ridges. North Moat is the king at 3,196 feet, followed by Middle Moat at 2,805 feet and South Moat at 2,770 feet.

To traipse the length of the mountains is a day well spent, traversing the summits with bald ridges because of a fire that burned the long narrow range years ago.

But another uplifting experience is hiking North Moat using the rugged loop comprised of the Moat Mountain and Red Ridge Trails.

North Moat is the chiseled stage from which to see many White Mountain highlights. Though far less tall than the mile-high peaks off in the horizon, from its ledgy crown the sky is loaded with hiking and tourist landmarks.

The rocky crag that is Mount Chocorua is easily spotted in the south, as is Conway Lake. The fire tower atop Kearsarge North stands in the west, as do the ski trails on North Conway's Cranmore Mountain The Presidential peaks and Carter Range reign to the north, while the sinuous Kancamagus Highway wiggles between the east and west.

But North Moat is not the only dais from which to ponder. The Red Ridge Trail has its

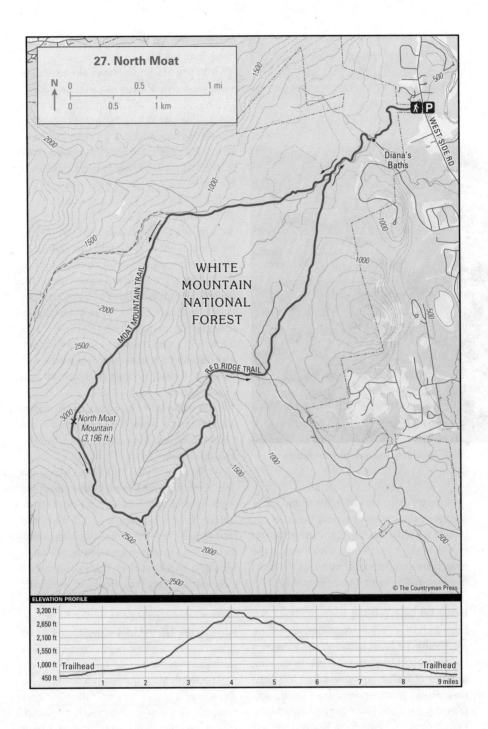

27. North Moat

N

0   0.5   1 mi

0   0.5   1 km

1500

500

2000

1000

WEST SIDE RD

Diana's
Baths

1000

1500

MOAT MOUNTAIN TRAIL

WHITE
MOUNTAIN
NATIONAL
FOREST

1000

1000

500

500

2000

2500

RED RIDGE TRAIL

3000

North Moat
Mountain
(3,196 ft.)

1500

1000

2500

1500

2000

500

2500

2000

© The Countryman Press

ELEVATION PROFILE

3,200 ft
2,650 ft
2,100 ft
1,550 ft
1,000 ft   Trailhead   Trailhead
450 ft

1   2   3   4   5   6   7   8   9 miles

North Moat contains a barren landscape.

own magnificent look at much of the same scenery via a windswept rocky expanse that is itself a worthy journey. Combining the two provides hikers with a magnificent look at the mountains and fields that make up the heart of the popular Mount Washington Valley.

HOW TO GET THERE

From Schouler Park in North Conway village and Route 16 (also called White Mountain Highway and Main Street), travel to the second set of traffic lights and turn left onto River Road, going under a train trestle and crossing the Saco River. Stay straight as the road becomes West Side Road. Turn left

into the trailhead for Diana's Baths about 2.5 miles from the traffic light.

A White Mountain National Forest Service Recreation Pass is required for parking.

The hike is in the White Mountain National Forest. White Mountain National Forest Headquarters, 71 White Mountain Drive, Campton, NH 03223; phone: 603-536-6100; web: www.fs.usda.gov/white mountain.

THE TRAIL

As with many loop hikes, this circuit can be done in either direction. Doing it counterclockwise, as is described here, tackles the steeps of the Moat Mountain Trail on the ascent instead of as a less forgiving descent.

The trek through the White Mountain National Forest starts with something of a suburban feel along the wide, well-manicured, and packed path under the evergreens with benches, fences, bridges, and picnic tables for the 0.6-mile journey to Diana's Baths. The rushing waterfalls, ledges, and potholes are at a former sawmill that operated in the 1800s. The seductive waters are a favored swimming hole.

At Diana's Baths, the Moat Mountain Trail turns right for a benign jaunt on an old logging road that flirts with the north bank of Lucy Brook for a spell. At 1.2 miles, the Red Ridge Trail—the pathway taken during the loop's descent—leaves left as the Moat Mountain Trail continues. Fairly soon there's a crossing of Lucy Brook that can be difficult during times of high water.

The relentless steeps up the northeast ridge to the North Moat summit are broken by a couple of vantage points before the final push to the summit at 4.3 miles.

The North Moat summit is a fine spot for a break and a look around. Often the only company is the wind, the clouds overhead, the incredible landscape, and stagnant

From North Moat, look down upon North Conway.

cairns. The trail soon dives back down into the coniferous forest and into a narrow knoll with sporadic widening ledges, followed by a junction marked by boulders and the Red Ridge Trail, which is the passageway for 3.6 miles before the trail returns to the junction with the Moat Mountain Trail.

Red Ridge is rather kind at the onset, soon leaving the cover of the forest before breaking out to a stunning, almost lunar landscape of rock ledges, with blueberries in season, pine, and spruce. There is a sense of being above treeline below the trees. It can be slow going along the Red Ridge.

There is some tricky footing to contend with while ogling the landscape.

The pathway returns to the trees with a few dips and a gravelly section. There's some zigging and zagging before crossing Moat Brook and a gravel forest road, then joining with the Moat Mountain Trail again at 8.8 miles. Turn right on the Moat Mountain Trail on what is now familiar ground. If Diana's Baths isn't that crowded, consider stopping there for a swim or splash before the final 0.5 mile or so to the trailhead. If you're hiking in July or August, chances are you won't be alone.

28

Mount Eisenhower

Difficulty: Moderate to Strenuous	
Time: 5 hours	
Distance (round trip): 6.6 miles	
Elevation gain: 2,750 feet	
Trails: Edmands Path, Mount Eisenhower Loop	
Map: USGS Mount Washington, Stairs Mountain, NH	
Trailhead GPS coordinates: N44° 14.94' W71° 23.48'	

The rounded dome crown atop Mount Eisenhower in the Southern Presidential Range is an alpine jewel. Smack in the middle of a regal neighborhood amidst New Hampshire's grandest mountains, Eisenhower has a reputation for providing a fair exchange to hikers: make the appropriate effort to reach the summit and be rewarded with first-rate looks at the brilliant White Mountains.

At 4,760 feet, Eisenhower is the twelfth-highest mountain in the state and contains a unique summit in that it is relatively flat. Though climbing any New Hampshire 4,000-foot mountain isn't easy, Eisenhower isn't all that difficult for the seasoned hiker.

It is named after Dwight D. Eisenhower, the thirty-fourth president of the United States. But that wasn't the peak's original name. It was first called Mount Pleasant or Pleasant Dome, the reason being that in 1820, a group of local hikers led by innkeeper Ethan Allen Crawford (also a pioneering guide in and above the notch that bears his last name) went on a mountain-naming expedition in the Presidentials. But at the time, only five presidents had taken office—Washington, Adams, Jefferson, Madison, and Monroe. After Eisenhower died in 1969, an effort was made to change the mountain's name to honor him. It wasn't until 1972, three years after the state legislature voted in a bill to change the name, that Mount Pleasant bore the name of the ex-president and World War II hero.

A US president isn't the only luminary associated with the mountain. Hikers can get there on the fairly forgiving Edmands

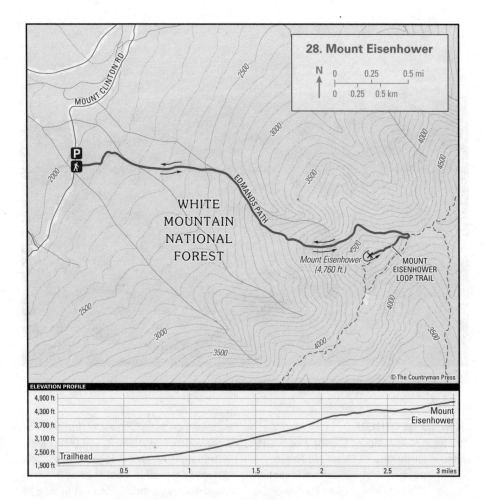

ELEVATION PROFILE

Path, named for early Presidential Range trailblazer J. Rayner Edmands. Edmands, who once worked in the Harvard College Observatory, was a founding member of the Appalachian Mountain Club in 1876, and its president in 1886. Known for working in the woods wearing a flannel shirt and knickers, Edmands now has hikers literally walking in his footprints. A memorial to him is located on a plaque affixed to a rock in Edmands Col (a saddle between Mounts Jefferson and Adams), and states: "The first to build continuous uniformly graded paths on the Presidential Range. Always rising but never steeply."

That holds true today, mostly. There really aren't long, steep sections, maybe just a short pitch or so, to Edmands Path, reconstructed in 1909. Generally, the footing is good and the trail has been well maintained over the years. The steep stuff is on the Mount Eisenhower Loop. Even though the pathway does form a loop over the mountain with the Crawford Path (also the Appalachian Trail) this hike is an out-and-back journey.

Mount Eisenhower's summit is well-marked with cairns.

HOW TO GET THERE

The trailhead on Mount Clinton Road is located near the top of Crawford Notch, off Route 302, by the Appalachian Mountain Club's Highland Center. From the top of the notch, turn onto Mount Clinton Road and drive about 2.3 miles to the trailhead.

A White Mountain National Forest Service Recreation Pass is required for parking.

The hike is in the White Mountain National Forest. White Mountain National Forest Headquarters, 71 White Mountain Drive, Campton, NH 03223; phone: 603-536-6100; web: www.fs.usda.gov/white mountain.

THE TRAIL

The blue-blazed trail begins benignly enough, even flat, as it crosses a few brooks, the first two on log bridges. Cross a bridge over the Abenaki Brook at 0.4 mile and then follow the trail right on an old logging road. The trail leaves left off the old road at 0.7 mile before starting a steady rise in the land of birches. As the 4,000-foot mark in elevation is reached, the trail zigs before passing through a small stone gateway at 2.2 miles. The path wanders by a stream flowing over some ledges at 2.5 miles that can be slippery when wet. That's followed by a short, rocky segment before the trail eases for a bit as teases of what's ahead can be seen through the trees.

The trail bursts out into the open and reaches the junction with the Mount Eisenhower Loop at 2.9 miles. Turn right on the Loop trail and follow the rocky switchbacks, steep at times, to the kindly summit along

The stunning vistas from the top of Mount Eisenhower are impressive.

carefully laid rock and wood corridors. The summit is marked by a large cairn. This is the alpine zone, so tread carefully, taking care not to stomp the fragile plants. Stay on the marked path. And also be cognizant of the weather.

But be sure to take a good look around the windswept summit. The mountain appears stuck in the middle of a giant staircase. To the southwest are big mountains—Pierce, Jackson, and Webster—that now appear smaller, while in the north Mounts Washington and Jefferson tower above. To the west in Vermont are peaks like Camel's Hump. Watch as the Cog Railway churns up Washington and spot the grand Mount Washington Hotel. Gaze upon the nearby village of Twin Mountain. Look to the south to find Mount Chocorua's rocky top.

The way back is along the same route. But linger on Eisenhower as long as possible.

29

Franconia Ridge

Difficulty: Strenuous

Time: 8 hours

Distance (round trip): 8.9 miles

Elevation gain: 3,900 feet

Trails: Falling Waters Trail, Franconia Ridge Trail (also the Appalachian Trail), Greenleaf Trail, Old Bridle Path

Map: USGS Franconia, NH

Trailhead GPS coordinates: N44° 8.52' W71° 40.87'

Hiking the stunning Franconia Ridge over Mounts Lincoln and Lafayette with an amazing above-treeline trek is one of the best hikes in New England. Plus, it's arguably one of the easiest to access, given that the trailhead in Franconia Notch State Park is off an interstate. There is also the Appalachian Mountain Club's Greenleaf Hut at 4,200 feet, which allows the opportunity to turn a day hike into an overnight. So put it all together, particularly on a weekend, and at times you have a bustling piece of exposed alpine real estate that is often at the whim of fierce (think lightning strikes) and windy weather. Being prepared with proper gear and the latest weather forecast is essential.

This classic loop, which can be done in either direction, ventures across the rocky spine of three mountains: Little Haystack (4,760 feet), Lincoln (at 5,089 feet, the seventh highest in NH), and Mount Lafayette at 5,260 feet, the sixth-highest Granite State peak. By hiking counterclockwise, the steeper sections are accomplished earlier on. Either way, the vistas are dramatic across Franconia Notch to the granite cliffs of Cannon Mountain in the west and the 45,000-acre Pemigewasset Wilderness Area in the east, beyond which lies the lofty Presidential Range.

HOW TO GET THERE

From the Franconia Notch Parkway (I-93), follow the signs for Lafayette Campground. The campground is on the southbound side. There is parking on both the southbound side (campground) and northbound side

Franconia Ridge strikes a dramatic pose in Franconia Notch State Park.

(accessed by a tunnel). The trail leaves the northbound side.

The route leaves from Franconia Notch State Park, 9 Franconia Notch Parkway, Franconia, NH, 03560; phone: 603-823-8800; web: nhstateparks.org.

Also more information at White Mountain National Forest Headquarters, 71 White Mountain Drive, Campton, NH 03223; phone: 603-536-6100; web: www.fs.usda.gov/whitemountain.

THE TRAIL

The trek begins in the hardwoods as the Old Bridle Path and Falling Waters Trail merge together. The Falling Waters Trail diverges right at 0.2 mile and crosses Walker Brook. In about a half mile, Dry Brook is crossed.

Don't be misled by its name. The brook is often rather wet following the spring melt and torrential rains. The pathway follows the brook as the footing becomes steeper, but hikers also come upon a series of waterfalls and cascades on the aptly named trail with its rocky steps. Rough footing continues up the 80-foot-high Cloudland Falls at about 1.3 miles. From the top of the impressive falls, look for a nice view of Mount Moosilauke. A couple of other waterfalls form the pool atop Cloudland Falls.

Continuing up Little Haystack, a short spur trail at 2.8 miles leads to Shining Rock, an incredible vantage point to Franconia Notch and the Kinsman Ridge, also in the west.

The trail bursts out at treeline with its

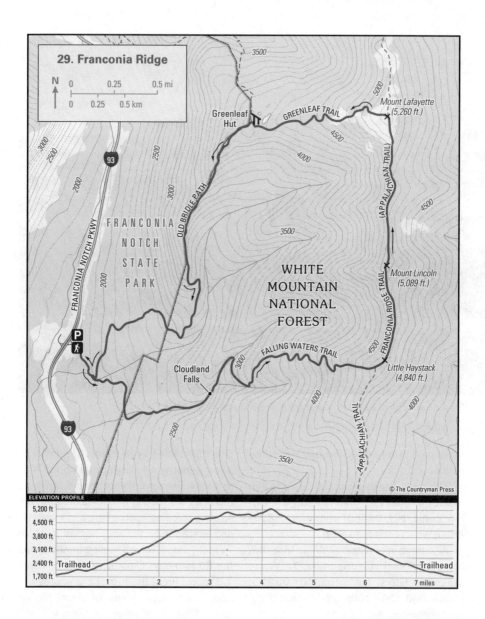

29. Franconia Ridge

N

| 0 | 0.25 | 0.5 mi |
| 0 | 0.25 | 0.5 km |

Greenleaf Hut

GREENLEAF TRAIL

Mount Lafayette (5,260 ft.)

(APPALACHIAN TRAIL)

FRANCONIA NOTCH PKWY

93

FRANCONIA NOTCH STATE PARK

OLD BRIDLE PATH

WHITE MOUNTAIN NATIONAL FOREST

Mount Lincoln (5,089 ft.)

FRANCONIA RIDGE TRAIL

P

Cloudland Falls

FALLING WATERS TRAIL

Little Haystack (4,840 ft.)

APPALACHIAN TRAIL

93

© The Countryman Press

ELEVATION PROFILE

5,200 ft
4,500 ft
3,800 ft
3,100 ft
2,400 ft Trailhead
1,700 ft

Trailhead

1   2   3   4   5   6   7 miles

jaw-dropping landscape near the intersection with the Franconia Ridge Trail on Little Haystack at 3.2 miles. Specks on the trail are hikers in the distance amidst the spectacular narrow ridge about to be hiked between Little Haystack and Lafayette. Turn left on the Franconia Ridge Trail to begin the northbound trek on the sublime passageway. The ridge is flat and stays that way until the base of craggy pyramid-shaped Mount Lincoln is reached at about 3.7 miles. It's a steep jaunt up the outcroppings to the summit at 3.9 miles. Knobby Lincoln is a place to perhaps linger longer as hikers tend to congregate a bit more on the next peak, Lafayette, a glorious mile away. Though smaller, the views are equally impressive.

The skyline hike presses across the ridge with a steep push up to Lafayette's majestic bare summit at about 4.9 miles. The mountain is the highest in the Franconia Range and contains fragile alpine plants, so stick to the path.

Mount Moosilauke is in the southwest with Vermont's Green Mountains rippling behind it running north–south. In the east are more of the White Mountain peaks above 4,000 feet, including notorious Owl's Head, with its precipitous slide, the wondrous Bonds, and observation-tower-topped Mount Carrigain. Find a spot along the massive stones if the wind is blowing strongly.

Turn left on the Greenleaf Trail as it descends gradually down into the scrub and then back up a bit to the Greenleaf Hut at about 6 miles. The hut opened in 1930 and was constructed using donkeys to haul in materials. It's was the AMC's first hut to have running water and indoor toilets (Madison Spring Hut was the organization's first White Mountain hut), and was renovated in 1989. Pop in for shelter or trail snacks.

Finish the loop by bearing left onto the Old Bridle Path, the trail that was used by those burros to get to the hut. But it isn't a carriage ride in the park. The trail serves up some fine viewpoints to Cannon and the Kinsmans, and across expansive Walker Ravine, while also navigating a few humps called Agony Ridge. Once the trail descends back into the trees, the end is near. At 8.7 miles, the trail joins forces with the Falling Water Trail once again and travels in tandem to the trailhead.

Franconia Ridge, seen from Lonesome Lake, is a formidable hike.

30

Mount Washington

Difficulty: Strenuous

Time: 9 hours

Distance (round trip): 9.2 miles

Elevation gain: 3,800 feet

Trails: Ammonoosuc Ravine Trail, Crawford Path (Appalachian Trail)

Map: USGS Mount Washington, NH

Trailhead GPS coordinates: N44° 16.02' W71° 21.65'

Mount Washington is the mother of all New England mountains. The highest peak in the northeastern United States at 6,288 feet, it is revered, beautiful, challenging, and deadly. It's known as the "home of the world's worst weather;" a mind-numbing wind gust of 231 miles per hour that blew across the wintry summit on April 12, 1934 (the highest ever recorded by man) provided the mountain's leap to notoriety. The summit is frequently in cloud and fog, and temperatures are generally a good twenty degrees lower than at the trailhead. Factor in wind and storm tracks—even a summer day can feel like winter on the rock pile. A handful of weather systems converge over Washington, creating its foul weather, sometimes without much warning.

But when the weather cooperates, the mountain is perhaps the greatest stage in all of New England to witness Mother Nature's glory, with views east to the Atlantic Ocean, north to Canada, west to Vermont and perhaps New York on the right day, and south to more wild New Hampshire.

The first recorded ascent, by Darby Field, happened in 1634, and visitors have been coming to the mountain ever since. Frankly, some die. There have been more than 140 fatalities on and around the mountain since 1849, ranging from falls to hypothermia. Hikers must absolutely be prepared, be aware of the weather, and be quick to turn around if things aren't going their way.

The summit is also a crossroads, allowing for a multitude of tourists to access the peak. In the east, the Mount Washington Auto Road winds its way to the summit. The

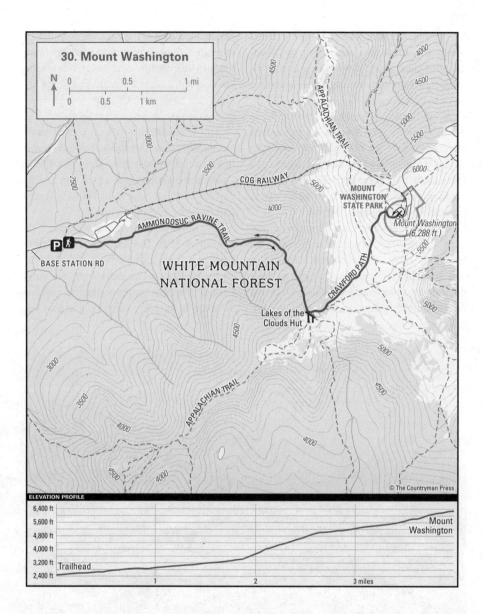

30. Mount Washington

N

| 0 | 0.5 | 1 mi |
| 0 | 0.5 | 1 km |

COG RAILWAY

APPALACHIAN TRAIL

MOUNT WASHINGTON STATE PARK

Mount Washington (6,288 ft.)

AMMONOOSUC RAVINE TRAIL

P

BASE STATION RD

WHITE MOUNTAIN NATIONAL FOREST

CRAWFORD PATH

Lakes of the Clouds Hut

APPALACHIAN TRAIL

© The Countryman Press

ELEVATION PROFILE

6,400 ft				Mount Washington
5,600 ft				
4,800 ft				
4,000 ft				
3,200 ft	Trailhead			
2,400 ft		1	2	3 miles

paved and dirt road also hosts a running race and two bicycle races. From the west, the Cog Railway chugs to the top.

Once on the summit, a New Hampshire state park, there's often a whirlwind of activity, with a host of buildings that house antennas, a cafeteria, a post office, an information desk, a gift shop, and Mount Washington Observatory, with its weather station and museum. Observers man the station year-round, working weeklong shifts to make hourly data collections. The Appalachian Trail crosses the summit, so expect thru-hikers in season.

The mountaintop is in the alpine zone, with rare plants, cairns, and footing on lichen-covered boulders that are sharp and often slippery when wet. Be cautious. Weather can obscure the trail markings.

Mount Washington also is home to Tuck-erman Ravine, a glacial cirque on its eastern shoulder known for holding snow well into spring and often year-round. Historic ski races were held there, and it is still a rite of passage for skiers and snowboarders who make the trek there every spring.

Mount Washington is also a rite of pas-sage for hikers, a serious challenge. All too often, hikers focus on the hike up the mountain. There is no easy way to or from the summit on foot, and the descent can be equally if not more arduous than the ascent,

especially if a hiker tires and the weather de-teriorates. Plan on spending a full day hiking Mount Washington, and factor in spending time on the summit if it suits you, since you really can hike, grab a burger, and go down. But never take this mountain lightly.

This classic hike winds up and down the mountain's western flank. The climb also goes to the Appalachian Mountain Club's Lakes of the Clouds Hut, which can turn the day hike into an overnight. There is shelter and trail snacks for purchase.

The hut makes this a popular way up the mountain. Plus, the Ammonoosuc Ravine Trail and Crawford Path combine for the shortest way up the peak from the west. Though the Ammonoosuc Ravine Trail has its share of scenic cascades, it is also very

Be prepared for every season on Mount Washington.

Winter transforms the summit of Mount Washington into beauty beyond words.

steep at times, with slippery wet rocks that can be problematic for hikers exceeding their abilities.

HOW TO GET THERE

From Twin Mountain and the junction of Routes 3 and 302, travel east on 302 about 4.5 miles, passing by Fabyans Station restaurant, and turn left on Base Road. Travel about 5.5 miles to the parking area on the right. If you find yourself in the Cog Railway parking area, you've gone too far.

A White Mountain National Forest Service Recreation Pass is required for parking.

The hike is in the White Mountain National Forest. White Mountain National Forest Headquarters, 71 White Mountain Drive, Campton, NH 03223; phone: 603-536-6100; web: www.fs.usda.gov/white mountain.

There is more information at Mount Washington State Park, Routes 16 and 302, Sargent's Purchase, NH; phone: 603-466-3347; web: www.nhstateparks.org.

THE TRAIL

The full-day outing starts out rather trouble-free by crossing Franklin Brook, entering a world of ferns and fir before rambling by the Ammonoosuc River. At about a mile, a connecting trail enters from the left. The jaunt is pleasant, but there are places where it's rough underfoot. The trail crosses Monroe Brook and skirts an area that looks like something of an avalanche rumbled through it. The sign of elevation gain is the diminishing height of the trees. That starts to happen, and at 2.1 miles, the emerald-colored Gem Pool sits at the foot of a waterfall. The stunning waters indicate it's huffing time as some severe steeps are ahead, some pitches aided by rock steps. The steeps go on for just under a half mile, often with slippery slabs of stone. At about 2.5 miles, there is a taste of what's ahead— Mount Washington. The trail lets up a bit and crosses several streams before more ledges are reached. Soon the trees shrink and the rock cairns seem to grow as the trail crosses into treeline shortly before the junction with the Crawford Path (AT) under the watch of Mount Monroe, the fourth-highest mountain in the state.

The popular Lakes of the Clouds Hut is also there, the largest (sleeps 90) and highest (5,050 feet) of the AMC's White Mountain network. Notice the glacial tarns that give the hut its name.

Turn left on the Crawford Path passing the hut. The Crawford Path is the oldest continuously used mountain trail in the country. It has its origin in 1819, was upgraded to a bridle path in 1840, and by 1870 was back to being a footpath to land among the clouds.

Stay on Crawford. It'll go by Davis Path, then zig and zag by the Gulfside Trail. The two paths become one and bear right for the final push to the summit (4.6 miles) that goes by the Yankee Building (communications based), the Tip Top House (old hotel), the Stage Office (Auto Road information and shop), the Cog Railway, and the Sherman Adams building, which contains the park offerings and observatory, before reaching the summit, marked by a large pile of rocks and a sign.

Leave time to take a look around the summit.

The descent is along the same trails. Pay close attention on the initial stretch back to the hut, with its many cairns.

Vermont

Introducing Vermont

Vermont is home to the Green Mountains, maple syrup, and cheese. Aptly named, Vermont is the Green Mountain State, with its prototypical villages with white-church steeples, quaint shops, old cemeteries, and striking mountains.

The Green Mountains run north–south the length of the entire state from Massachusetts to Quebec, with notable peaks such as the state's highest, Mount Mansfield, and the oddly named Camel's Hump. The Long Trail runs the length of the state too, and coincides with the Appalachian Trail at times.

Vermont is also home to the more than 400,000 acres of the Green Mountain National Forest, largely in the southern and central parts of the state. Location is everything, and some 70 million people are said to be within a day's drive of it. Not only are there about 900 miles of multiuse trails for hiking, cross-country skiing, and cycling, but the forest is also home to a handful of alpine and Nordic skiing areas.

Though much of the focus is on the Green Mountains, there are plenty of other peaks to climb, from Wheeler in the bucolic Northeast Kingdom to Mount Hunger outside Waterbury.

Vermont also has a wealth of state parks with a wide offering of terrain, from easy short walks to challenges.

31

Mount Tom

Difficulty: Easy	
Time: 1½ hours	
Distance (round trip): 3.2 miles	
Elevation gain: 600 feet	
Trails: Faulkner Trail	
Map: USGS Woodstock North, VT	
Trailhead GPS coordinates: N43° 37.44' W72° 31.49'	

Mount Tom is perhaps the best in-town hike in all of New England. Little mountain with big views: from its south peak summit at 1,250 feet, a canvas of rural Vermont is spread for all to see. Located in the tiny village of Woodstock, the hike should also be combined with exploring the village streets for their quaint general store, shopping opportunities, smartly trimmed green, inns, B&Bs, covered bridge, and eateries.

The mountain was once a small ski area, and though its low-lying elevation may make it a leg-stretcher for veteran hikers, Mount Tom is a glorious family and multigenerational hike. The mountain itself is on some precious real estate. Portions of the peak are on town-owned land, while others are part of the Marsh-Billings-Rockefeller National Historical Park, with its 20 miles of attractive trails and carriage roads. Laurance S. Rockefeller once owned the estate at the base of Mount Tom. He and his wife, Mary Billings, gave the mansion and its 550 acres to the government in the spirit of conservation. It became a national historical park in 1998 and also contains a 14-acre manmade pond—The Pogue—between Mount Tom's north and south peaks.

In winter, the mountain is transformed into a winter wonderland as part of the 60-kilometer Woodstock Ski Touring Center that maintains and tracks the trails for cross-country skiing and snowshoeing.

Mount Tom's a pretty popular place, with lots of trails for all seasons. There are a handful of access points to the mountain, including from the national historical park, but the

The hike up Mount Tom in Woodstock, Vt. begins in town at Faulkner Park.

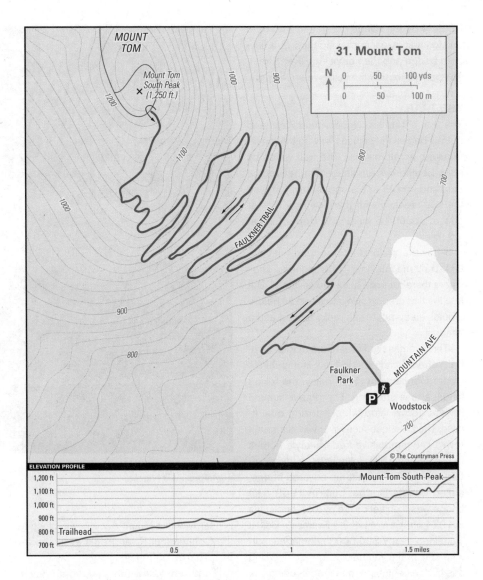

31. Mount Tom

quickest access is from town on the civilized switchbacks of the Faulkner Trail from Faulkner Park on Mountain Avenue.

The obvious Faulkner Trail is in a lovely residential area, so respect those who call the street home. The trail is readily accessible from the park, and starts off very gently, but the last pitch is a tad steep and rocky, with a cable rail to make the going easier.

There's an Old World–atmosphere to the trail, with its benches and array of zigs and zags—more than twenty of them along the way.

HOW TO GET THERE

From I-89, take Exit 1 for Woodstock, Rutland, and Route 4. Travel west on Route 4 for some 10 miles to Woodstock. Stay on

Route 4 by the village green and turn right on Mountain Avenue, passing through a covered bridge and then crossing River Street. The park is about 0.5 mile down on the right.

THE TRAIL

The trail enters the woods, bears left, and quickly begins the sinuous way up the mountain with an alpine feel. The trail winds by huge boulders, even squeezing between a pair, and comes to a stone archway. Twice the trail crosses with the Link Trail (Lower Link at about 0.5 miles and Upper Link at 1.2 miles).

After the second intersection with the Link Trail, the Faulkner Trail reaches a knoll where there's a taste of the views ahead. But first the trail drops down into a saddle before a quick steep pitch with rocky footing and a handrail.

Then comes the Mount Tom magic. Central Vermont and east to New Hampshire's Upper Connecticut River Valley, the rolling landscape is stunning. The grassy summit towers above Woodstock, oozing quaintness. The Ottauquechee River winds through town. The impressive Federal-style homes look something like dollhouses ready for afternoon tea. Try to spot the covered bridge, called Middle Bridge, built in 1969. The bridge was then set on fire by local hooligans in 1974 on the night of the Firemen's Ball. It sustained nearly $90,000 in damages, and a handful of the youths who were of working age had to contribute to the repair costs.

Okemo Mountain is spotted in the south while Killington Peak takes up the northwest. Mount Peg, Woodstock's other in-town hike,

The well graded path up Mount Tom contains numerous switchbacks.

is nearby, while Mount Ascutney is close to the Connecticut River. Peg's even shorter than Tom at 1,060 feet.

To return, follow the same route down. And if you didn't use any of the benches on the way up, be sure to do so before returning to the car. There's no rush on Mount Tom.

32

White Rocks Overlook and Ice Beds Trail

Difficulty: Easy

Time: 1½ hours

Distance (round trip): 1.8 miles

Elevation gain: 450 feet

Trails: Ice Beds Trail

Map: USGS Wallingford, VT

Trailhead GPS coordinates: N43° 27.06' W72° 56.61'

Looking for a hike to just chill? Then head to the Ice Beds Trail in south-central Vermont for an easy jaunt to the base of a huge boulder field that is known to hold snow and ice into summer and even year-round on occasion. The snow and ice is contained deep within the spaces between the boulders, and because of the type of rock, it gives them a white sheen.

The trail is in the White Rocks National Recreation Area, a big place no one knows about. Unless, as Yogi Berra might chime in, you already do.

Located in the Green Mountain National Forest, the 36,000-acre area stretches through several towns, including Weston, Wallingford, and Dorset, and a pair of wilderness areas. There are cliffs for climbing and bouldering, trails for hiking, and ponds for paddling and fishing. Pieces of the Appalachian and Long Trails wind through it, and there is a smattering of shelters maintained by the Green Mountain Club as well. In winter, snowmobilers travel on snowy corridors while free-heel skiers have a section of the Catamount Ski Trail to explore.

According to the US Forest Service, during the last Ice Age glaciers scored and exposed the Cheshire quartzite that makes up the cliffs at White Rocks. Native Americans quarried stone from the site for tools, followed by settlers in the 1850s who cleared the land for grazing. This was followed by logging.

An easy way into the area is from the White Rocks Picnic Area in Wallingford, between Ludlow and Rutland. It is the

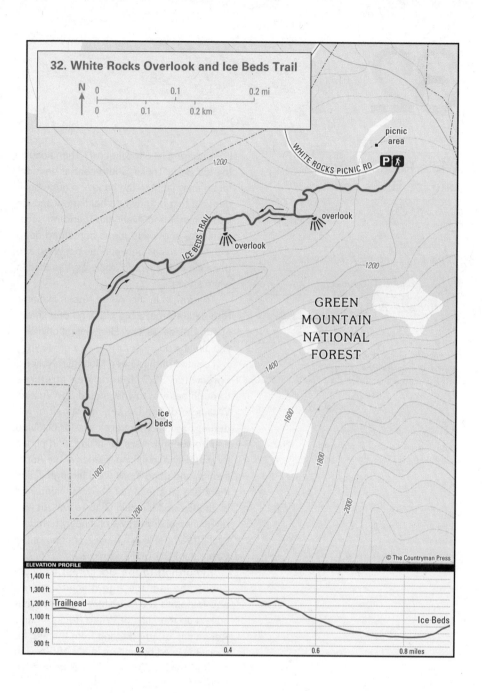

32. White Rocks Overlook and Ice Beds Trail

N

| 0 | | 0.1 | | 0.2 mi |
| 0 | 0.1 | | 0.2 km | |

picnic area

WHITE ROCKS PICNIC RD

1200

ICE BEDS TRAIL

overlook

overlook

1200

GREEN
MOUNTAIN
NATIONAL
FOREST

1400

1600

ice
beds

1800

1000

2000

1200

© The Countryman Press

ELEVATION PROFILE

1,400 ft				
1,300 ft				
1,200 ft Trailhead				
1,100 ft				Ice Beds
1,000 ft				
900 ft				
	0.2	0.4	0.6	0.8 miles

Scenic ledges along the way to the Ice Beds display Vermont's charm.

launching point for a benign but beautiful hike, first to a view from the White Rocks Overlook of the massive pile of talus, and then to the base of the rock pile, with its cool air and frigid stream.

Part family hike, part leg-stretcher for the fitness freak, the Ice Beds are a lovely destination. The Ice Beds are one of those peculiar New England finds where cold reigns year-round and the boulder graveyard creates caves that are cool, literally.

HOW TO GET THERE

From Wallingford, travel about 2 miles east on Route 140 and turn right on Sugar Hill Road. Soon, turn right on Forest Road 52

and drive about 0.5 mile to the parking area with its picnic area.

The White Rocks Recreation Area is in the Green Mountain National Forest. Green Mountain National Forest Headquarters, 231 North Main Street, Rutland, VT, 05701; phone: 802-747-6700; web: www.fs.usda .gov/greenmountain.

THE TRAIL

The blue-blazed Ice Beds Trail leaves the parking area and pierces the woods. Immediately there are wooden footbridges followed by an ascent up a rocky ridge on a series of switchbacks that afford several spur trails to precipitous drop-offs. Stick to the trail until about 0.25 mile, when the White Rocks Overlook is reached. The overlook provides a stunning look at the sharp peak, cliffs that have been known to host peregrine falcons, and the dramatic rockslide of White Rocks, as well as glimpses out to Otter Creek Valley.

Staying on the Ice Beds Trail, the pathway goes under hemlocks, and at about 0.5 mile allows for another vantage out to White Rocks. The trail then drops off a bit with a couple of quick zigs and zags before a woods road comes in by a fork at about 0.7 mile. The trail curves left downhill and soon a brook comes into view, with footbridges. The water is the signal the rock pile is soon. Enjoy the blasts of cold air. That little stream tends to be a crisp 40 degrees or so from all that runoff.

The base of the rockslides is reached at about 0.9 mile. In winter, ice forms in the wide places. If you are tempted to climb the rocks, pay attention. And if you have something to eat, find a flat one and enjoy the natural air conditioning before returning along the same pathway.

33

Gile Mountain

Difficulty: Easy	
Time: 1 hour	
Distance (round trip): 1.4 miles	
Elevation gain: 400 feet	
Trails: Gile Mountain Tower Trail	
Map: USGS South Strafford, VT	
Trailhead GPS coordinates: *N43° 47.37' W72° 20.57'*	

Tiny Gile Mountain is one of those hikes locals love. If it's all about location, then the 1,873-foot hill is in a prime Upper Connecticut River Valley spot, close to active Hanover, NH, with Dartmouth College on the Granite State side of the long, wide river while standing above countrified Norwich on the Vermont side.

Gile, because of a fire tower with an observatory platform on its wooded summit, is a big little mountain offering commanding panoramic views into Vermont and over to New Hampshire on a clear day. It sees extensive year-round use and is often a destination for sunset and full-moon excursions (done by carrying appropriate equipment like a headlamp).

According to Vermont's venerable Green Mountain Club, nearly 40 fire towers once stood in Vermont, dating back to the early 1900s when the state was seeing a lot of logging activity. Modern progress marched on, and airplane surveillance replaced the watchers in the fire towers. Still, more than a dozen fire towers and observation platforms remain through the Green Mountain State.

It's easy to wax eloquent about these high-standing wood and steel structures. Simply, they provide a stage above the trees. Those with roofs can be shelters to wait out inclement weather.

Be ready for the steps, better than any fitness center StairMaster. Actually, Gile is one of those little hikes that locals like to use as a bit of a workout. Since there is limited real estate on the towers, be sure to share. Use the railings going both up and down,

Feel like a bird atop the fire tower on Gile Mountain.

particularly if you are a hiker who is a bit fearful of heights. As a matter of fact, fire towers can sway in high winds, but the view will probably take your mind off that. The effort is worth it to be that much closer to the birds surfing the thermals. Then there's the alfresco opportunity of having a mountaintop lunch above the mountain.

HOW TO GET THERE

From Norwich and Main Street, travel north out of town on Main for about 0.6 mile and turn left on Turnpike Road for about a 5.5-mile drive to the trailhead. Stay left at the intersections with New Boston Road and Lower Turnpike Road (dirt).

The trails are maintained by Town of Norwich Trails Committee, PO Box 376, Norwich, VT 05055; phone: 802-649-1419; web: www.norwich.vt.us.

THE TRAIL

The trail leaves the parking area on something of an old logging road and soon starts to gently climb through the hardwoods as

it turns right off that pathway. At about 0.3 mile the trail goes under a power line that offers pretty views across to the rippling hills in New Hampshire before returning to the woods with its nice old birches followed

The fire tower is a popular Upper Valley hike.

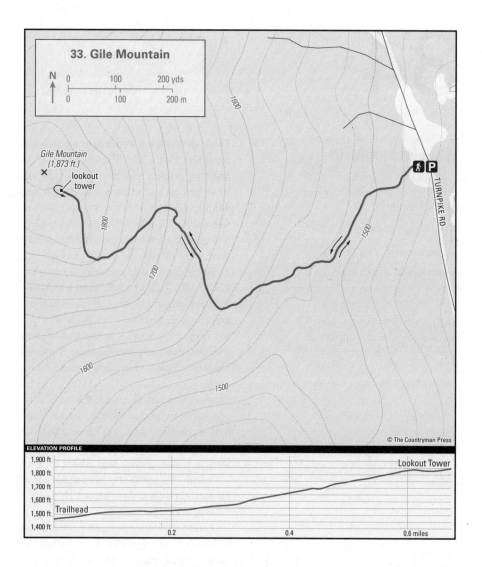

33. Gile Mountain

N
0   100   200 yds
0   100   200 m

1600

Gile Mountain (1,873 ft.)
× lookout tower

1800

1700

1600

1500

TURNPIKE RD

© The Countryman Press

ELEVATION PROFILE

			Lookout Tower
1,900 ft			
1,800 ft			
1,700 ft			
1,600 ft			
1,500 ft	Trailhead		
1,400 ft			
	0.2	0.4	0.6 miles

by switchbacks that wiggle across the side of the hill. The pitch steepens close to the top.

Near the summit is the old fire ranger's cabin. Soon enough, there is the fire tower with its approximately 90 steps standing atop a rocky ledge. Climb up and be treated to the stunning panorama of the White Mountains standing to the east with brawny Mount Ascutney in the south and the backbone of the Green Mountains holding court in the west. A closer look finds the ski trails of Killington in the southeast. In the east is also a ridge containing Mount Cube and the Appalachian Trail.

The return trip is along the same trail. Be sure to pack a lunch and linger a bit on the fire tower for its two-state views. Just because the hike is quick doesn't mean the stay at the top has to be too.

34

Wheeler Mountain

Difficulty: Moderate

Time: 2½ hours

Distance (round trip): 2.6 miles

Elevation gain: 715 feet

Trails: White Trail, Red Trail

Map: USGS Sutton, VT

Trailhead GPS coordinates:
N44° 43.68' W72° 5.80'

Think of Wheeler Mountain as the little mountain that could. Except you'll be the one chugging up, saying "I think I can." And when you get to the top of the smooth open ledges of Wheeler Mountain and then the spectacle of Eagle Cliff, towering over the grandeur of Vermont's rural Northeast Kingdom, you'll tell yourself you're glad you did.

Don't dismiss this spunky mountain at 2,371 feet. This is a hike with a myriad of rock scrambles handing off to smooth outcroppings. From them, take the time to gaze out upon an incredible landscape of ponds and mountains and into Canada. The Green Mountain State's gloriously bucolic corner, sandwiched between New Hampshire and Quebec, is an idyllic place. It is an interwoven northern land of working farms, hearty forests, pristine lakes, and formidable mountains. The jewel is dramatic Lake Willoughby, with its towering cliffs that attract rock and ice climbers, and hefty peaks like Mount Pisgah, Bald Mountain, Mount Hor, and of course, Wheeler.

And though there is much natural beauty to be seen, there is also a visible windmill farm along the way.

HOW TO GET THERE

From West Burke and the junction of US 5 and VT 5A, drive north toward Barton about 8.2 miles and turn right on dirt Wheeler Mountain Road. Travel 2 miles to the small trailhead on the left.

From I-91, take Exit 25. Turn right on Route 16 going north for 1 mile. Turn right on

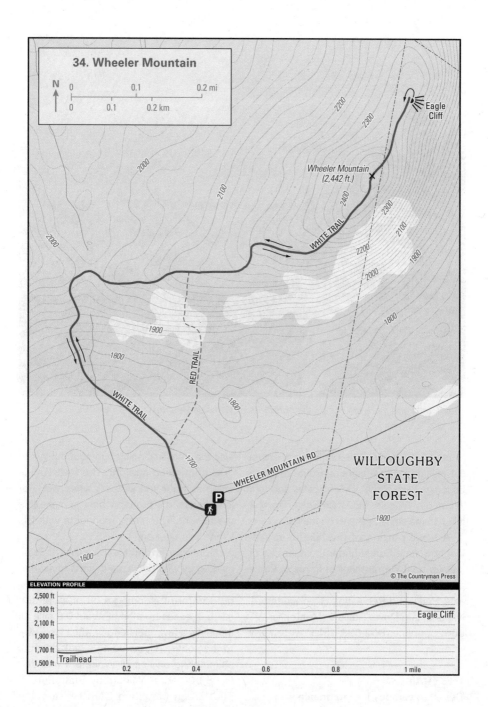

34. Wheeler Mountain

N

| 0 | | 0.1 | | 0.2 mi |
| 0 | 0.1 | | 0.2 km | |

Eagle Cliff

Wheeler Mountain
(2,442 ft.)

WHITE TRAIL

RED TRAIL

WHITE TRAIL

WHEELER MOUNTAIN RD

WILLOUGHBY
STATE
FOREST

© The Countryman Press

ELEVATION PROFILE

2,500 ft					
2,300 ft					Eagle Cliff
2,100 ft					
1,900 ft					
1,700 ft					
1,500 ft	Trailhead				
	0.2	0.4	0.6	0.8	1 mile

Forest, field and more roll out on the horizon from Wheeler Mountain.

Routes 5/16 (Main Street in Barton). Travel 0.1 mile and stay straight on Route 5, which becomes Lake Street. Drive 5 miles and turn left on dirt Wheeler Mountain Road. Travel 2 miles to the small trailhead on the left.

A small portion of the hike is in Willoughby State Forest under the auspices of the Vermont Department of Forests, Parks and Recreation. Vermont Department of Forests, Parks and Recreation Headquarters, 1 National Life Drive, Davis 2, Montpelier, VT 05620; phone: 802-828-1531; web: www.vtfpr.org.

THE TRAIL

The short scrappy hike to granite slabs begins easily enough by maple and apple trees, dips down, crosses a field, and soon splits,

with the Red Trail going right and the White Trail continuing straight. The Red Trail is much steeper and slippery when wet. For loop lovers, it's probably best to make this the ascent. The path reconnects with the White Trail later on.

Continue straight on the White Trail, marked by white dots, as it starts to ascend among the hardwoods and then makes a right before beginning a bit of a spirited climb. It eases up a bit at about 0.5 mile as it passes a few open ledges with nice views to the southeast, including a look down at shimmering and small Wheeler Pond and the 8,000-acre Willoughby State Forest. The Green Mountain Club has a camp there with two rustic cabins built in the early 1970s. The camp was once owned by

The ledges on Wheeler Mountain are good places to take it all in.

the Appalachian Mountain Club. The GMC bought it in 2004.

Willoughby State Forest was established in 1928 and includes the cliff-heavy peaks of Mounts Hor and Pisgah, the cliffs receiving National Natural Landmark status in 1967. The original state forest was a checkerboard of about 1,700 acres but has grown over the years and includes the towns of Newark, Westmore, and Sutton.

The trail returns to the woods, and at about 0.7 mile reconnects with the Red Trail with both colors blazed on the trees. The trail eventually leads to open ledges with outstanding views as the climb continues to the summit of Wheeler Mountain and its southeastern cliffs, with an outstanding look above 1,600-acre Lake Willoughby, with its trout, perch, and landlocked salmon.

The edgy and ledgy summit at about 1.2 miles–take care up there–is an amazing place. The Green Mountains stand in the west led by Jay Peak and its ski trails, and Mount Mansfield. The eastern sky contains Burke Mountain (another ski area) plus Bald Mountain (fire tower), Mount Hor, and Pisgah. If the day's clear, try to spot the Franconia Ridge in New Hampshire.

Though the summit is outstanding, there is another fine perch ahead, Eagle Cliff. Continue through the spruce to the dizzying open ledge of Eagle Cliff, towering above the pastoral scenes below.

Then return along the same way.

35

Lye Brook Falls

Difficulty: Moderate

Time: 3 hours

Distance (round trip): 4.6 miles

Elevation gain: 740 feet

Trails: Lye Brook Trail, Lye Brook Falls Trail

Map: USGS Manchester, VT

Trailhead GPS coordinates: N43° 9.53' W73° 2.48'

Waterfalls are tantalizing and moody. After a rain or during spring melt, they gush, seemingly taking on a powerful and imposing presence. But when there's no rain in the middle of summer, they are but a trickle, Mother Nature's leaky faucet.

Lye Brook Falls is such a place.

One of Vermont's highest waterfalls, the thick horsetail of water plunges some 125 feet or so down the seemingly terraced rocky wall in the Green Mountain National Forest.

Lovely Lye Brooks Falls is fed by Lye Brook. It was once called the Trestle Cascade as a testament to a trestle that spanned near the falls during a time when logging and railroads ruled stylish Manchester.

The fashionable and lively village attracts the outdoor world with its hiking, fly-fishing, and proximity to ski areas, but now the falls are under the auspices of the nearly 18,000-acre Lye Brook Wilderness.

That's what makes the moderate trek to the falls so remarkable, that true wilderness is so close to town. The trailhead is just a couple of miles from downtown and its free Wi-Fi opportunities and strolling streets for shopping.

The Green Mountain National Forest says the 4.6-mile out-and-back adventure along the blue-blazed Lye Brook and Lye Brook Falls Trails uses old logging railroad grades and old woods roads, as time was the area was heavily logged, with sawmills and charcoal kilns scattered about. The way is generally steady, but there are some pitches where a bit more energy is expended to

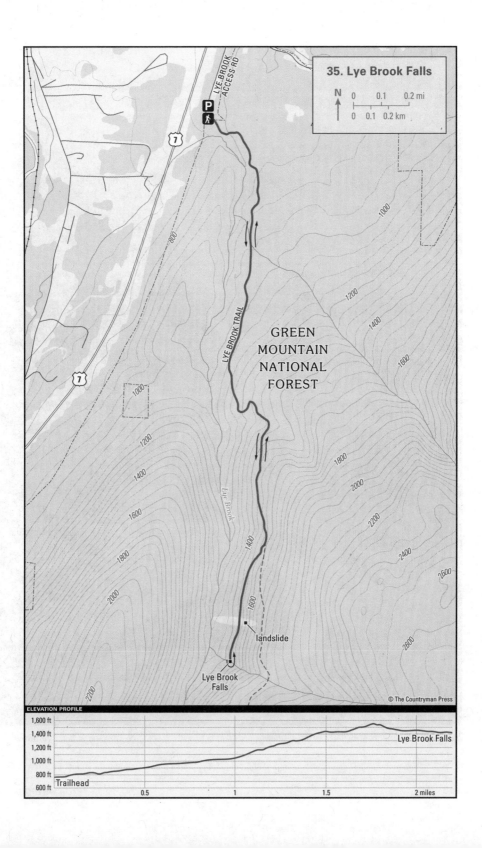

35. Lye Brook Falls

N

| 0 | 0.1 | 0.2 mi |
| 0 | 0.1 | 0.2 km |

LYE BROOK ACCESS RD

7

7

LYE BROOK TRAIL

Lye Brook

GREEN
MOUNTAIN
NATIONAL
FOREST

landslide

Lye Brook
Falls

© The Countryman Press

ELEVATION PROFILE

1,600 ft	
1,400 ft	Lye Brook Falls
1,200 ft	
1,000 ft	
800 ft	
600 ft	Trailhead

0.5   1   1.5   2 miles

Lye Brook Falls is one of Vermont's highest.

chug up. Plus, be cognizant of the plentiful stream crossings.

Also know that a small section of the trail passed right through an impressive landslide created by the finicky and powerful fingers of Hurricane Irene passing through in 2011.

HOW TO GET THERE

From Manchester and the junction of US Route 7 and VT Routes11/30, travel east about 0.5 mile on Routes 11/30 before turning right on East Manchester Road. Drive about a mile and turn left on Glen Road. Bear right at the fork on Lye Brook Access Road and go about 0.5 mile to the trailhead parking.

For more information, try Green Mountain National Forest Headquarters, 231 North Main Street, Rutland, VT 05701; phone: 802-747-6700; web: www.fs.usda.gov/green mountain.

THE TRAIL

The hike begins easily enough from the circular parking area on level ground through the hardwoods, with signs telling visitors of only foot travel. The trail parallels the brook en route to the falls, though it's not always possible to see it. Maybe 100 yards into the journey there's an unmarked trail junction that invites exploration of the waters, giving a bit of a closer look.

Soon enough there's a trail registry, and at about 0.4 mile the wilderness boundary is reached. The trail is forgiving, showing up smooth and rocky stretches with some interesting rock formations along the way. There are also those multiple stream crossings, the first one not terribly far after entering the wilderness.

In about a mile, the trail shows off a

The hike to Lye Brook Falls passes through an impressive slide.

bit, heading up into an area known as Lye Brook Hollow with some steepish drop-offs down to the waters. Pass through a hemlock stand and then more intermittent patches of smooth and stones. Along the way are small clutters of rocks that tumbled down the hillside, foreshadowing what is to come.

At 1.8 miles, bear right on the Lye Brook Falls Trail as the Lye Brook Trail continues on to the left. The trail narrows and begins a slight descent through a wet rocky area before coming upon the slide. The slide is startling, as if an entire piece of the woods was just knocked out. Trees, rocks, and more fell some 500 feet or so down the hill, creating a look down across a valley. The trail is easily navigated some 20 yards across, and then it's back into the woods.

The falls are soon reached at about 2.2 miles into the hike with its web of trails heading down to a large sunning rock or up along a goat path. Turning left affords fall lovers a fine perch to marvel at the spectacle no matter the season.

Return the same way to the trailhead.

36

Mount Ascutney

Difficulty: Moderate

Time: 5 hours

Distance (round trip): 6.4 miles

Elevation gain: 2,400 feet

Trails: Brownsville Trail, Windsor Trail

Map: USGS Windsor, VT

Trailhead GPS coordinates:
N43° 27.91' W72° 26.41'

Mount Ascutney is a major feature of southeastern Vermont's landscape. A monadnock, in essence a lone mountain or hill, the peak at 3,150 feet is a familiar sight towering over the Connecticut River Valley, visible from both the Green Mountain State and New Hampshire.

From a nearly 25-foot observation tower at its summit, hikers can gaze out upon a dizzying panorama that takes in Vermont, New Hampshire, Massachusetts, and New York. The tower isn't the mountain's original. That one was built in 1920 and was used for fire lookout until 1952. Eventually it was taken down, as it fell into disrepair. The state of Vermont built the present-day tower in 1989 using portions of the old tower. Talk about recycling.

With some 2,000 acres of protected land around it, Ascutney is an active place for recreation as it is located in Mount Ascutney State Park, which also has a campground. There's a toll road some 3.7 miles in length that goes shy of the summit, a hang-glider launch, and four major hiking trails going to the top from various trailheads. The western slope was home to a ski area that first began operating in the late 1940s and closed in 2010. Ascutney was also known for its logging operations and four granite quarries that operated around the 1,500-foot level, according to the Ascutney Trails Association. The first trail up Ascutney, an old volcano core cone, was constructed in 1825.

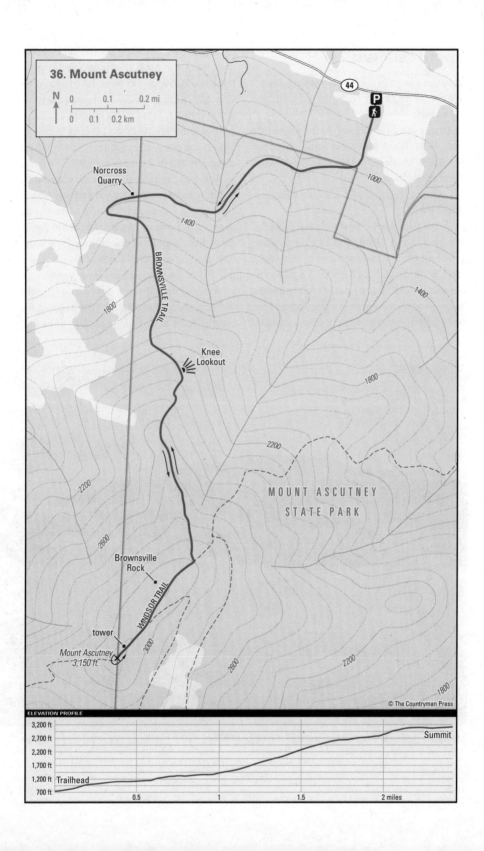

36. Mount Ascutney

N

| 0 | 0.1 | 0.2 mi |
| 0 | 0.1 | 0.2 km |

44

P

Norcross
Quarry

1000

1400

BROWNSVILLE TRAIL

1800

1400

Knee
Lookout

1800

2200

2200

MOUNT ASCUTNEY
STATE PARK

2600

Brownsville
Rock

WINDSOR TRAIL

3000

2600

2200

tower

Mount Ascutney
3,150 ft.

1800

© The Countryman Press

ELEVATION PROFILE

					Summit
3,200 ft					
2,700 ft					
2,200 ft					
1,700 ft					
1,200 ft	Trailhead				
700 ft		0.5	1	1.5	2 miles

HOW TO GET THERE

From the village of Windsor, travel about 4.5 miles west on Route 44 to the parking area on the left.

The route is in Mount Ascutney State Park, 1826 Black Mountain Road, Windsor, VT 05089; phone 802-674-2060; web: www .vtstateparks.com.

THE TRAIL

Start the hike on the white-blazed Brownsville Trail cut in 1898. The trail rises along a hill and climbs fairly steadily and steeply. The trail moderates a bit about 0.3 mile in as it meets an old quarry road. At 1.1 miles the trail passes by the remains of the former Norcross granite quarry. Huge boulders, tangled

rusting cables, decaying booms, and wasted rock mark the area. If you decide to climb the rock slabs for the view, take it easy. Of Ascutney's quarries, this one was the most substantial. It is said the largest chuck of granite cut there weighed 20 tons. A boarding house once stood at the quarry, which closed in 1910.

The trail presses on upward, sometimes through some rougher terrain and sometimes zigzagging. At about 1.2 miles there's an overlook to pastoral farms, while at the 2-mile mark there's another opportunity for a vista. At Knee Lookout take a look at Windsor and the rest of the Connecticut River Valley.

At 2.4 miles there's some foot-friendly flats signifying the arrival at the mountain's North Peak at 2,660 feet. Up ahead is

Mount Ascutney is a noted landmark in the Upper Valley.   JAN BASCH

Clouds come in off the horizon from Mount Ascutney.

another viewpoint that encompasses ski areas like Killington and Okemo.

The trail dips before reaching the junction to join the Windsor Trail (about 2.9 miles), which enters from the left. The summit's not that far away. Hike by the foundation of the Stone Hut site at 3 miles, a former shelter. There's a short spur trail by the Hut that leads to Brownsville Rock, a vantage point to see outstanding views of Camel's Hump and Killington. Take a closer look at the rock and notice the split. Apparently some local college students on the other side of the Connecticut River made a hole in the rock, filled it with black powder, and set it off. The rock remains, as does the split.

It's a quick 0.2 mile from there to the summit (3.2 miles) and the tower. Climb it to be closer to the birds and perhaps hang gliders playing in the thermals. From it, see Vermont's Green Mountains, New Hampshire's White Mountains, the Berkshires of Massachusetts, and the Taconics in New York State. Some mountains stand out more than others. Mount Monadnock with its bare ledgy summit is the prominent peak in the south, with ski trails of Killington and Okemo to the south beyond the Connecticut River. But those aren't the only ski areas out there. Look closely in the southwest for Mount Snow, Stratton, and Magic.

Descend by the same route.

37

Mount Hunger

Difficulty: Strenuous
Time: 4 hours
Distance (round trip): 4 miles
Elevation gain: 2,290 feet
Trails: Waterbury Trail
Map: USGS Stowe, VT
Trailhead GPS coordinates: N44° 24.15' W72° 40.52'

From its rock summit crown, Mount Hunger offers some of the most incredible views in Vermont. The vistas may be dazzling, but there's some effort involved in getting there, with handfuls of ledges to scramble, boulders to navigate, and streams to cross.

Be like a turtle: take it slow and steady up the blue-blazed Waterbury Trail. It's the elevation gain that's making those muscles cry out.

Mount Hunger is in a fine hiking neighborhood, and another local favorite. Route 100, part of the drive to the trailhead, is the state's most labeled roadway, mostly called the "Skier's Highway." It is more. It's also an excellent way to bicycle the state tip-to-tail, but to the hiker, the meandering north–south road near the wonderful resort mecca of Stowe also acts as a demarcation line for a couple of major-league Vermont mountain ranges. The Green Mountains are in the west, with such prominent peaks as Mount Mansfield (the state's highest at 4,393 feet), another 4,000 footer in Camel's Hump (4,083 feet) and 3,684-foot Bolton Mountain. To the east of Route 100 stands a wall of mountains called the Worcester Range, home to popular climbs like Stowe Pinnacle, Worcester Mountain, and the classic rounded knoll of Mount Hunger above Waterbury Center, which leaves from a Loomis Hill Road trailhead a few miles from the town's gazebo on the green.

Mount Hunger stands 3,538 feet tall and is an alpine porch for viewing hulking Camel's Hump in the south, the storied White Mountains of New Hampshire in the east,

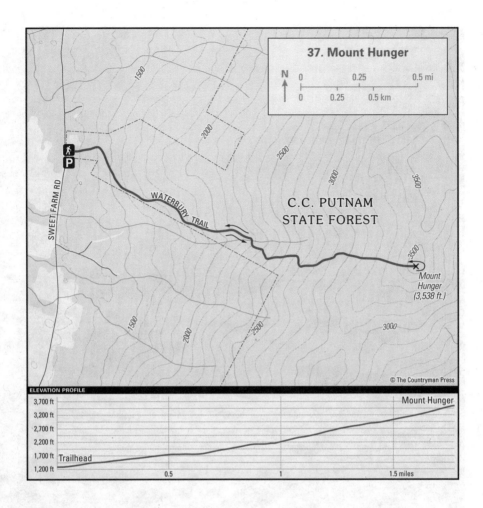

37. Mount Hunger

N

| 0 | 0.25 | 0.5 mi |
| 0 | 0.25 | 0.5 km |

SWEET FARM RD

WATERBURY TRAIL

C.C. PUTNAM
STATE FOREST

Mount
Hunger
(3,538 ft.)

© The Countryman Press

ELEVATION PROFILE

3,700 ft · Mount Hunger
3,200 ft
2,700 ft
2,200 ft
1,700 ft · Trailhead
1,200 ft

0.5   1   1.5 miles

and mighty Mansfield in the northwest. The Waterbury Trail is a two-plus-mile path to the summit. Mellow at the start through the forest and large boulders, the trail increases in difficulty as it climbs a ravine, crosses a boulder- and tree-strewn brook, and eventually comes to some rock scrambles before bursting out onto the ledgy peak. There are opportunities for other hikes, including a diversion to the ledges of White Rock Mountain or a rugged and longer excursion to the spectacle of Stowe Pinnacle and Worcester Mountain.

HOW TO GET THERE
From I-89, take Exit 10 and head north on VT 100. In about 2.7 miles, near Waterbury Center, turn right onto Howard Avenue. In about 0.75 mile, turn left onto Maple Street. Travel 0.2 mile and make a right onto Loomis Hill Road. Stay on Loomis Hill Road—which eventually turns to dirt—for about 3.6 miles to the trailhead on the right.

The hike is in the C.C. Putnam State Forest under the auspices of the Vermont Department of Forests, Parks and Recreation. Vermont Department of Forests, Parks

The hike up Mount Hunger contains some rock scrambles.

and Recreation Headquarters, 1 National Life Drive, Davis 2, Montpelier, VT 05620; phone: 802-828-1531; web: www.vtpr.org.

THE TRAIL

The trail pierces through the 13,470-acre C.C. Putnam State Forest. Follow the initially wide path that soon winds and rises through the woods, eventually coming to a series of switchbacks. There's a bit of relief about midway through the trek as it levels off and reaches a series of small cascades—nice on a hot summer day—before increasing in steepness, with a few rocky walls with plenty of cracks for hands and feet.

Well-placed blazes on the Waterbury Trail are hikers' friends.

At about 2 miles and just below the summit, the White Rock Trail enters from the right. It's about 0.5 mile to White Rock, with stunning slab rock below its summit.

Continuing up Mount Hunger, it's time for the final push up to the top, the mountain's bare south peak surrounded by some low-lying evergreens.

The loaded, jaw-dropping, sweeping panorama is a bit like a "who's who" of the Green and White Mountains. The western sky is home to the long Green Mountains, with prominent Camel's Hump southwest and Mansfield rising high too. The two reign over a glorious patchwork of fields and forest. In the south, the interstate wiggles along.

In the east stand the White Mountains. Depending on the weather—and Hunger, despite its moderate elevation, does see its share of cloud, wind, and fog—it's possible to see the Presidential Range, Mount Moosilauke, and the massive wall that is Franconia Ridge. If doing this hike in the fall, the view may be accented by the possibility of snow-capped peaks signaling the transition into winter.

For those with sharp eyes (or binoculars), spend a little time looking to the northwest. That's where the Trapp Family Lodge in Stowe is located; its storied family was made famous in the musical and movie *The Sound of Music*. Standing on the summit of Mount Hunger, it's easy to see the hills are alive here too.

Return to the trailhead using the same trail.

38

Okemo Mountain (Ludlow Mountain)

Difficulty: Moderate

Time: 4 hours

Distance (round trip): 6 miles

Elevation gain: 1,900 feet

Trails: Healdville Trail

Map: USGS Mount Holly, VT

Trailhead GPS coordinates:
N43° 25.95' W72° 45.71'

Okemo Mountain is heralded for its ski slopes, but hikers can head to the summit at 3,343 feet and a tower to take in a rich panorama of the Green Mountains, White Mountains, and New York's Adirondacks.

Also called Ludlow Mountain, the mountain's summit was used from about 1920 onward in the fight against forest fires. According to the Green Mountain Club, the Civilian Conservation Corp (CCC) constructed a steel tower from 1932 to 1934. The tower was manned until about 1970 and was later named to the National Historic Lookout Register in 1998.

The trail is also linked to the railroad, as the well-blazed Healdville Trail, the path to the summit, is named after the defunct train station that once operated there. The train tracks are for the working Green Mountain Railroad.

Thank the Vermont Youth Conservation Corp, an organization that puts youth to work on conservation projects throughout the state, for constructing the trail under the guidance of the Vermont Department of Forests, Parks and Recreation during the summers of 1991–1993.

The trail winds through the 7,300-acre Ludlow State Forest, through Ludlow, Mount Holly, Andover, and Weston. The CCC constructed not only the fire tower but also an access road and ranger's cabin (near the summit stone remains are still there, and a tall chimney).

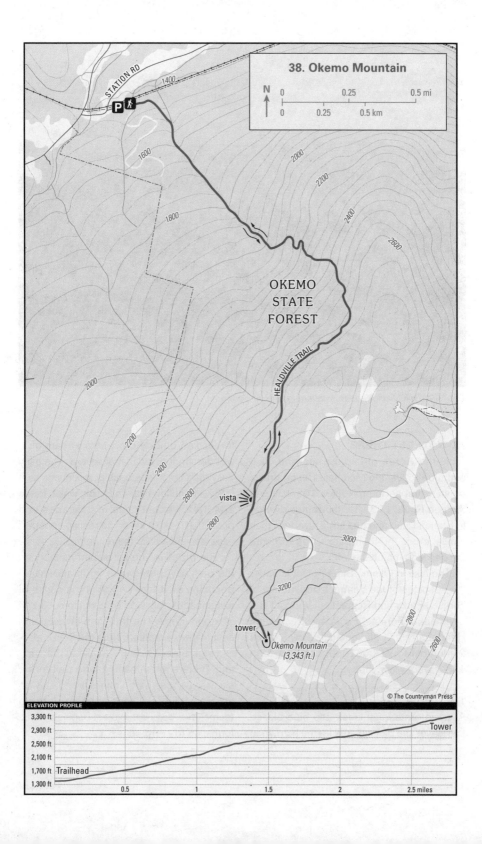

38. Okemo Mountain

N

| 0 | | 0.25 | | 0.5 mi |

| 0 | 0.25 | | 0.5 km |

STATION RD

1400

1600

1800

2000

2200

2400

2600

OKEMO
STATE
FOREST

HEALDVILLE TRAIL

2000

2200

2400

2600

2800

vista

3000

3200

tower

Okemo Mountain
(3,343 ft.)

2800

2600

© The Countryman Press

ELEVATION PROFILE

3,300 ft					Tower
2,900 ft					
2,500 ft					
2,100 ft					
1,700 ft	Trailhead				
1,300 ft					
	0.5	1	1.5	2	2.5 miles

The Healdville Trail leads to a stunning look at Vermont.

HOW TO GET THERE

From the village of Ludlow near the main entrance to Okemo Mountain Resort, travel 4 miles, first north on Routes 103/100 and then on Route 103 after the routes diverge to Station Road and turn left. Travel less than a mile, cross the train tracks, and turn into the parking area on the left.

The hike in Okemo State Forest is under the auspices of the Vermont Department of Forests, Parks and Recreation. Vermont Department of Forests, Parks and Recreation Headquarters, 1 National Life Drive, Davis 2, Montpelier, VT 05620; phone: 802-828-1531; web: www.vtfpr.org.

THE TRAIL

At an informational kiosk, the blue-blazed trail leaves the parking area for the hardwood forest and quickly crosses a stream on a wooden bridge, the first of several. The early easy start soon increases in steepness as it follows tumbling Branch Brook, which forms a tantalizing collection of cascades and pools that make a welcome resting spot perhaps best suited for the return trip.

The brook is soon a distant memory as the pathway through the birch and maple becomes a bit forgiving during a series of switchbacks, followed by a welcome length of stone steps. The trail then eases some as it follows a plateau. Near the 2-mile mark is a sign that signals it's a mile to the summit. There's an unmarked side trail to the ski area access road. Ignore it and stay on the Healdville Trail, soon crossing a stream (sometimes dry) as the forest begins a transformation to evergreens.

The hike to the tower on Okemo Mountain is rewarded with long-ranging vistas.

At 2.3 miles, the trail comes to an overlook with views north to Killington and west to the Taconics along with a peek at Vermont's agrarian lifestyle. The trail then climbs steeply and comes upon a vantage point to the Green Mountain National Forest's undeveloped Wallingford Pond. The trail gives some relief as it soon reaches the summit, first passing by the chimney and what's left of that cabin among the moss.

At 2.9 miles, the trail comes to its final junction, where a right turn leads to the summit and tower at 3 miles into the journey.

Clamber up the tower above the trees and immediately be above the ski area on the mountain's eastern shoulder, where a chairlift is easy to spot as part of the 360-degree vista; look for Mount Monadnock beyond it. Mount Ascutney is to the east, while Mount Washington stands high in the northeast. Stratton and Mount Snow sit in the south, while the west is a nice look at the spine of the Green Mountains.

Spend some time before heading down the same way, and don't forget about those lovely waterfalls near what is now trail's end.

39

Camel's Hump

Difficulty: Strenuous

Time: 4 hours

Distance (round trip): 4.8 miles

Elevation gain: 2,300 feet

Trails: Burrows Trail, Long Trail

Map: USGS Huntington, VT

Trailhead GPS coordinates:
N44° 18.30' W72° 54.46'

Distinctive Camel's Hump is a hiker's mountain. At 4,083 feet high, it is one of Vermont's highest. The rocky summit has an alpine feel and a dizzying panorama of the Champlain Valley, New York's Adirondacks in the west, the chain of Green Mountains stretching north to south, and even the White Mountains to the east in New Hampshire.

Located in the 21,000-acre Camel's Hump State Park across five towns, the double-humped mountain is very popular with not only hikers but also Vermonters. The much-loved peak was included on the state's millennial quarter—the United States Mint's 50 State Quarters Program started in 1999. The white-blazed Long Trail also crosses its summit.

There aren't any cell towers or ski lifts on Camel's Hump, but it is something of a natural history museum and laboratory—it's called Camel's Hump Natural Area—in that it supports one of the state's few alpine vegetation areas. Hikers can threaten the rare plants with footprints, so sticking to the trail is important.

Removing rocks is discouraged. The environment hosts species like the white flowered mountain sandwort and grassy Bigelow's sedge. This Arctic-like environment is fragile, with shallow soils. These are plants that are built to withstand harsh weather conditions. Keep that in mind when planning to hike Camel's Hump too. The mountain is also used to study environmental influences like acid rain.

The mountain was called "Tah-wak-be-dee-ee-wadso" by Native Americans. That

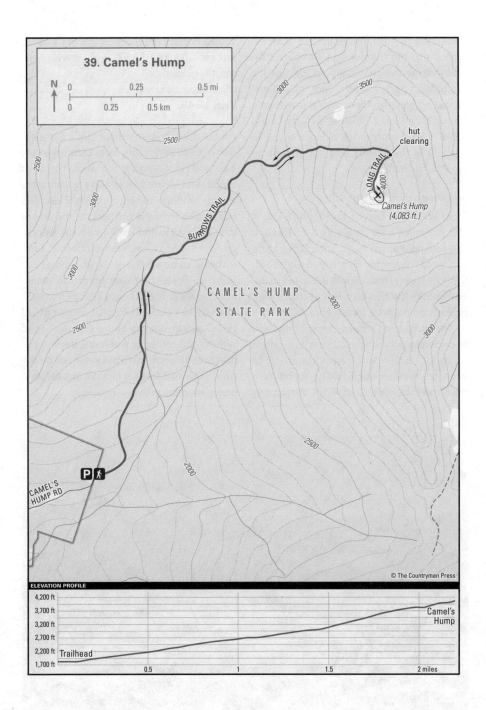

39. Camel's Hump

N

| 0 | 0.25 | 0.5 mi |
| 0 | 0.25 | 0.5 km |

3000
3500
hut
clearing
2500
2500
LONG TRAIL
4000
Camel's Hump
(4,083 ft.)
3000
BURROWS TRAIL
CAMEL'S HUMP
STATE PARK
3000
3000
3000
2500
2500
2000
P
2500
CAMEL'S
HUMP RD

© The Countryman Press

ELEVATION PROFILE

| 4,200 ft |
| 3,700 ft |
| 3,200 ft |
| 2,700 ft |
| 2,200 ft | Trailhead |
| 1,700 ft |

Camel's
Hump

0.5   1   1.5   2 miles

translates to "the mountain like a seat." French explorer Samuel de Champlain traveled through the area in the 1630s, and his exploration party called it "lion couchant" or resting lion. Ira Allen, one of the state's founders, called it "Camel's Rump" on a 1798 map. Somewhere along the line in the 1830s, the name Camel's Hump came around. The name stuck.

HOW TO GET THERE

From I-89, take Exit 11 for Richard. Travel about 2 miles east on Route 2 to Richard and turn right at the traffic light. Drive some 9 miles to Huntington Center and turn left on Camel's Hump Road. Travel 3.5 miles to the trailhead for the Burrows Trail at road's end, passing the trailhead for the Forest City Trail.

The route is in Camel's Hump State Park, an undeveloped state park. There is no phone or visitor center; web: www.vtstateparks .com. More information can be found from the Green Mountain Club, 4711 Waterbury-Stowe Road, Waterbury Center, VT 05677; phone: 802-244-7037; web: www.green mountainclub.org.

THE TRAIL

Hikers can climb the mountain from a series of trails originating from Duxbury in the east and Huntington in the west. The most direct, and shortest, route to the summit is along the blue-blazed Burrows Trail. The trail begins from the trailhead at the end of dirt Camel's Hump Road, enters the woods, crosses a bridge, and comes upon an informational kiosk with hiker registration as the Burrows–Forest City Connector Trail enters from the right. The Burrows Trail increases in difficulty as it ascends to a flat section called Hut Clearing just shy of the summit. Laced with an array of rocks and roots, there aren't many views when the leaves are still on the trees. The trail follows a small stream as it steepens, often with loose rocks.

Hikers soak up the sun on the ledgy summit of Camel's Hump.

Camel's Hump has a number of trail options including the simple-to-follow Burrows Trail to the Long Trail.

The end is near when the trail descends into a saddle in Hut Clearing at 2.1 miles with a number of trails—Monroe and Long. Be sure to stick to the Burrows Trail on the return leg.

The clearing has a bit of a storied past. A hotel once stood there in the mid-1800s and was eventually consumed by fire. In the early 1900s, the flat spot hosted several tents, precursors to a hut that stood until the 1950s.

In the col, turn right on the Long Trail for the final 0.3-mile scramble to the summit. There are incredible views near the top, but also be prepared to share that precious real estate with other hikers.

The summit, which has some of the finest views in New England, is also a spot where on the right day it's possible to see the highest mountains in three states. New York's Mount Marcy stands in the west with Mount Washington in the Granite State to the east. Vermont's Mount Mansfield is north.

Other noted mountains include Killington and Pico in the south, and the Franconia Ridge over in New Hampshire.

On the return route, be cognizant of those steep rocks that can be slippery when wet.

40

Mount Mansfield

Difficulty: Strenuous	
Time: 4½ to 5 hours	
Distance (round trip): 5.6 miles	
Elevation gain: 2,550 feet	
Trails: Eagles Cut, CCC Road, Sunset Ridge Trail, Long Trail	
Map: USGS Mount Mansfield, VT	
Trailhead GPS coordinates: N44° 31.76' W72° 50.56'	

Mount Mansfield is the highest peak in Vermont, at 4,393 feet high. The Green Mountain Club says some 40,000 hikers trek to its summit every year. Not only does it host a spectacular ridge line that is home to rare plants, but the mountain is also accessible to the masses. A toll road from the Stowe Mountain Resort gets visitors to within about a mile of the summit, while a scenic gondola whisks them to a scenic platform in the glorious alpine real estate.

The mountain is easily distinguished from miles away, especially the east and west, as it looks like a profile of a person's face. There are even names to go along with these landmarks. Hikers refer to various features as the Adam's Apple, Chin, Upper Lip, Lower Lip, Nose, and Forehead. The Chin is the highest point. Between the Adam's Apple and Forehead on the summit ridge is a glorious section of the Long Trail, about 2 miles long, that is mostly all above treeline.

There are several ways to explore Mansfield, but this mountain is exposed to some serious weather that makes it more like a trek to New Hampshire's Mount Washington or Maine's Katahdin. There are also some incredible views of the Green Mountains from north to south. Lake Champlain is in the west followed by New York's Adirondacks with New Hampshire's White Mountains in the eastern sky.

The summit is in the alpine zone, with a collection of rare plants. There are plants like diapensia flowers and mossy lichen on the rocks, but also harder stuff to find like Creeping Snowberry and Old Man's

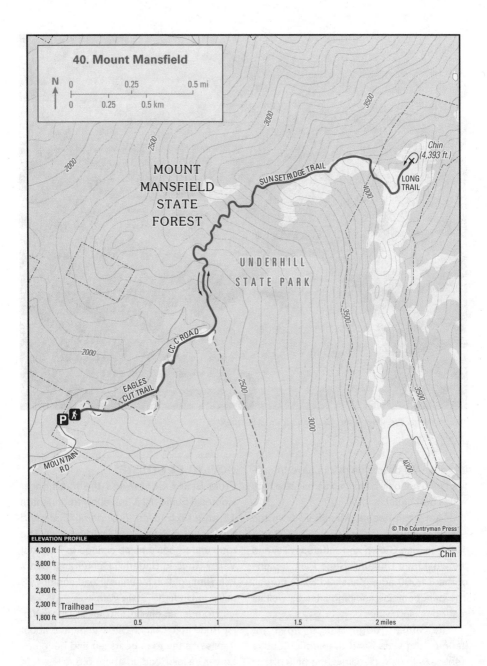

40. Mount Mansfield

MOUNT
MANSFIELD
STATE
FOREST

UNDERHILL
STATE PARK

SUNSET RIDGE TRAIL

Chin
(4,393 ft.)

LONG
TRAIL

CC C ROAD

EAGLES
CUT TRAIL

MOUNTAIN
RD

© The Countryman Press

ELEVATION PROFILE

Chin

Trailhead

Beard. The GMC actively protects the alpine zone. The Long Trail crosses a handful of 4,000-plus-foot mountains (Camel's Hump and Mount Abraham too). On Mansfield are string rails, if you will, tied to rocks, which act as a boundary. Stay within the confines and off the rocks and plants. The club says the growing season in the alpine zone is

A sign points the way to the Chin on Mount Mansfield.

less than 90 days. The plants have to contend with not only hikers' soles but also high winds and brutal cold.

Hikers can access Mansfield from the east through Smugglers' Notch and Route 108 between Stowe and Jeffersonville, and the west from Underhill State Park, a piece of the 34,000-acre Mansfield State Forest. The park contains camping sites as well as restrooms and water.

The Sunset Ridge Trail is known for its stunning vistas and the section above treeline with its rock cairns and blue blazes showing the way. There is also a chance to take a side trip (and add 0.4 mile to the hike) to a huge balancing rock called Cantilever Rock.

HOW TO GET THERE

From Essex Center and the junction of Routes 15 and 128, travel north on Route 15 about 6.5 miles to Underhill Flats and turn right on River Road heading east. The road undergoes a name change to Pleasant Valley Road in Underhill Center as it bears left. Turn right on Mountain Road and drive 3 miles to Underhill State Park.

From Jeffersonville, turn left on Upper Valley Road from Church Street and travel about 4 miles as the road bears left and becomes Lower Valley Road. In about 5.5 miles, turn left on Mountain Road (sign for Underhill State Park) and travel 3 miles to park.

The route goes through Underhill State Park, 352 Mountain Road, Underhill, VT

05490; phone: 802-899-3022; web: www.vtstateparks.com. Small fee.

More information can be found from the Green Mountain Club, 4711 Waterbury-Stowe Road, Waterbury Center, VT 05677; phone: 802-244-7037; web: www.green mountainclub.org.

THE TRAIL

The route begins from the parking lot, with its informational kiosk and weather forecast by the park ranger's office. The trail leaves the lot and soon turns right on the blue-blazed Eagles Cut, a fall line trail built by Boy Scouts. The wide trail by stands of birch crosses the winding CCC Road three times before turning left at 0.3 mile and following it for about 0.2 mile to an informational kiosk with trail register.

The kiosk marks 0.5 mile into the hike. Bear left on the Sunset Ridge Trail and soon cross a bridge constructed in 1988 by the Vermont Youth Conservation Corps and Vermont Parks and Recreation. The Sunset Ridge Trail crosses more bridges and continues as the Laura Cowles Trail soon enters at 0.6 mile. Stay left on Sunset Ridge as it ascends some rock steps, and at 1.3 miles the spur trail to Cantilever Rock is reached. The trail continues through some interesting boulders, even cave-like at times. The trail steepens with the occasionally scramble and bursts out onto ledges. Take a look around. The rocky crown in the foreground is the Chin while the other distinctive peak is Camel's Hump. Look down upon the Champlain Valley.

The trail bears right at the West Chin Natural Area and soon bears left as the Laura Cowles Trail enters again.

A hiker navigates the slab on Mount Mansfield.

At 2.6 miles, the Sunset Ridge Trail ends. Turn left on the white-blazed Long Trail heading north for the 0.2-mile jaunt to the Chin. The trail crosses over bog bridges and also has the strings designating the alpine zone.

The Chin is reached at 2.8 miles. Look out upon the vast expanse with Canada to the north, New York in the west, and New Hampshire to the east, and then retrace the route to the trailhead.

Introducing Maine

The largest state in New England, Maine has vast mountains and forests. Remoteness is easy to find, and so is diversity. Most visitors in the non-snow months head for the coast, making the mountains less populated.

Maine's distinguished mountains are part of the Appalachian chain and stretch all the way from the White Mountain National Forest and its border with New Hampshire in the western section of the state all the way to Baxter State Park with rugged Mount Katahdin.

There is much to hike in Maine, but in these pages the hikes are in the western mountains and lakes, the seacoast of 40,000-acre Acadia National Park, and burly Baxter State Park with more than 200,000 acres.

The White Mountain National Forest extends into Maine and holds many opportunities for hiking while using North Conway, NH (or Gorham, NH), as base camp. But travel maybe an hour north and west to Bethel and from there explore brawny Grafton Notch State Park.

Acadia may be one of the smallest national parks, but Mount Desert Island is a coastal gem, while Baxter State Park outside Millinocket is a wild hiking experience unlike any other in New England.

41

Table Rock

Difficulty: Easy to Moderate

Time: 2 hours

Distance (round trip): 2.4 miles

Elevation gain: 900 feet

Trails: Table Rock Trail, Appalachian Trail

Map: USGS Old Speck Mountain, ME

Trailhead GPS coordinates: N44° 35.42' W70° 56.78'

Table Rock isn't a mountain. It's a well-known granite ledge on Baldpate Mountain in Grafton Notch State Park. From it, hikers overlook the notch that slices through the Mahoosuc Range in western Maine, or scramble carefully among its slab caves and tunnels as a bit of a spunky spelunker. Use metal rungs. This is a popular family excursion, so keep on eye on the kids both at the caves and on the ledge.

The 3,000-acre park serves up some uneven terrain along with spectacular scenery. The Appalachian Trail winds through and is part of this loop, which is on the harder side of easy because of the steepness getting up to the ledge. Along Route 26—also known as the Grafton Notch Scenic Byway—which goes between Newry and Upton, are trails for hikers, gorges, and waterfalls. Bird-watchers might want to turn the binoculars to the sky, as the notch is a section of the Maine Birding Trail. Keep an eye out for roadside wildlife as well.

Before or after the hike to Table Rock, consider spending more time in the notch discovering its cascades. The trailhead for this hike is near the 23-foot-high Screw Auger Falls, located in a tight gorge. There's also a local swimming hole, the Bear River, with many welcoming shallow pools. The V-shaped chasm that houses Mother Walker Falls can be cool in hot times. The gore is nearly 1,000 feet long. There's also Moose Cave, reached during a 0.25-mile-long loop.

But first get above it all to Table Rock using the orange-blazed Table Rock Trail and white-blazed Appalachian Trail. In

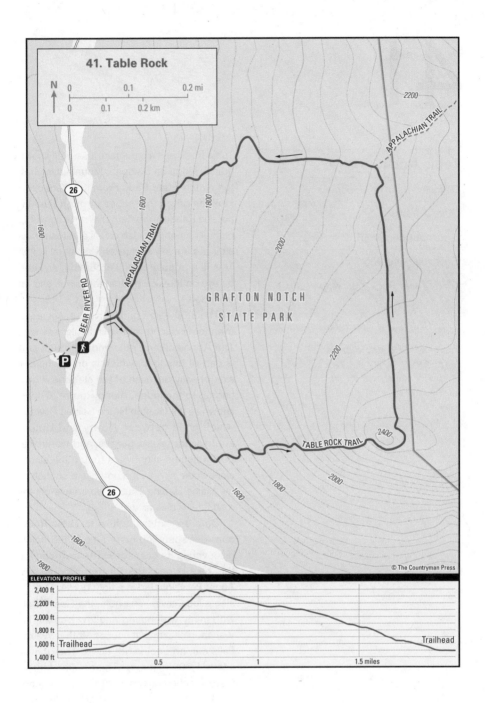

41. Table Rock

N
0   0.1   0.2 mi
0   0.1   0.2 km

26

APPALACHIAN TRAIL

2200

1600

1800

1600

2000

BEAR RIVER RD

APPALACHIAN TRAIL

GRAFTON NOTCH
STATE PARK

2200

P

2400

TABLE ROCK TRAIL

2000

26

1600   1800   2000

1600

1800

© The Countryman Press

ELEVATION PROFILE

2,400 ft
2,200 ft
2,000 ft
1,800 ft
1,600 ft   Trailhead   Trailhead
1,400 ft
           0.5   1   1.5 miles

summer, AT hikers doing the entire trail, called thru-hikers, will be on the trail. They have come a long way; the men tend to have beards, and they might sport a particularly rank aroma. Regardless, they all have tales to tell, and you will literally be walking in their footsteps.

HOW TO GET THERE
From Bethel, travel east on Route 2 to junction with Route 26 in Newry. Turn left and travel 12 miles to trailhead parking on the left.

The route is in Grafton Notch State Park, 1941 Bear River Road, Newry, ME 04261; phone: 207-824-2912; web: www.maine .gov. Fee.

THE TRAIL
The hike leaves a trailhead (same as the Old Speck hike, small fee) on Route 26 with an informational kiosk and toilet. Either cross the road or take the AT to the right of the kiosk to the road where on the other side is a huge AT sign. The AT quickly enters the woods and utilizes a series of wooden bog bridges to cross the Bear River and wet and muddy sections. At 0.1 mile, there is a junction with the AT bearing left and the Table Rock Trail leaving right. Take a right on the Table Rock Trail. The trail begins to climb gradually with some stone staircases, but after about 0.3 mile, the trail steepens sharply (note it's possible to climb to the ledges following this loop clockwise on the AT to Table Rock Trail and return the same way as an out-and-back journey) as it goes up the side of a hill and a mossy-stony area after a little more than 0.5 mile. Follow the switchbacks and squeeze into the ravine before stopping at an outlook near the base of the slab caves at about 0.9 mile. Be very careful if deciding to explore the caves, familiar to area rescue teams called in to help

The huge AT alongside Route 26 in Grafton Notch State Park signals Table Rock is near.

injured fallen hikers. Of course, there's also the wooden ladders and metal rungs to use as well in approaching Table Rock.

At 1 mile, there's the short side trail on the left leading out to Table Rock.

Flat like a table, the ledge provides a look out to Old Speck across the road and the cliffs of the Eyebrow. See Route 26 wiggle and look down through the notch to the back of one of the Sunday River ski area peaks.

To complete the loop, take the upper portion of the Table Rock Trail, now blazed in blue, about 0.5 mile to the white-blazed

Wooden planks help hikers on their way to Table Rock.

AT along a fairly Plain Jane section of trail—a wonderful relief compared to the chutes and ladders of Table Rock.

At 1.5 miles, turn left at the junction on the white-blazed AT again and follow it just shy of a mile back to the trailhead, where it might be time to find those cooling waters of Grafton Notch.

42

Cadillac Mountain

Difficulty: Moderate

Time: 3 hours

Distance (round trip): 4.4 miles

Elevation gain: 1,450 feet

Trails: Cadillac North Ridge Trail

Map: USGS Seal Harbor and Southwest Harbor, ME

Trailhead GPS coordinates: N44° 22.71' W68° 13.76'

Cadillac Mountain isn't the highest mountain in Maine, but it has to be the most visited.

Standing at a mere 1,530 feet, Cadillac is located in a stunning piece of Maine—Acadia National Park. The mountain is the first place in the country to watch a sunrise during select months and is the highest point on the North Atlantic seaboard.

It is where the mountains meet the sea.

Not only do visitors hike up Cadillac, with its outstanding vistas from mountains to sea, they can also drive up along the auto road, making the summit a very happening place in the heart of summer.

Nonetheless, the mountain's a must-do.

The park is absolutely stunning, with much to do. Plan on taking a few days to explore. Hiking, with about 125 miles of trails, is but one activity. Walkers and cyclists enjoy the splendid carriage roads financed by philanthropist and equestrian John D. Rockefeller Jr., who constructed motor-free pathways for his enjoyment. The terribly scenic Park Loop Road attracts motorists and cyclists, who should know it's narrow, winding, and often crowded. Rock climbers scale seaside cliffs. Birders look for shore birds, and of course the popular nesting peregrine falcons on the Precipice in spring and summer. There's also swimming, boating, fishing, and more. In winter, cross-country ski and snowshoe.

The first national park east of the Mississippi River, Acadia encompasses a vast 49,000 acres or so with some 36,000 owned by the National Park Service and thousands of acres of privately owned lands

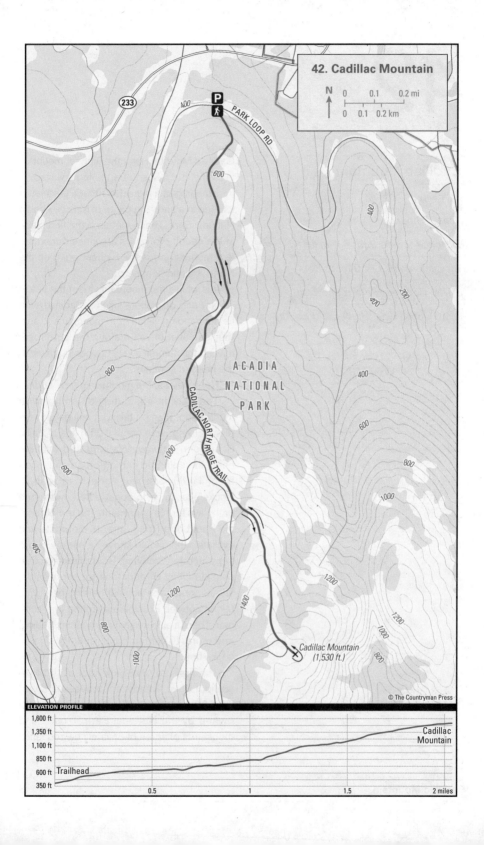

42. Cadillac Mountain

N
0   0.1   0.2 mi
0   0.1   0.2 km

233

P

PARK LOOP RD

600

400

400

200

400

ACADIA
NATIONAL
PARK

600

800

CADILLAC NORTH RIDGE TRAIL

800

1000

1000

600

1000

400

1200

1200

1200

1400

800

1000

800

1000

Cadillac Mountain
(1,530 ft.)

© The Countryman Press

ELEVATION PROFILE

1,600 ft			Cadillac
1,350 ft			Mountain
1,100 ft			
850 ft			
600 ft	Trailhead		
350 ft			

0.5   1   1.5   2 miles

under conservation easements managed by the park service.

With its scenic ridge lines, cliffs, coastal landscape, and footpaths, Acadia is one of the most visited US parks, with about two million visitors annually. First dubbed Sieur de Monts National Monument in 1916, Acadia became a park in 1919, but was called Lafayette National Park. The name changed to Acadia on January 19, 1929.

Most of the park is on Mount Desert Island, once part of the mainland. Explorer Samuel de Champlain journeyed along the coast in 1604 and is credited with naming the island.

But it wasn't until about 200 years later that the island was discovered again, this time by summer residents able to anchor their stately small ships in the harbor and then stay in their even statelier cottages, which were more like mansions.

From the top of pink granite Cadillac, it's easy to see the ideal of the maritime and mountain landscape. Get there via the blue-blazed Cadillac North Ridge Trail on the peak's north side, with stunning vistas to Bar Harbor, Frenchman Bay, Eagle Lake, and 1,265-foot Dorr Mountain, the second-highest peak in the park, which is named after the "Father of Acadia," George Dorr, noted for his passion and vision.

The trail doesn't offer much protection from the elements and generally climbs rather steadily (even some steps along the way) from the limited parking trailhead. From portions of granite to whimsical stretches

Cadillac Mountain in Acadia National Park is where the mountains meet the sea.

Cadillac Mountain

through the spruce and pine woods, the trail doesn't skimp on views. It doesn't take long for the vistas to show Bar Harbor, long Eagle Lake in the west, and Cadillac up ahead.

HOW TO GET THERE

From the Hulls Cove Visitor Center in Acadia National Park off Route 3, travel south on the Park Loop Road for about 3 miles. Turn left on the Park Loop Road for about 0.5 mile to trailhead parking on the left.

The hike is within Acadia National Park, PO Box 177, Bar Harbor, ME 04609; phone: 207-288-3338; web: www.nps.gov. There is an entrance fee to the park in season. The park contains two campgrounds on Mount Desert Island, Seawall and Blackwoods. Blackwoods is closest to this hike.

THE TRAIL

The trail really isn't very far from the 3.5-mile-long auto road, staying to its east.

The easy-to-follow way also contains cairns the higher one progresses. They too become part of the landscape, often looking magical. But they are there for a reason. They are instrumental markers should fog roll in and obscure the way.

The cairns on Cadillac and other Acadian peaks are made in what's called a Bates style. Named after a twentieth-century trail builder named Waldron Bates, the figures consist of four rocks. There are two base stones that look like legs supporting a long flat stone topped with a small rock that gives it a headlike appearance.

Also, blueberries like growing by the rocks.

After 2 miles, the trail reaches pavement near the top. Hikers turn left for the summit by a trail sign and placard following a paved way, which also has some steps near the end.

Spend some time at the summit. Cadillac,

The cairns on Cadillac Mountain take on a magical quality.

called Green Mountain until 1918 and then changed to honor the French explorer Antoine de La Mothe Cadillac, is not a place for solitude, but at times it is found there. What *are* found there are 360-degree views, a gift shop, and restrooms.

There is also a short 0.3-mile loop hike for those who have a bit of pep remaining in their step.

The top isn't above treeline, but it may appear that way as the resilient vegetation there must contend with strong winds and freezing temperatures to survive. Twisted pines often have haunting appearances.

Given the mountain's view, it was a prime spot for a hotel that stood for a spell in the late 1800s, only to succumb to fire. A cog railway also once graced its summit.

The beauty of the return trip along the same way is having that salty landscape smack in your face.

43

The Bubbles

Difficulty: Moderate

Time: 2 hours

Distance (round trip): 1.6 miles

Elevation gain: 550 feet

Trails: Bubbles Divide Trail

Map: USGS Southwest Harbor, ME

Trailhead GPS coordinates:
N44° 20.47' W68° 15.03'

Short, steep, and stunning. That about sums up the popular hike to a pair of rounded pink granite hills collectively called the Bubbles.

Certainly the name is playful, but do expect to exert energy to climb 872-foot North Bubble and 766-foot South Bubble. The two are an Acadia landmark, nearly identical-looking domes on the north end of Jordan Pond. The Bubbles are the money shot, their reflections in the pond a photo mainstay for many park visitors.

The playful Bubbles tower over the 45 miles of carriage roads in the park, with their trailheads passed en route to the hike. Thank John D. Rockefeller for those roads. For 27 years, from 1913 to 1940, his construction efforts resulted in roads with sweeping ocean vistas. The roads of broken stone that wind through the eastern half of the island, past lakes and mountains, are now enjoyed by travelers on foot, bicycle, and horseback. Gently graded and lined with gravel, the carriage roads are somewhat mazelike, but well marked.

There was a time when the Bubbles were covered heavily with tree growth, but a 1947 fire created the open vistas that draw today's hikers.

Though a compact hike, there are options here. Choose just one Bubble if you don't want to do both. Views are exceptional from both, but South Bubble has something North Bubble doesn't—a huge glacial erratic named Bubble Rock well worth the visit.

The Bubbles are a landmark along the shores of Jordan Pond.

HOW TO GET THERE

From the Acadian National Park Visitor Center, travel south on the Park Loop Road for a little more than 6 miles, staying straight at the Sand Beach and Cadillac Mountain junction. Look for the Bubble Rock trailhead on the right.

The hike is within Acadia National Park, PO Box 177, Bar Harbor, ME 04609; phone: 207-288-3338; web: www.nps.gov. There is an entrance fee to the park in season. The park contains two campgrounds on Mount Desert Island, Seawall and Blackwoods. Blackwoods is closest to this hike.

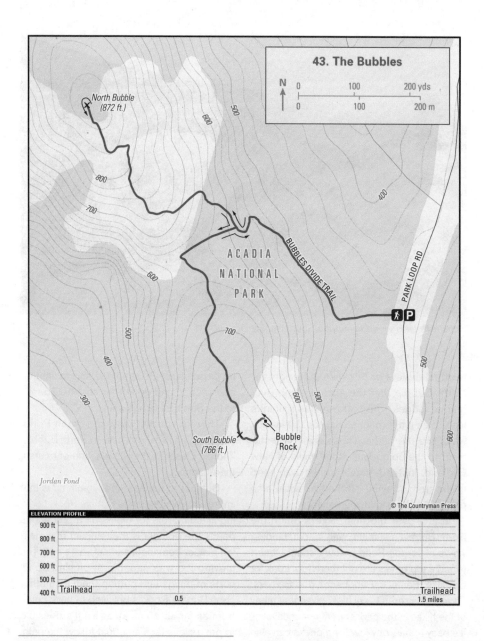

43. The Bubbles

N

| 0 | 100 | 200 yds |
| 0 | 100 | 200 m |

North Bubble
(872 ft.)

600

500

800

700

ACADIA

NATIONAL

PARK

BUBBLES DIVIDE TRAIL

PARK LOOP RD

600

500

400

700

400

300

500

600

500

South Bubble
(766 ft.)

Bubble
Rock

Jordan Pond

© The Countryman Press

ELEVATION PROFILE

900 ft
800 ft
700 ft
600 ft
500 ft
400 ft

Trailhead

Trailhead
1.5 miles

0.5   1

THE TRAIL

Leave the parking area on the blue-blazed Bubbles Divide Trail, passing the weathered Acadian trail signs and a kiosk with a map and description of what is ahead. In essence, stay on the Bubbles Divide Trail until it forks and then decide which (or both) Bubbles are for you. Proceed rather easily through the hardwood forest and come to that junction in about 0.2 mile. There are log and stone steps to the left that go to South Bubble, while to the right the way goes to

The Bubbles

Bubble Rock is an oddity on the South Bubble summit.

North Bubble. For this hike, turn right for North Bubble and the abrupt climb over granite ledges. The pathway has a unique feature as it approaches the top. Little rock walls line the paths. These aren't a testament to the ubiquitous stone walls of New England. Instead, these are ways to keep hikers from straying off the trail while also protecting the fragile vegetation.

In just over 0.5 mile, hikers reach the North Bubble's summit, with its outstanding views of Jordan Pond below. Mount Desert Island's top peaks are out there too. Look for Cadillac, Pemetic, Penobscot, and Sargent. Though they aren't very high, given that many of the hikes in the park start at near sea level, it's easy to see why low-lying peaks can also be a challenge.

Now it's time for South Bubble. Return down the same way, back to the now-familiar fork. At the junction, make a right and head

up those stairs. Go about 0.1 mile to another intersection and go left for about 0.25 mile to the South Bubble summit.

There's another view of Jordan Pond. Spot Eagle Lake. Look over to North Bubble. There's Cadillac, the islands, and of course, the Atlantic.

But just to the east of the summit is that impressive white granite Bubble Rock. Looking like a marble for giants on a precarious perch, the boulder is the remnant of a melting glacier from thousands of years ago. The moving ice was capable of picking up all sorts of things and putting them in another spot. Bubble Rock is believed to have come from as far as 40 miles away. It's possible to get a close look at it. Just follow the path, but also note the cordoned-off areas to keep away from.

Return to the trailhead the same way.

44

Pleasant Mountain

Difficulty: Moderate

Time: 4 hours

Distance (round trip): 5.8 miles

Elevation gain: 1,800 feet

Trails: Southwest Ridge Trail (also called MacKay Pasture), Ledge Trail

Map: USGS Pleasant Mountain, ME

Trailhead GPS coordinates:
N44° 0.43' W70° 51.19'

Just a tad over 2,000 feet in elevation, Pleasant Mountain is the highest peak in southern Maine. Surrounded by a colorful palate of ponds, lakes, fields, and farms, the 2,006-foot broad mass rises above Maine's Lakes Region and offers excellent vistas back to New Hampshire's Presidential Range as well as summit ledges with blueberries in season during this fine ridge outing.

Pleasant Mountain is roughly 4 miles long, running north–south in Denmark and Bridgton. Ten miles of hiking trails ensure hikers will come to the mountain near the Granite State border, and being on protected land ensures they will do so for some time.

The mountain has few residents beyond the scurrying chipmunks, partridges, and squirrels. An unmanned fire tower, one of more than 140 in the state, stands atop the summit. At one time, a hotel stood there as well, from 1873 to 1907. There are now a host of communication towers at the summit, which was once burned by fire in 1860.

A partnership between the Nature Conservancy and Loon Echo Land Trust (LELT) conserves 3,400 acres of the land with its ledgy summit, called the Pleasant Mountain Preserve. LELT was formed in 1987 to protect woodlands in the northern Sebago Lake area.

On its northern front sits the laid-back Shawnee Peak ski area. The ski area first opened with a rope tow in 1938 and was once called Pleasant Mountain. But over the years there have been several owners, and the name change has stuck.

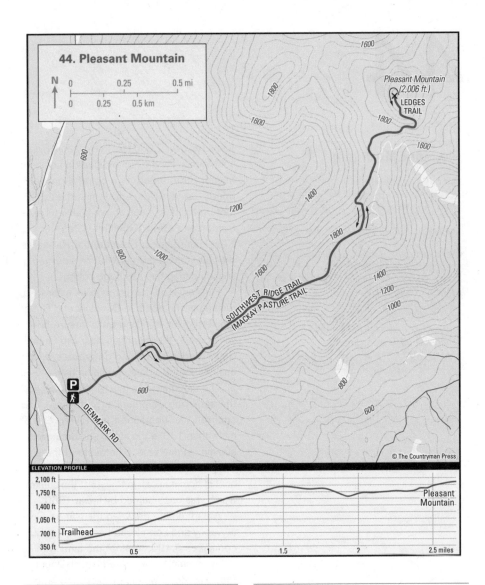

HOW TO GET THERE

From Fryeburg, travel about 6 miles east on Route 302. Turn right on Denmark Road (which will turn to dirt) for some 3.4 miles to the parking area.

The trails are managed by Loon Echo Land Trust, 8 Depot Street, Bridgton, ME 04009; phone: 207-647-4352; web: www.lelt.org.

THE TRAIL

The hike does have its undulations but is generally on the easier side of moderate. The yellow-blazed Southwest Ridge Trail, also referred to as the MacKay Pasture by some, contains a number of cairns along the way too and does cross private land. It begins as an old woods road under the forest's cover, bends to the right by the pines,

Hikers on Pleasant Mountain might find an unusual structure.

ascends the side of a hill, bears left, and then after about 0.5 mile, serves up the first of its treats: Maine's world of inland water. Throughout the hike, Beaver Pond, Long Pond, and Moose Pond are frequently spotted. Finger-shaped Moose Pond is of particular interest. The 1,700-acre waterway is bisected by Route 302 near the ski area with its fine roadside vista.

As the trail follows the mountain's southwest ridge, there is an unusual site marking the southwest summit at around 1,900 feet—a teepee. It's a weather-beaten house of old, about 1.7 miles along, that's more suited for child-size people than adults.

Lunch might be an option. From the ledges there are nice looks at the waterways and the mountains east in New Hampshire, like Kearsarge with its fire tower and the Moat Mountain Range.

The trail follows the ridge a bit before dipping down into a col that eventually rises steadily up to a junction at which the blue blazes of the Ledges Trail enter from the right. Turn left on the Ledge Trail and follow it the remaining 0.2 mile to the summit on a pathway that sees a mingling of ledges and low-lying vegetation.

At the summit, find a sunny spot. To the west is the Saco River Valley, with its

From the Pleasant Mountain summit, an array of waterways are spotted.

popular sinuous river that flows from the top of New Hampshire's Crawford Notch to the Atlantic. There are many ponds, some pleasant for paddling, like Lovewell and Pleasant Ponds and Lower Kimball Pond. Highland Lake and Long Lake shimmer to the west, while Sebago Lake is among the waterways in the south. All showcase the Lakes Region seemingly contained by the White Mountains in the west.

On the return trip, follow the same trail, and be sure to sample more blueberries.

45

Tumbledown Pond

Difficulty: Moderate

Time: 3 hours

Distance (round trip): 3 miles

Elevation gain: 1,500 feet

Trails: Brook Trail

Map: USGS Roxbury, ME

Trailhead GPS coordinates:
N44° 43.75' W70° 31.89'

Western Maine's rocky Tumbledown Mountain should not be ignored. It seems to stand taller than its 3,090 feet, and from its trio of peaks—East, West, and North—the landscape ripples with mountains from the lesser known Tumbledown Range all the way back to New Hampshire's White Mountains.

Though its rounded hulking humps attract hikers, the much-loved high elevation Tumbledown Pond is itself an excellent destination. With a host of wide ledges to soak up the sun, an island in the middle, and an awe-inspiring 700-or-so-foot cliff over its shores, the pond is sheer alpine beauty.

But it is also a prime picnic spot in summer, so plan accordingly.

North of Rumford and Mexico, the trailhead is sandwiched by a couple of fairly close summer hot spots. To the east is Mount Blue State Park in Weld, featuring its campground and stunning Webb Lake. To the west in Byron is Coos Canyon, an often-overlooked yet spectacular gorge. Treasure seekers are drawn to it to pan for gold in the Swift River.

Fascinating Tumbledown Mountain is part of a range than includes 2,962-foot Blueberry Mountain, 3,568-foot Jackson Mountain, and 3470-foot Little Jackson Mountain. Tumbledown gets the most attention and has several trails to its summit. It has also been the object of some tender loving care over the years, due to continuing conservation efforts. In 2002, it was announced that more than 11,600 acres, including the top of Tumbledown Mountain, were now protected as part of a team effort

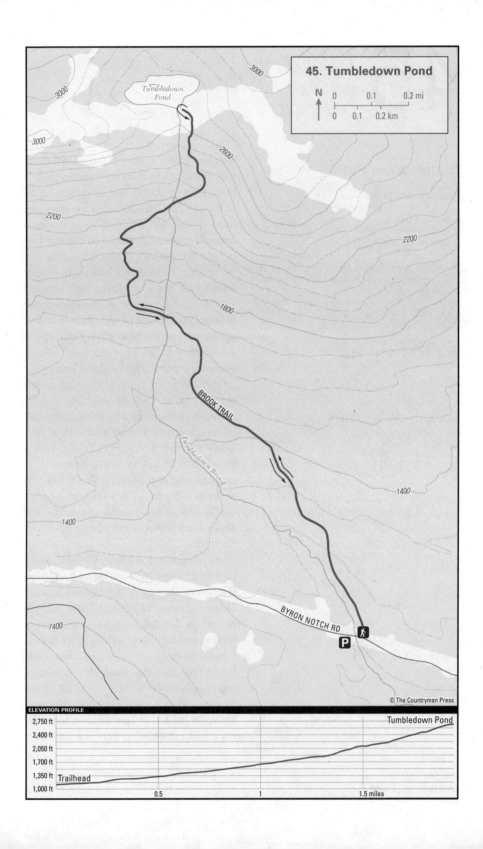

45. Tumbledown Pond

N

| 0 | 0.1 | 0.2 mi |
| 0 | 0.1 | 0.2 km |

Tumbledown Pond

3000

3000

3000

2600

2200

2200

2200

1800

BROOK TRAIL

Tumbledown Brook

1400

1400

1400

1400

BYRON NOTCH RD

P

© The Countryman Press

ELEVATION PROFILE

	Tumbledown Pond
2,750 ft	
2,400 ft	
2,050 ft	
1,700 ft	
1,350 ft	Trailhead
1,000 ft	

0.5   1   1.5 miles

Tumbledown Pond is not to be missed.

by the Maine Department of Conservation, Trust for Public Land, and Tumbledown Conservation Alliance. Some 30,000 acres of forests, alpine vistas, and hiking trails in the Tumbledown and Mount Blue State Park area are now protected.

There are several trails up Tumbledown—rock climbers frequent the mountain for its granite slabs and buttresses—and none of them are easy. The Parker Ridge Trail, the oldest pathway up the mountain, follows an open ridge with outstanding views, while the difficult Loop Trail (it doesn't make a loop) climbs steeply to the col or saddle between the peaks. A new trail, the 1.1-mile-long Little Jackson Connector, was constructed late in the twenty-first century's first decade, and

allows for a challenging 4.4-mile circuit of the pond using it and the Park Ridge and Brook Trails.

HOW TO GET THERE

Starting in Weld, drive 2.3 miles north and turn left on Westside Road. Bear right in 0.5 mile onto wide dirt Byron Notch Road (closed in winter). At about 2.3 miles, bear right to stay at Byron Notch Road and in about 1.7 miles turn left into trailhead parking for the Brook Trail. There is also some parking along the road. At the trailhead is an informational kiosk and toilet. If coming from Byron, take Byron Notch Road about 6 miles to the trailhead. The road is very steep in portions in this direction.

Tumbledown Pond

Sand around Tumbledown Pond makes for inviting places for relaxing.

More information can be found at Maine's Division of Parks and Public Lands Headquarters, 22 State House Station, Augusta, ME 04333; phone: 207-287-3821; web: www .maine.gov/doc/parks/.

THE TRAIL

The 1.5-mile-long blue-blazed Brook Trail is the most direct route to the pond. Though it initially follows a relatively wide former logging road with a forgiving grade along a brook that flows down from the pond, the footing at times is like hiking on marbles. Smoother lines are found on both sides of the trail that crosses the brook and also some culverts with well-placed stones to navigate.

After about a mile, the trail enters deeper into the woods on welcome and well-trodden dirt as it begins to climb steeply along huge boulders that appear to have tumbled down from the mountain. The trail generally follows alongside the brook and also crosses it. The trail goes along sweeping hairpin curves around the boulders. There are also many down branches to dissuade hikers from venturing onto old sections of the trail that have been rerouted.

The boulders, and many roots, may prove challenging to some hikers. Scramble with caution, looking for hand- and footholds. They are there.

After scrambling up, over, and around the boulders, the shores of the stunning pond are soon reached.

Heed the blue paint on the rocky ledges and look for the word "Brook" that acts as a trail sign in the splendid alpine environment. Explore the ledges with their sandy splotches and low-lying bushes, and find a spot to relax.

The 9-acre pond is about 20 feet deep at its deepest. There are a couple of small springs that enter its shores, while its outlet, Tumbledown Brook, flows south into West Brook and on to Webb Lake, says a Maine Department of Inland Fisheries and Wildlife survey from 1998. Fly-fishing hikers might want to try their luck angling for stocked brook trout.

The return trip to the trailhead along the Brook Trail involves traveling over those roots and big rocks again. There's no shame in doing a little butt-sliding to make it back safely.

46

Old Speck

Difficulty: Strenuous
Time: 6 to 6½ hours
Distance (round trip): 7.6 miles
Elevation gain: 2,650 feet
Trails: Appalachian Trail (also called Old Speck Trail), Mahoosuc Trail
Map: USGS Old Speck Mountain, ME
Trailhead GPS coordinates: N44° 35.40' W70° 56.83'

Old Speck Mountain, at 4,170 feet, is the fourth-highest mountain in Maine and forms the western wall of rugged Grafton Notch. The brawny peak with the wooded top hosts an observation tower with a metal ladder that, when climbed, affords excellent views of the notch it calls home, and West and East Baldpate in the north. In the southern sky, the massive Mahoosuc Range ripples out on the horizon, followed by the handsome Presidential Range.

At one time the abandoned tower was unsafe to climb, but it was overhauled and is now a glorious perch for commanding scenery.

Old Speck is part of the burly Mahoosucs, a chain of 14 mountains along the Maine–New Hampshire border. Old Speck is the tallest among them. The collection of peaks is oft overshadowed by the Presidentials, but they are impressive pieces of real estate. Included in the Mahoosucs is what is considered the toughest mile of the Appalachian Trail. Also in the neighborhood is the nearly 40-mile Grafton Loop Trail, which meanders on both sides of the notch. It's a shining example of new trails being established across the region. Built by the Appalachian Mountain Club and a group called the Grafton Loop Trail Coalition–Maine Bureau of Parks and Lands, Maine Conservation Corps, Maine Appalachian Trail Club, Sunday River Ski Resort, and others–over six years, the eastern half opened in 2003 and the west section in 2007.

Also located in Grafton Notch State Park, the challenging trek to Old Speck includes

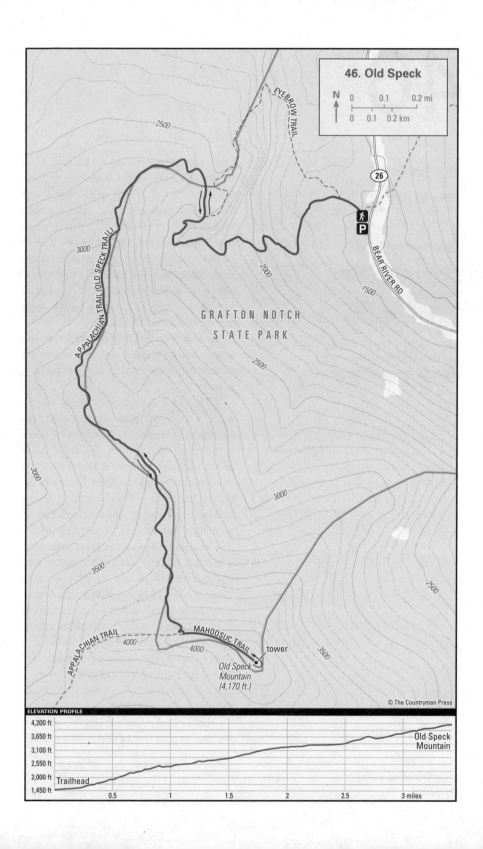

46. Old Speck

N

0   0.1   0.2 mi

0   0.1   0.2 km

EYEBROW TRAIL

26

P

BEAR RIVER RD

2500

3000

2000

1500

A.P.PALACHIAN TRAIL (OLD SPECK TRAIL)

GRAFTON NOTCH
STATE PARK

2500

3000

3500

4000

APPALACHIAN TRAIL

MAHOOSUC TRAIL

4000

3500

2500

tower

Old Speck
Mountain
(4,170 ft.)

© The Countryman Press

ELEVATION PROFILE

4,200 ft						Old Speck
3,650 ft						Mountain
3,100 ft						
2,550 ft						
2,000 ft	Trailhead					
1,450 ft						
	0.5	1	1.5	2	2.5	3 miles

hiking on the AT and is part of the Loop, so expect to see AT thru-hikers, AT section-hikers, Loop hikers, and day trippers all on the rocky and rooty trail.

Don't be fooled by its name though. Old Speck isn't some tame pet. It's got quite a bite.

HOW TO GET THERE

From Bethel, travel east on Route 2 to junction with Route 26 in Newry. Turn left and travel 12 miles to trailhead parking on the left.

The route is in Grafton Notch State Park, 1941 Bear River Road, Newry, ME 04261; phone: 207-824-2912; web: www.maine .gov. Small parking fee.

THE TRAIL

The white-blazed AT (also called Old Speck Trail) leaves from a parking area that includes a toilet, an informational kiosk, and a hiker registry. The trail sees its fair share of use and is in very good shape but is also steep, craggy, and at times somewhat greasy. The trail starts more or less gently and in 0.1 mile comes to a junction with the Eyebrow Trail which leads to the right. The Eyebrow is an 800-foot cliff (closed to climbers; it is seen from the trailhead) reached along a steep trail that includes cable handrails, iron rungs, and a ladder to help get to ledges with nice views. The trail eventually comes out by the AT again.

To continue to Old Speck, turn left at the junction and soon cross a brook that signals the beginning of a tough mile, including a series of switchbacks, rock steps, and wooden ladder steps. The trail soon follows Cascade Brook through the forest of ferns, beech, and moss. At times there are vantage points to the brook, including a multitiered waterfall.

Reaching a ledge (blueberries in season) with views up to pointed Old Speck, the pathway shortly leads to the junction at 1.1

The summit tower atop Old Speck lifts hikers above the landscape in Grafton Notch State Park.

miles, where the Eyebrow Trail enters right. Continue left on the Old Speck Trail as it ascends the mountain's north ridge. The forest undergoes a bit of a personality change, the high-elevation woods becoming a land of fir and spruce. There are some ledgy spots and occasional ups and downs as the trail ascends. A steep and rocky pitch means a junction is near. The trail bursts out to a stunning north-looking vantage point before re-entering the woods and eventually coming to the junction at 3.5 miles with the blue-blazed Mahoosuc Trail and Old Speck's end.

Turn left on the forgiving Mahoosuc Trail

Mountains seem to ripple on forever from the top of Old Speck.

for a bit of a playful romp that travels over a couple of wooden planks en route to the forested summit, with its high rock cairns and observation tower. For those who don't want to climb the tower, there are still views available from its base including impressive mountains, lakes, and the new kid in town on the New England landscape, a wind farm. This one is in Roxbury, with 22 turbines stretching along a 4-mile ridge on Flathead Mountain that opened in late 2011.

But from the tower, gaze north and see Lake Umbagog straddling the Maine–New Hampshire border, Lower and Upper Richardson Lakes in Maine near the town of Rangeley, and into Canada. Nearby in the east are Puzzle Mountain and Sunday River Whitecap, while the Sunday River ski area is to the south. The west holds views to New Hampshire and on clear days, Vermont.

On the return trip along the same trails, spend some time admiring the cascades on the Old Speck Trail if you didn't do it on the way up.

47

Blueberry and Speckled Mountains

Difficulty: Moderate to Strenuous

Time: 6 hours

Distance (round trip): 8.6 miles

Elevation gain: 2,550 feet

Trails: Bickford Brook Trail, Blueberry Ridge Trail

Map: USGS Wild River and Speckled Mountain, ME

Trailhead GPS coordinates: N44° 16.03' W71° 0.22'

To borrow from poet Robert Frost, Evans Notch is the road less traveled. Though New Hampshire is largely celebrated as the focal point of the White Mountain National Forest, there's a legion of wondrous woods, spectacular mountains, and rushing waterways in western Maine's 49,000-acre portion of the WMNF.

When hikers converge to the mountain passes in the Granite State during the popular days of summer, the winding canopied notch that wiggles between the two states is often less busy, particularly for those hitting the trails midweek.

At 2,906 feet, Speckled Mountain is no giant. On its ledgy summit are the remains of a fire tower that stands no more. It was used until the mid 1960s and was removed in 1986. One doesn't need any more steps to gaze out to better-known mountains, such as Adams, Washington, or Madison. Long-distance hikers know the Mahoosucs, and there they are, a line heading north. Not to be confused with Old Speck to the northeast, Speckled's hardwoods give it a freckled face in the fall.

Speckled is also one of the two anchor mountains of the Caribou Speckled Mountain Wilderness, designated as a protected area by the 1990 Maine Wilderness Act. All of its 14,000 acres are in Maine. The other mountain, 2,840-foot Caribou Mountain, is about 4 miles north of Speckled.

Then there's Blueberry Mountain, which is the real sweet spot in the pair. Not even 2,000 feet high, the 1,781-foot peak is one

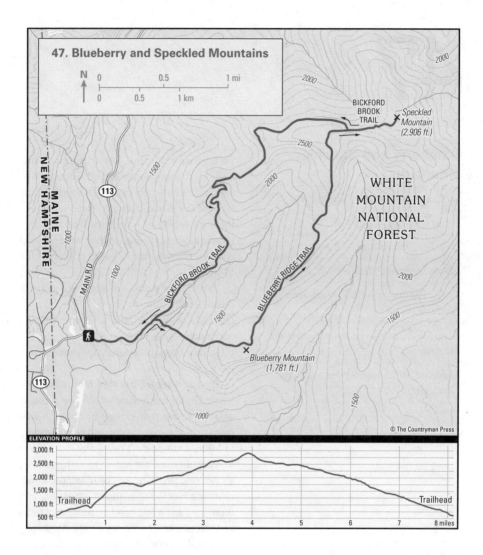

47. Blueberry and Speckled Mountains

N

0   0.5   1 mi
0   0.5   1 km

BICKFORD
BROOK
TRAIL

Speckled
Mountain
(2,906 ft.)

WHITE
MOUNTAIN
NATIONAL
FOREST

MAINE
NEW HAMPSHIRE

113

MAIN RD

BICKFORD BROOK TRAIL

BLUEBERRY RIDGE TRAIL

Blueberry Mountain
(1,781 ft.)

113

© The Countryman Press

ELEVATION PROFILE

3,000 ft
2,500 ft
2,000 ft
1,500 ft
1,000 ft   Trailhead   Trailhead
500 ft
1   2   3   4   5   6   7   8 miles

long open ledge loaded with sublime spaces that look out to The Basin below, the rocky outcroppings of North and South Baldfaces, Mount Meader, cliffs, and more.

And it's got loads of blueberries too.

HOW TO GET THERE

From Fryeburg and Route 302, drive north on Route 113 for about 20 miles to the trailhead. From Gilead and Route 2, drive south just over 10 miles to the trailhead. The parking area is located at the Brickett Place Wilderness Information Center. Much of Route 113 is closed during winter.

A White Mountain National Forest Service Recreation Pass is required for parking.

The hike is in the White Mountain National Forest. White Mountain National Forest Headquarters, 71 White Mountain Drive, Campton, NH 03223; phone: 603-

The top of Speckled Mountain contains remnants of what once was.

536-6100; web: www.fs.usda.gov/white mountain.

THE TRAIL

The circuit begins on the Bickford Brook Trail outside the Brickett Place Wilderness Information Center, housed in an 1800s brick farmhouse. Inside is an interpretive display detailing the area's history, including that of the Brickett family who dwelled there.

The trail was the path used by rangers to access the fire tower atop Speckled during its heyday. It quickly enters the wilderness area. It rises gradually to a right turn on the Blueberry Ridge Trail at 0.7 mile and dips down to Bickford Brook. Soon, a spur path offers view of a slide. Then the Bickford Slides Loop offers another detour, to slides and a swimming hole. (This loop trail leads to the Blueberry Ridge Trail and might be better for a look on the way down).

Staying on the Blueberry Ridge Trail, the path crosses Bickford Brook with its moss-covered rocks (can be tough in times of high water) and continues steeply at times upward for about 0.75 mile up the ridge of Blueberry Mountain, passing a junction with the White Cairn Trail (nice optional look to view), then Overlook Loop before reaching the summit at about 1.3 miles. This mountain's a sleeper in the hiking community, and those who make the trip will see why. It is there on the open ledges filled with blueberries in season that hikers will hear the sound they have come to experience—nothing.

Enjoy the time spent on Blueberry Mountain. Turn around on those open ledgy rocks for the Evans Notch and Cold River Valley views. Follow the many cairns. Linger over some blueberries. Pass the junction with the Stone House Trail as the trail darts in and

The views from Speckled Mountain ripple from Maine into New Hampshire.

out of the spruce and fir, sometimes like going through a tunnel with limbs overhead.

The Blueberry Ridge Trails ends at the upper reaches of the Bickford Brook Trail at 3.5 miles. Turn right on the Bickford Brook Trail for the 0.5-mile climb to the summit at 4 miles on the trail that fluctuates from wide to almost single-track-like. Spot where the fire tower used to stand to gaze upon the Mahoosucs and Saddleback Mountain, plus familiar peaks in the south. But also look down, as there are many open ledges with an array of geologic hallmarks, such as glacial potholes and notches.

Retrace your path for 0.5 mile (4.5 miles) and wind around Ames Mountain before a junction with the Spruce Hill Trail at 5.2 miles. The Bickford Brook Trail is forgiving as it widens for the march back down.

When the Bickford Slides Loop enters, consider taking it to the pool, but it's a tad rough in stretches. The Bickford Brook Trail leads back to the parking area, where popping into the Brickett House isn't a bad idea.

48

South Turner Mountain

Difficulty: Moderate to Strenuous

Time: 4 hours

Distance (round trip): 4 miles

Elevation gain: 1,700 feet

Trails: Chimney Pond Trail, Russell Pond Trail, Sandy Stream Pond Trail, South Turner Mountain Trail

Map: USGS Mount Katahdin, ME

Trailhead GPS coordinates: N45° 55.18' W68° 51.44'

Maine's highest peak, Katahdin, is often the grand target of many a visitor to Baxter State Park.

But many peaks in the park are worthy of hikes—including South Turner Mountain, which arguably has some of the finest views over to that great peak when the weather cooperates.

South Turner Mountain doesn't even reach the 3,500-foot mark. Yet its craggy top hat affords a view to a thrill, the entire Katahdin massif from the east side.

Though the mountain is just 3,122 feet high, it can be a strenuous hike for some to get to the summit. Don't be fooled by the paltry 2-mile hike to the top. There's some scrambling to do too.

Plus, you might see a moose on the way there. That's no guarantee, but the muddy area ripe with vegetation around the shores of Sandy Stream Pond is prime moose territory and also ducky for waterfowl.

Actually, the hike just to Sandy Stream is an easy undertaking and should be considered for those who have no desire to mountain climb but want to see them.

HOW TO GET THERE

From I-94, take Exit 240 and travel west on Route 11 for just over 11 miles. Turn right on Katahdin Avenue. In about 0.25 mile, turn left on Bates Road, which becomes Baxter Park Road. Travel some 16.5 miles to the Togue Pond gatehouse. From there turn right, and drive nearly 8 miles to the day-use area on the left by the Roaring Spring Campground.

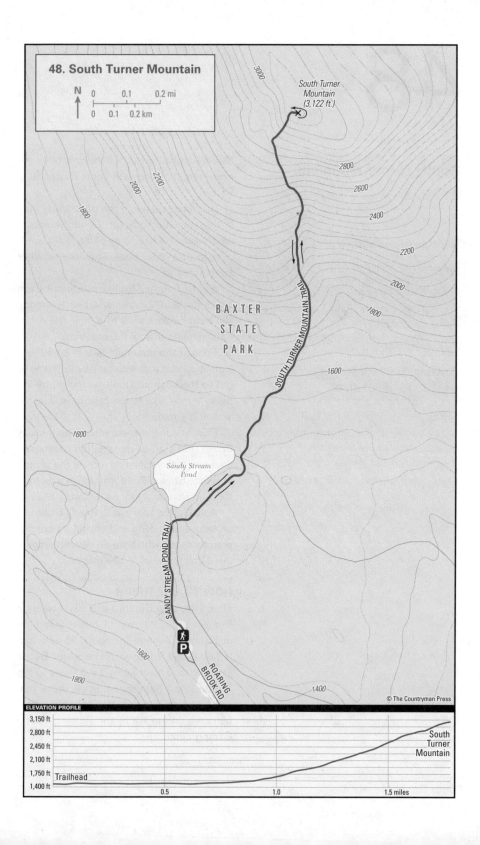

48. South Turner Mountain

N 0   0.1   0.2 mi
   0 0.1 0.2 km

South Turner
Mountain
(3,122 ft.)

3000

2800

2600

2400

2200

2000

1800

2200

2000

1800

1600

BAXTER
STATE
PARK

SOUTH TURNER MOUNTAIN TRAIL

1600

Sandy Stream
Pond

1600

SANDY STREAM POND TRAIL

1600

1800

1400

ROARING BROOK RD

© The Countryman Press

ELEVATION PROFILE

				South
3,150 ft				Turner
2,800 ft				Mountain
2,450 ft				
2,100 ft				
1,750 ft Trailhead				
1,400 ft				
	0.5	1.0	1.5 miles	

The ledgy summit of South Turner Mountain is among Baxter State Park favorites.

Katahdin is in Baxter State Park. More information is available through the Baxter State Park Authority, 64 Balsam Drive, Millinocket, ME 04462; phone: 207-723-5140; web: www.baxterstateparkauthority.com. (The hike to Mount Katahdin has more information on Baxter State Park as well).

THE TRAIL

Basically the South Turner Mountain Trail leads to the mountaintop, but it also uses fractions of a few other pathways—Chimney Pond Trail, Russell Pond Trail, and Sandy Stream Pond Trail.

The trek begins by a ranger cabin with a sign pointing to Sandy Stream Pond (and a place for hikers to register) on the Chimney Pond Trail and leaves the Roaring Brook Campground by crossing a bridge (it's now the Russell Pond Trail) over the namesake stream. Soon thereafter stay straight on the Sandy Stream Pond Trail, which leads to the shores of the pond with its exceptional views of the massif. Keep an eye out for moose prints. There are boardwalks leading to closer looks of the pond, Katahdin, and South Turner. Moose can often be spotted on a munch break in the still waters. Those boardwalks and log bridges are excellent examples of the work trail crews do along pathways.

The trail continues along the pond's eastern side. At 0.7 mile, turn right on the South Turner Mountain Trail, which will climb up the mountain's southwestern side.

The pathway starts out rather easily but soon reaches a labyrinth of small boulder fields with cairns, ledges, and painted markings also leading the way. The footing gets better, but the trail also steepens. Don't worry, stone steps help out too. A spring is passed before the last 0.5 mile or so with

Sandy Stream Pond, on the way to South Turner Mountain, is a wild, remote, and scenic wonderland.

its expansive views and sometimes loose rocks underfoot. But up top, enjoy that commanding 360-degree view over to landmarks like Katahdin Lake in the south and Traveler Mountain, some 3,541 feet high. The 640-acre Katahdin Lake contains a private traditional sporting camp on its southern shores.

Traveler Mountain is an under-the-radar peak, but it's said to be the highest volcanic mountain in New England, as well as the highest in Maine north of Katahdin.

Return to the trailhead along the same pathways, paying attention to the loose rocks and steepness.

49

The Bigelows

Difficulty: Strenuous
Time: 10 hours or multi-day
Distance (round trip): 13.5 miles
Elevation gain: 3,600 feet
Trails: Fire Warden's Trail, Appalachian Trail, Horns Pond Trail
Maps: USGS The Horns, Sugarloaf Mountain, ME
Trailhead GPS coordinates: N45° 6.59' W70° 20.23'

The Bigelows are big, bad, and beautiful. Big because Bigelow Mountain with its two peaks—4,145-foot West Peak and 4,090-foot Avery Peak—is one of Maine's ten mountains of over 4,000 feet in elevation. Bad because there's no easy way to hike them, and after a long, hard day outdoors, a hiker's likely to be smelling bad. And beautiful for its summits and ridges with breathtaking views of mountains and astonishing waterways, such as incredible 20,000-acre Flagstaff Lake to the north.

About 40 miles north of Farmington, east of the tiny village of Stratton and south of the Canadian border, the nearly 12-mile-long east–west running Bigelow Range is protected by 36,000 acres of public land in the impressive Bigelow Preserve.

Bigelow Mountain is across the valley from the state's second-highest peak, pyramid-shaped Sugarloaf with its ski trails. It is in a remote land of abundant wildlife, sizable logging trucks, and active recreation. Flagstaff Lake is part of the Northern Forest Canoe Trail, which extends 740 miles through New York, Vermont, Quebec, New Hampshire, and Maine. The mountain is in the neighborhood of Maine Huts and Trails, a nonprofit organization constructing a 180-mile-long network of trails with lodges in western Maine. The Appalachian Trail, part of this rugged circuit, runs through it.

This tough loop is the longest hike in this guidebook. But it can also be broken up into an overnight or extended hike of a few days for those looking for a solid and well-liked backpacking adventure. There are three

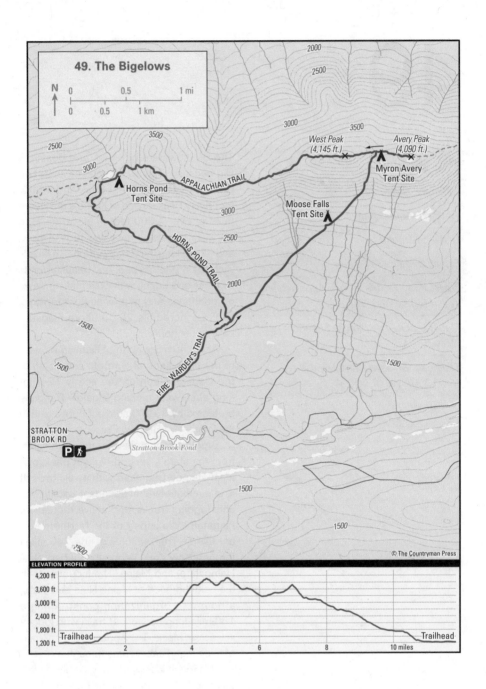

49. The Bigelows

N

0   0.5   1 mi

0   0.5   1 km

2000

2500

2500

3500

3000

3000

3500

West Peak
(4,145 ft.) ✕

Avery Peak
(4,090 ft.) ✕

Myron Avery
Tent Site

APPALACHIAN TRAIL

Horns Pond
Tent Site

Moose Falls
Tent Site

3000

2500

HORNS POND TRAIL

2000

1500

1500

1500

FIRE WARDEN'S TRAIL

STRATTON
BROOK RD

Stratton Brook Pond

1500

1500

1500

© The Countryman Press

ELEVATION PROFILE

| 4,200 ft |
| 3,600 ft |
| 3,000 ft |
| 2,400 ft |
| 1,800 ft |
| 1,200 ft |

Trailhead

Trailhead

2   4   6   8   10 miles

A hiker ascends Mount Avery with West Peak as the backdrop.

campsites at elevation: Moose Falls, Myron Avery, and Horns Pond. All have outhouses and natural water sources along the heart of the circuit, while another primitive site—Stratton Brook Pond—is near the beginning.

HOW TO GET THERE

From the blinking light in Carrabassett Valley by Routes 16/27 and the access road to the Sugarloaf ski area, travel north on Routes 16/27 for 3.3 miles. Turn right on dirt Stratton Brook Road (also called Stratton Brook Pond Road). Drive 1.6 miles (crossing the Appalachian Trail in about a mile) and park by the Appalachian Trail kiosk. The road—often iffy in spots—continues left for about 0.5 mile before it dead-ends by Stratton Brook Pond, with its primitive campsites

and severely limited parking. Parking there shaves about a mile off the hike.

More information can be found at Maine's Division of Parks and Public Lands Headquarters, 22 State House Station, Augusta, ME 04333; phone: 207-287-3821; web: www.maine.gov/doc/parks/.

THE TRAIL

Start the trek by following the rough dirt road left from the parking area, coming to an outlet by Stratton Brook Pond at about 0.5 mile that is easily crossed by rock-hopping up to the blue-blazed Fire Warden's Trail. At the pond, take in the views of Sugarloaf to the south and Bigelow from the Horns (South and North Horns) and West Peak in the north. The road passes by the primitive

Flagstaff Lake is a stunning part of the landscape.

camping areas on a gentle grade by balsam fir, and bears left at a fork at 0.7 mile. Continue the gradual way and pass a sign for the Fire Warden's Trail at 1 mile. The Fire Warden's Trail ascends, increasing in difficulty, with rocky terrain that includes rock slabs. There is some relief crossing bog bridges and a small stream before reaching the junction with the Horns Pond Trail at 2.3 miles. Horns Pond is the trail used on the return trip, and there is a check-in box run by the Maine Appalachian Trail Club affixed to a tree. Bear right on the Fire Warden's Trail as it continues to rise over tiny streams and brooks.

The trail soon takes a sinisterly steep bite. In the course of about 1.5 miles, the trail gains some 1,700 hurtful feet in elevation.

The Moose Falls Campsite under the maples, complete with trailside privy, is reached at 3.6 miles for some relief, but there's still those merciless steps before reaching the flats of Bigelow Col, with its areas of revegetation, and the Myron Avery Tent Site. Avery was a Mainer with a US Navy career but loved the mountains. He was the first president of the Appalachian Trail Conference and helped develop the AT in Maine. He was one of the first to complete hiking the trail in its entirety, but in sections over time.

At 4.6 miles, the junction with the white-blazed Appalachian Trail marks the end of the Fire Warden's Trail. Turn right on the AT for the 0.8 mile out-and-back trip to tag Avery Peak, passing a caretaker's cabin before crossing a boulder field up to the summit, with its commanding views. Flagstaff Lake, formed by a dam, sits in the north, a dazzling jewel, with Canada behind it. Beyond it is Spring Lake. Across to the south is Sugarloaf and Crocker and the long Carrabassett Valley. In the east is an abandoned fire tower intentionally burned on April 15, 2011, by the Maine Forest Service. West Peak is the next stop. Return down to the col (5.4 miles) and begin the 0.3-mile leg up along the AT heading south by some stony outcrops to West Peak at 5.7 miles into the journey.

The summit has its low-lying krummholz and thin rocky ridge along the oft-windy crown. Enjoy the views once again before the 3-mile section to glorious Horns Pond. From the West Peak summit, drop down along a rocky ridge and into the cover of the forest as it swells through the evergreens with occasional views. The trail continues a downward migration before rising once again, sometimes steeply, to another ledgy stage, this time with 3,805-foot South Horn marking the 7.8-mile mark. Gaze down at Horns Pond and across the alpine landscape. South Horn and North Horn are called the Horns. Descending from South Horn, there is an opportunity for a side trip, 0.2 mile each way, to North Horn and its panorama.

It's a 0.8-mile trek along a sometimes rocky way down to the junction of the AT and Horns Pond Campsite, marked by a caretaker's tent. Spend a little time there walking the short spur path to twinkling 3-acre Horns Pond, stocked with trout, on the western side of the Horns. Get out of the sun in the lean-to, with its wooden seat and rocks on the floor, built by the Civilian Conservation Corp in the 1930s. It's now used for day use. There are tent sites, platforms, and three-sided overnight lean-tos.

The toughest part of the journey is now over, but there's still plenty of terrain to navigate. Continue south on the AT briefly to the junction with the blue-blazed Horns Pond Trail at the 8.6-mile mark. The trail soon plummets down rock steps and comes upon many boulders, including a massive one complete with cave. The trail eases a bit and leads to a boggy area that just calls for moose and includes a look up at South Horn. There's a return to some rockier terrain followed by a nice outlook out to Sugarloaf and Crocker. Continue to descend, crossing a series of small brooks before reaching the junction with the Fire Warden's Trail at 11.1 miles. From there it's time to retrace familiar terrain for 2.3 miles back by the campsites and enchanting Stratton Brook Pond, with a new appreciation for the Bigelows.

50

Mount Katahdin

Difficulty: Very Strenuous	
Time: 9 to 10 hours	
Distance (round trip): 10.4 miles	
Elevation gain: 4,200 feet	
Trails: Appalachian Trail, Hunt Trail	
Map: USGS Mount Katahdin, ME	
Trailhead GPS coordinates: N45° 53.21' W68° 59.97'	

The Penobscots called Mount Katahdin the "Greatest Mountain." Humbling and gratifying, Katahdin is the most challenging, strenuous, and remote of New England's high points.

Glacial cirques called basins, vast flats on the tablelands, steep pitches, and razor-like ridges make up Katahdin's domain of forest, lakes, ponds, and rivers in Baxter State Park outside Millinocket. The mountain stretches for 4 miles, and it is Katahdin's Baxter Peak at 5,276 feet that is the roof of Maine. Okay, so a towering cairn at the summit makes it a mile high.

Not much is easy about Katahdin. Not climbing it, not even getting there. There is no train, no van, no toll road to the top. Forget about ordering a burger at the summit cafeteria, because there isn't one. No road, no building has graced its summit. It's pure sweat, done the old-fashioned way on foot. Maybe it was Pamola, the eagle-moose Penobscot storm god, who beat back Henry David Thoreau when he tried to climb it in 1846, foul weather knocking out his attempt. The weather can change dramatically and drastically. Severe winds above treeline can stop travel.

Today, hikers can be squashed even before they enter the park, as once Baxter's parking lots are filled—and they can get that way early on summer and fall weekends—entry is curtailed. On days of hazardous weather, rangers have closed trails to the top. There are cutoff times for ascending the peak.

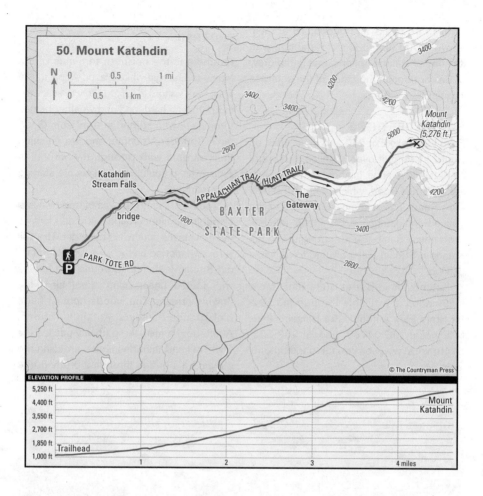

The 200,000-plus-acre park has narrow dirt roads and no running water or electricity. The many campgrounds fill up quickly. Reservations are absolutely, positively a must!

Leave the pets at home, and the long RV too. They're restricted. There's also a carry in/carry out policy in the park, which is also home to lots of wildlife, including moose, black bear, and deer.

In 2013, the park also set a limit for the maximum number of hikers in a group—12. Have more? Make smaller groups.

For the park, bring a water-treatment system, plenty of trash bags, and all the food you'll need, and make sure you fill your gas tank in Millinocket before going to the park.

It was Percival P. Baxter who worked to protect Katahdin and its surrounding lands. In 1930, the former governor (1921–25) made the first of his land purchases, donating it to the state. Baxter State Park was named in his honor in 1933.

Baxter once wrote: "Man is born to die. His works are short-lived. Buildings crumble, monuments decay, wealth vanishes, but Katahdin in all its glory shall remain the mountain of the people of Maine."

He nailed it.

With 46 peaks and ridges, 18 of them above 3,000 feet, it is still Katahdin, with its array of summit options, that is the draw of Baxter through the gates of the southern Togue Pond entrance.

HOW TO GET THERE

From I-94, take Exit 240 and travel west on Route 11 for just over 11 miles. Turn right on Katahdin Avenue. In about 0.25 mile, turn left on Bates Road, which becomes Baxter Park Road. Travel some 16.5 miles to the Togue Pond gatehouse. From there turn left, drive nearly 8 miles, and turn right into the Katahdin Stream Campground for day-use parking.

Katahdin is in Baxter State Park. More information is available through the Baxter State Park Authority, 64 Balsam Drive, Millinocket, ME 04462; phone: 207-723-5140; web: www.baxterstateparkauthority.com.

THE TRAIL

Katahdin is the northern terminus of the Maine to Georgia white-blazed Appalachian Trail. Park visitors in fall are likely to share the footpath with hardened and weather-beaten thru-hikers who started in April from Georgia's Springer Mountain and are finishing their intrepid walk through the woods; in June, excited southbound hikers are starting their journey.

The AT or Hunt Trail was blazed by camp owner Irving Hunt around 1900 and follows the mountain's southwest shoulder. The trail is readily spotted on the west side of Katahdin Stream in the campground and begins with a rather unassuming takeoff along the flowing stream. The woods contain huge pink granite boulders, Katahdin fixtures. After about a mile, the pathway passes the Owl Trail and then descends, crossing the stream on a bridge through a pretty gorge

The massif called Mount Katahdin is Maine's highest peak.

The stone steps along the AT are a boon to many hikers to and from Katahdin.

Mount Katahdin

with a nice view of Katahdin Stream Falls, reached by a short spur path. Near the bridge is an outhouse, and notice near the falls the fine stone steps that go through shrubbery, giving a wilderness place an almost cultivated look.

Onward through the spruce and fir, the trail soon steepens for a taxing climb that leads to a couple of huge rocks that form a cave at 2.7 miles. This is the last place for shelter on the hike. If the weather takes on a nasty persona, turn back here, because the trail steepens even more and breaks out above treeline. There are iron rungs and ladders ("monkey bars" as Baxter rangers often call them) to help navigate the steep outcroppings, as the views widen the higher one goes.

This is Hunt Spur, and follows the exposed ridge with its towering boulders and community of cairns. Climb, squeeze, grab, and scrape through the sardine tin of rocks.

Two granite slabs at about 3.7 miles marks what's called "The Gateway" into "The Tablelands." There's something otherworldly about this section of the mountain, which has some very level real estate at times. But the well-traveled path also winds through very exposed areas too.

At 4.5 miles, the trail comes to Thoreau Spring (an unreliable water source that is often more of a puddle) and the junctions of the Abol Trail and Baxter Peak Cutoff. Stop for a spell before making that final push to the summit, which still has some 600 feet of elevation gain ahead in about a mile.

The Katahdin summit is a joyous place, not only for AT hikers, but for anyone who has made it to the top and seen the massive cairn. Take in the incredible views of rippling mountains and shimmering lakes and ponds. Look out to South Basin, Chimney Pond, and of course the precarious mile-long relationship-busting Knife Edge connecting Pamola and Chimney Peaks.

To return, it's the same way down. But know that the trail will be difficult, perhaps even more so. Weariness and pain may appear so the way down, which may take more time than anticipated.

But once back down, you'll know why the Penobscot called Katahdin the greatest.

Resources

These organizations are most helpful on and off the trails:

Appalachian Mountain Club
5 Joy Street
Boston, MA 02108
Phone: 617-523-0636
E-mail: information@outdoors.org
Web: www.outdoors.org

Appalachian Trail Conservancy
799 Washington Street
PO Box 807
Harpers Ferry, WV 25425-0807
Phone: 304-535-6331
E-mail: info@appalachiantrail.org
Web: www.appalachiantrail.org

Green Mountain Club
4711 Waterbury-Stowe Road
Waterbury, VT 05677
Phone: 802-244-7037
E-mail: gmc@greenmountainclub.org
Web: www.greenmountainclub.org

Green Mountain National Forest
231 N. Main Street
Rutland, VT 05701
Phone: 802-747-6700
Web: www.fs.usda.gov/greenmountain

Greenways Alliance of Rhode Island
31 Stanchion Street
Jamestown, RI 02835
Web: www.rigreenways.org

Leave No Trace Center for Outdoor Ethics
PO Box 997
Boulder, CO 80306
Phone: 1-800-332-4100
E-mail: info@LNT.org
Web: www.lnt.org

Maine Appalachian Trail Club
PO Box 283
Augusta, ME 04332
E-mail: info@matc.org
Web: www.matc.org

Mount Washington Observatory
2779 White Mountain Highway
North Conway, NH 03860
Phone: 603-356-2137
Web: www.mountwashington.org

Randolph Mountain Club
PO Box 279
Gorham, NH 03581
Web: www.randolphmountainclub.org

White Mountain National Forest
71 White Mountain Drive
Campton, NH 03223
Phone: 603-536-6100
Web: www.fs.usda.gov/whitemountains

Bibliography

The following books are valuable resources in the world of New England hiking:

360 Degrees: A Guide to Vermont's Fire and Observation Towers, Green Mountain Club, 2005.

4000-Footers of the White Mountains, The (2nd ed.), Steven D. Smith and Mike Dickerman, Bondcliff Books, 2008.

Day Hiker's Guide to Vermont (6th ed.), Green Mountain Club, 2011.

Maine Mountain Guide (10th ed.), Appalachian Mountain Club, AMC Books, 2012.

Massachusetts Trail Guide (9th ed.), Appalachian Mountain Club, AMC Books, 2009.

Scudder's White Mountain Viewing Guide (2nd ed.), Brent E. Scudder, High Top Press, 2005.

White Mountain Guide (29th ed.), Appalachian Mountain Club, AMC Books, 2012.